100 Series Presents: Shades
Stories from the Quad Cities

by Jaawan Arrington

www.hundredseries.com

WWW.HUNDREDSERIES.COM

COVER DESIGN BY: KRIS KUENING FACEBOOK.COM/KEUNINGARTS

PUBLISHED BY PARADISIAC PUBLISHING IN DAVENPORT, IOWA.
WWW.PARADISIACPUBLISHING.COM

FOR MORE INFORMATION, PLEASE CONTACT:
PARADISIACPUBLISHING@GMAIL.COM

PRINTED IN THE UNITED STATES OF AMERICA.

BISAC CATEGORY: PHOTOGRAPHY > PHOTOESSAYS & DOCUMENTARIES

ARRINGTON, JAAWAN (AUTHOR)
THE 100 SERIES
ISBN: 978-0692959558

FIRST EDITION PUBLISHED IN THE UNITED STATES, OCTOBER 2017.

DISTRIBUTED BY CREATESPACE, AN AMAZON COMPANY.

THIS BOOK IS DEDICATED TO MY MOTHER, SHIRLEY.

WHAT MAKES US UNIQUE?

WHAT DO WE HOLD DEAR TO OUR HEARTS?

WE ALL HAVE THINGS, TALENTS, AND TRAITS THAT HELP MAKE US SPECIAL AND STAND OUT FROM EVERYONE ELSE. HOWEVER THERE ARE THINGS THAT MAY DEFINE US AS A PERSON THAT OTHER MAY NOT KNOW ABOUT, EVEN IF THEY SEE US EVERYDAY.

FOLLOWING MY FIRST PROJECT FOR THE 100 SERIES AND THIRD OVERALL, "100 DAYS OF AWESOME PEOPLE," I WAS OVERWHELMED BY THE POSITIVE RECEPTION I HAD RECEIVED FROM THE QUAD CITIES COMMUNITY. I KNEW I WANTED TO CONTINUE TO HIGHLIGHT EVERYDAY PEOPLE WITH INCREDIBLE STORIES, BUT I WANTED TO DO IT IN A COMPLETELY DIFFERENT WAY.

FOR THIS PROJECT I ASKED 100 PEOPLE TO FIND AN OBJECT THAT HAS SENTIMENTAL VALUE AND SHARE WHY THEY CHOSE THAT ITEM AND WHY IT HOLDS SO MUCH SIGNIFICANCE IN THEIR LIVES. THE GOAL IS TO SHOW OFF THAT UNIQUENESS AND INDIVIDUALITY AND HELP PEOPLE IN THE QUAD CITIES CONNECT WITH THOSE WHO LIVE WITH THEM IN THIS COMMUNITY.

I APPRECIATE EVERY SINGLE MAN, WOMAN, AND CHILD I MET WITH FOR SHARING SOME OF THE MOST MEANINGFUL, THOUGHTFUL, AND SOMETIMES HEARTBREAKING STORIES THAT HAVE GONE TO DEFINE THEM AS PEOPLE. IF I LEARNED ONE THING FROM DOING THIS PROJECT IT'S THAT IT'S DIFFICULT TO DISLIKE SOMEONE WHEN YOU LEARN WHAT MAKES THEM TICK.

THIS PROJECT, CALLED 100 SHADES, BEGAN ITS INITIAL RUN ON FEBRUARY 6, 2017 AND ENDED ON JUNE 25, 2017.

SINCERELY, JAAWAN

KASEY

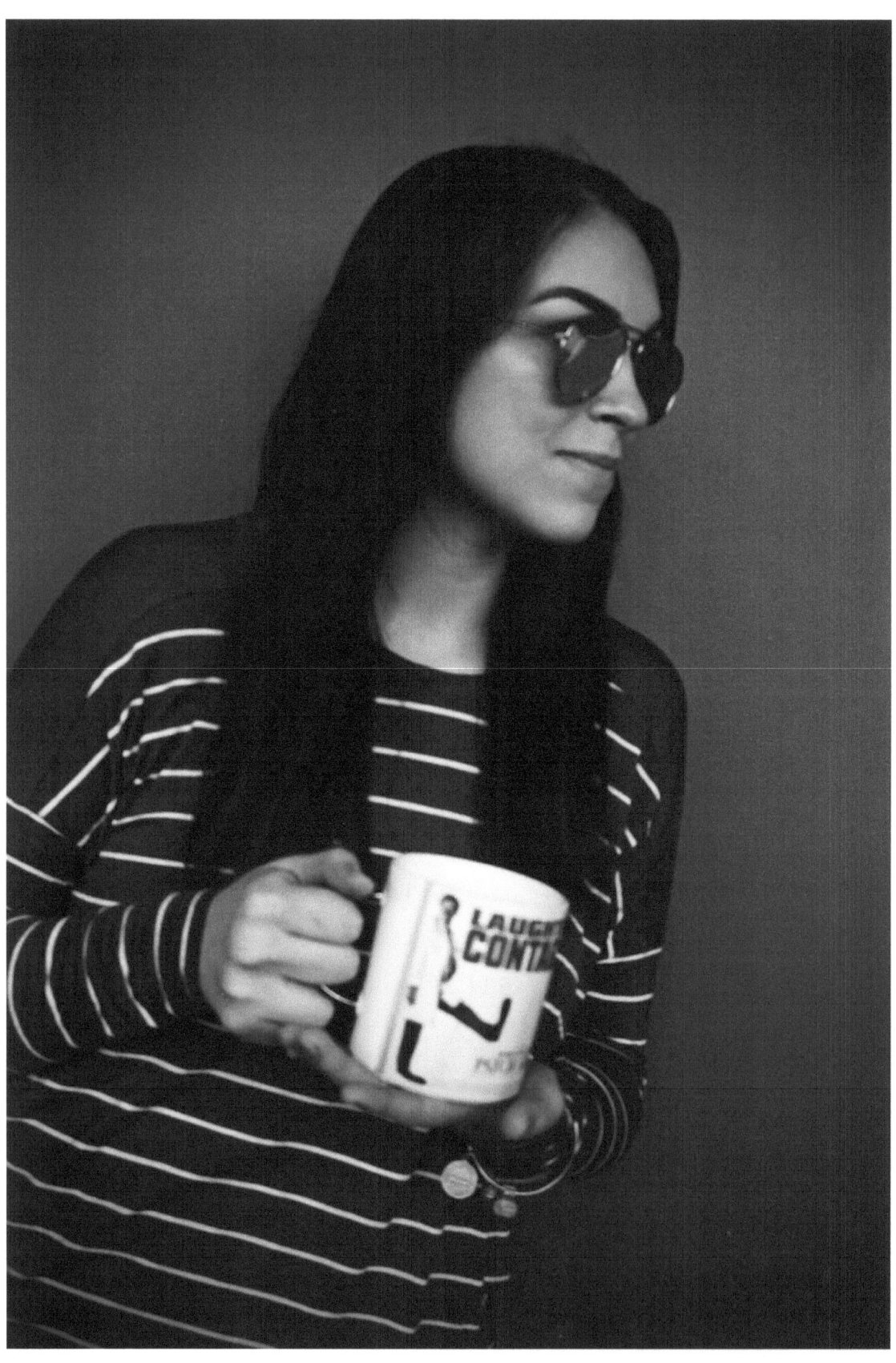

OBJECT:

Coffee mug with an image of the movie, "Patch Adams"

WHY IS IT IMPORTANT TO HER?

"I just bought this mug at and I transferred this image on it. This movie is hands-down my favorite movie. I would say that it's probably the closest thing that describes me as a person. At the beginning of the movie, he goes through a hard time in his life and he finds his way out by helping others through the medical field and that's what I hope to do. So I think that describes me the best!"

GREG

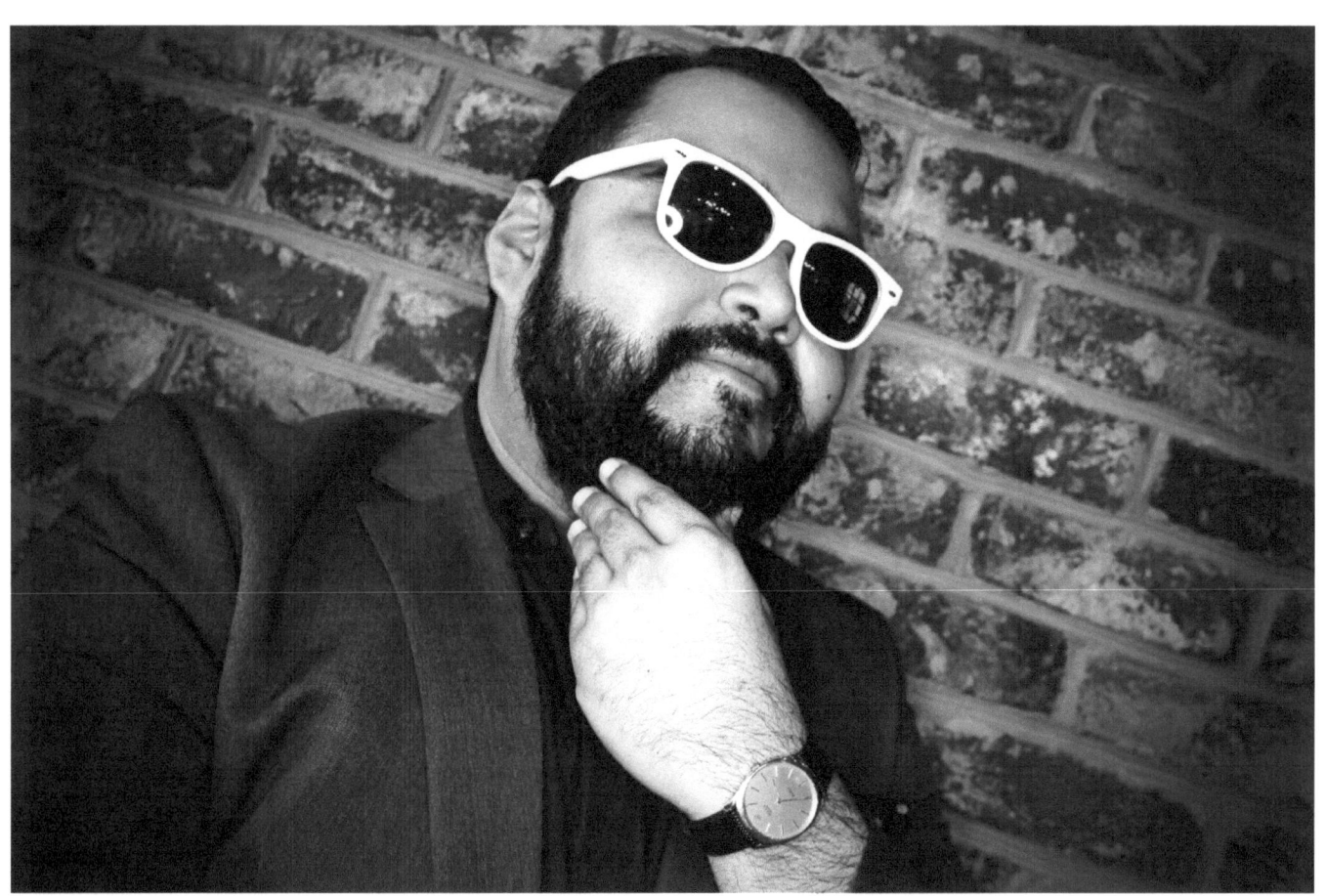

OBJECT:

Watch

WHY IS IT IMPORTANT TO HIM?

"When I was eight years old, I lost an uncle to cancer. He was someone that everyone in our family, on my mom's side, that we were all very proud of because my mom came from a very rural community in Mexico where there was even limited access to electricity. So my uncle left his rural community, pursued education in Mexico, graduated from the University of Guadalajara, and eventually moved to the United States and became very successful in Aurora, Illinois.

Well, he passed away when I was eight years old. This watch was left for my grandmother and my grandmother held it out in front of me and she said, 'Mijo, when you graduate from college, this watch will be yours.'
So I'm eight years old and I was like, 'Man, I'm going to be 22 by then. I'm going to be so old.' It just seemed like forever away when you're eight years old. And then my grandmother passed away when I was in junior high, but then my mom got the watch. And when I graduated college, that day she was like, 'Here's your watch!'

It now reminds me of three different things. First, it reminds me of my uncle. Who came from a rural community in Mexico and found success in the United States. Was able to learn a new language. Learn a new culture. And he never let where he came from limit him. In fact he used that to develop his character, which granted him great success and the hard work that came with it.

Second thing. Because it's a watch, it reminds me that our time is limited. One of these days these hands on this watch will stop for my life and for me, it will all be over. So, it's a reminder that the clock is always ticking.

The final thing that it kind of defines me is because I believe time is a tool and I use that tool and I invest it. I invest it with others. I invest it in activities that I enjoy doing. And I invest it in things that are going to improve either my life or the lives of others. And I believe in investing time, especially in people. Investing time in relationships, and investing time in developing individuals so that they can become the best that they can be.

That's kind of who I am. If I'm interested in something or somebody, I'm going to commit the time to ensure that whatever it is we're trying to do together is going to be successful. I don't want to waste that because to me time is a form of currency and I don't want to waste it. I want to make sure it's invested properly so that it grows."

TAYVIAN

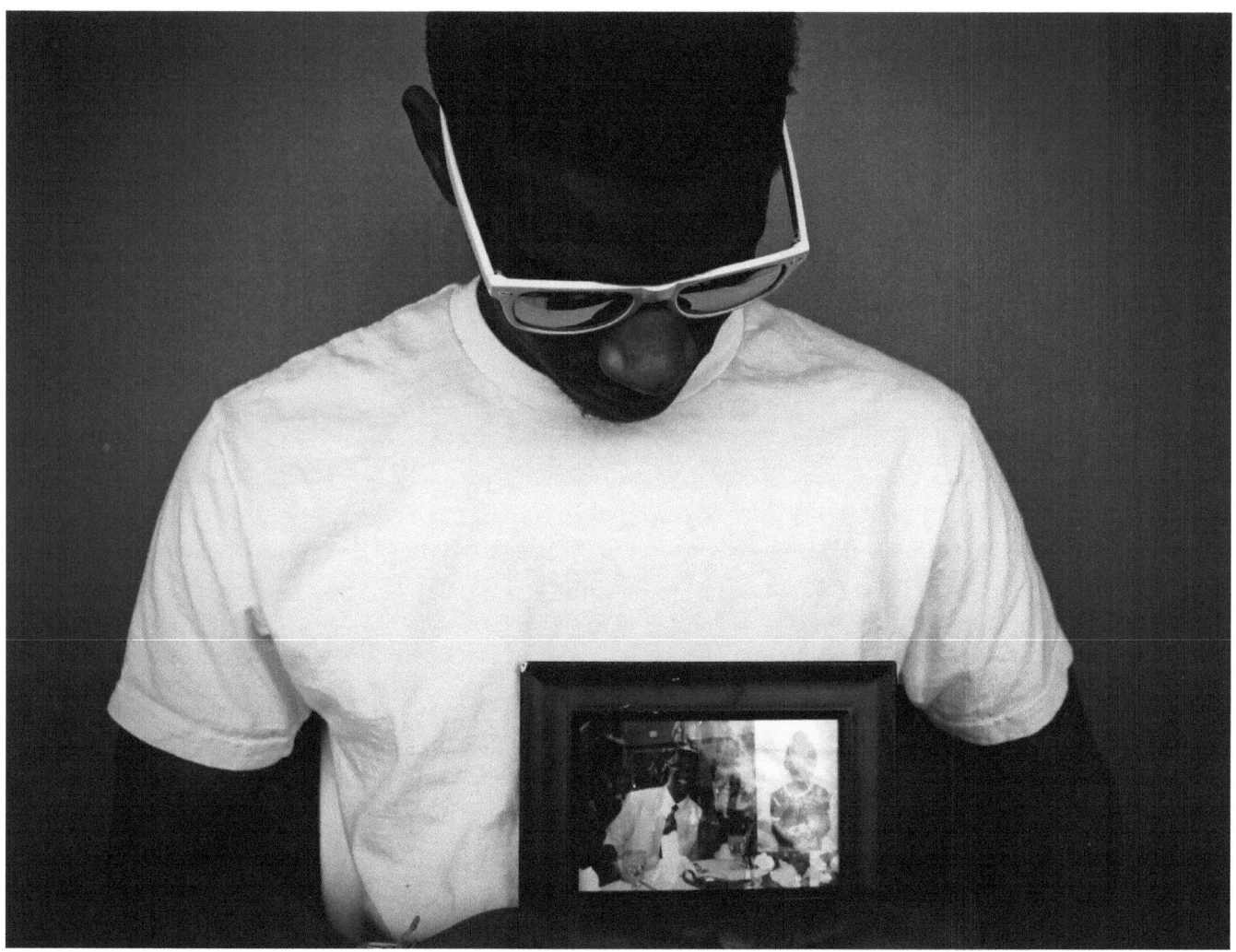

OBJECT:

PICTURE FRAME WITH TWO PHOTOS; ONE OF HIM AND HIS MOTHER, AND ANOTHER OF HIS SISTER

WHY IS IT IMPORTANT TO HIM?

"I PICKED THIS FOR A COUPLE REASONS. THE MOST OBVIOUS ONE IS PROBABLY A GIVEN. IT'S MY MOM AND MY SISTER AND THAT'S MY MOTIVATION EVERYDAY TO GO OUT AND DO WHAT I NEED TO DO. SO I CAN MAKE THEM PROUD AND GIVE BACK TO THEM AND SHOW THEM I LOVE THEM. BUT, I ALSO PICKED THIS PICTURE AND THIS FRAME BECAUSE WHEN I WENT OFF TO COLLEGE, THIS IS THE PICTURE FRAME THAT I PUT THESE PICTURES IN AND I KEPT THIS PICTURE FRAME UP SINCE I LEFT HOME. SO I GOT TO SEE THEM EVERYDAY EVEN THOUGH I DON'T GET TO SEE THEM EVERYDAY WHICH IS PRETTY AWESOME."

MARTIN

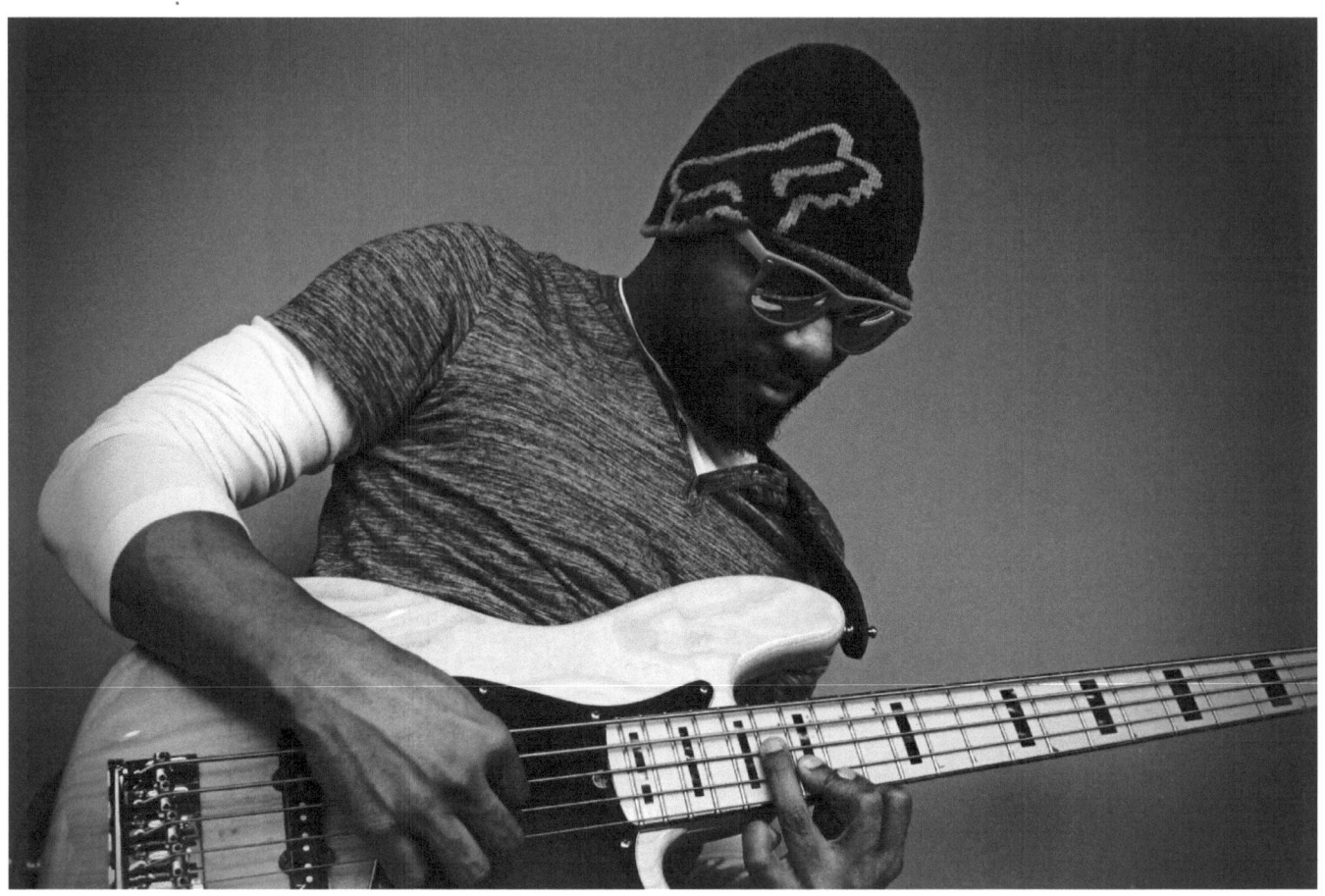

OBJECT:

Bass Guitar

WHY IS IT IMPORTANT TO HIM?

"I've been playing the bass officially since June of 2014. So about two and a half years. It's something that kind of represents the second half of my life since I started after I graduated college. Most people who know me, know me as a drummer. Only the people who know me as a bassist are the people who have met me since I moved to the Quad Cities in 2013. So it's kind of a newer thing for me and a lot of other people in my life, and I actually really enjoy playing it a lot.

I'm a drummer of 22 years and playing the bass for these two and a half years, I can honestly say I'll probably like the bass for than the drums. So, it's one of my favorite instruments."

ALYSSA

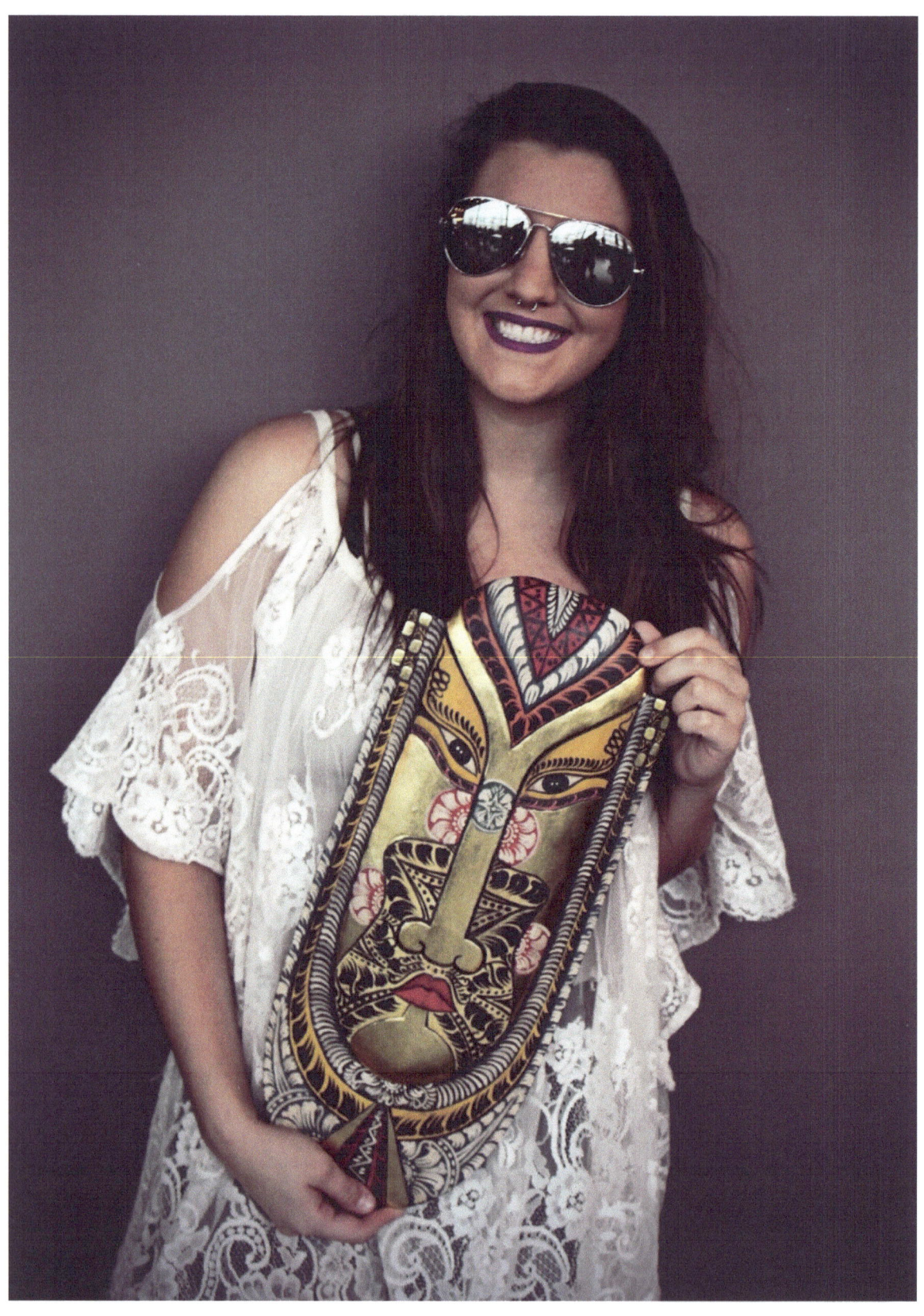

OBJECT:

TRIBAL FACE SCULPTURE.

WHY IS IT IMPORTANT TO HER?

"I BOUGHT IT AT A GARAGE SALE AND THE LADY SAID THAT SHE THINKS THAT IT CAME FROM NEW ORLEANS AFTER THE HURRICANE HAPPENED DOWN THERE, AND THEY WERE FINDING A BUNCH OF STUFF WASHED UP AND THIS SOMETHING THAT SHE HAD FOUND AND BROUGHT BACK TO HER HOUSE. SO WHEN I WAS BUYING IT AT THE GARAGE SALE, BECAUSE IT WAS ONLY 50 CENTS AND I WAS LIKE, 'WHY IS THIS ONLY 50 CENTS? THIS IS SO COOL!' SHE WAS LIKE, 'WELL, EVER SINCE I BROUGHT IT INTO MY HOUSE, BAD THINGS HAVE BEEN HAPPENING. IT'S CURSED.'
SHE WAS JUST TELLING ME HOW NEGATIVE HER LIFE WAS AND HOW SHE THINKS THAT IT WAS BECAUSE OF THIS. SO BEING THE SUPERSTITIOUS PERSON I AM, I'M LIKE, 'WELL, I'M GOING TO BUY IT! I'M GOING TO PUT IT IN MY ROOM!'

SO, ESSENTIALLY I WANTED TO SEE IF ANYTHING WOULD HAPPEN, AND THEN I STARTED THINKING VERY DEEPLY ABOUT IT AND I REALLY THINK IT WAS ALL IN HER HEAD BECAUSE WHEN I BROUGHT THIS INTO MY ROOM, I STARTED NOTICING A LOT MORE POSITIVE THINGS WERE HAPPENING IN MY LIFE AND I THINK MAYBE IT WAS BECAUSE OF MY PERSPECTIVE VERSUS ME THINKING, 'OH, SOMETHING BAD IS GOING TO HAPPEN.

I THINK A LOT OF PEOPLE THINK SO NEGATIVELY AND THEY'RE ALWAYS LOOKING AT THE NEGATIVE THINGS THAT ARE HAPPENING IN THEIR LIFE. THEY'RE DWELLING ON THE NEGATIVE THINGS AND I THINK THAT'S WHY THEY THINK THEIR LIFE IS SO BAD AND SUCKS AND THEY CAN'T REALLY SEE THE POSITIVES THAT ARE HAPPENING AND THEY'RE NOT LEARNING FROM WHAT THEY THINK IS THEIR NEGATIVE EXPERIENCES. THEY'RE JUST DWELLING ON THEM.

SO THIS MADE ME THINK OF PERSPECTIVE IN LIFE. SO I JUST STARTED LOOKING AT THINGS MUCH MORE POSITIVELY AND I WAS A LOT MORE OPTIMISTIC AND IT'S MADE ME SO MUCH HAPPIER. I WAS LIKE, 'LADY, YOUR LIFE DIDN'T GET BAD BECAUSE THIS WAS BROUGHT INTO YOUR HOUSE. YOUR LIFE IS BAD BECAUSE OF YOUR PERSPECTIVE IN LIFE.

MARISA

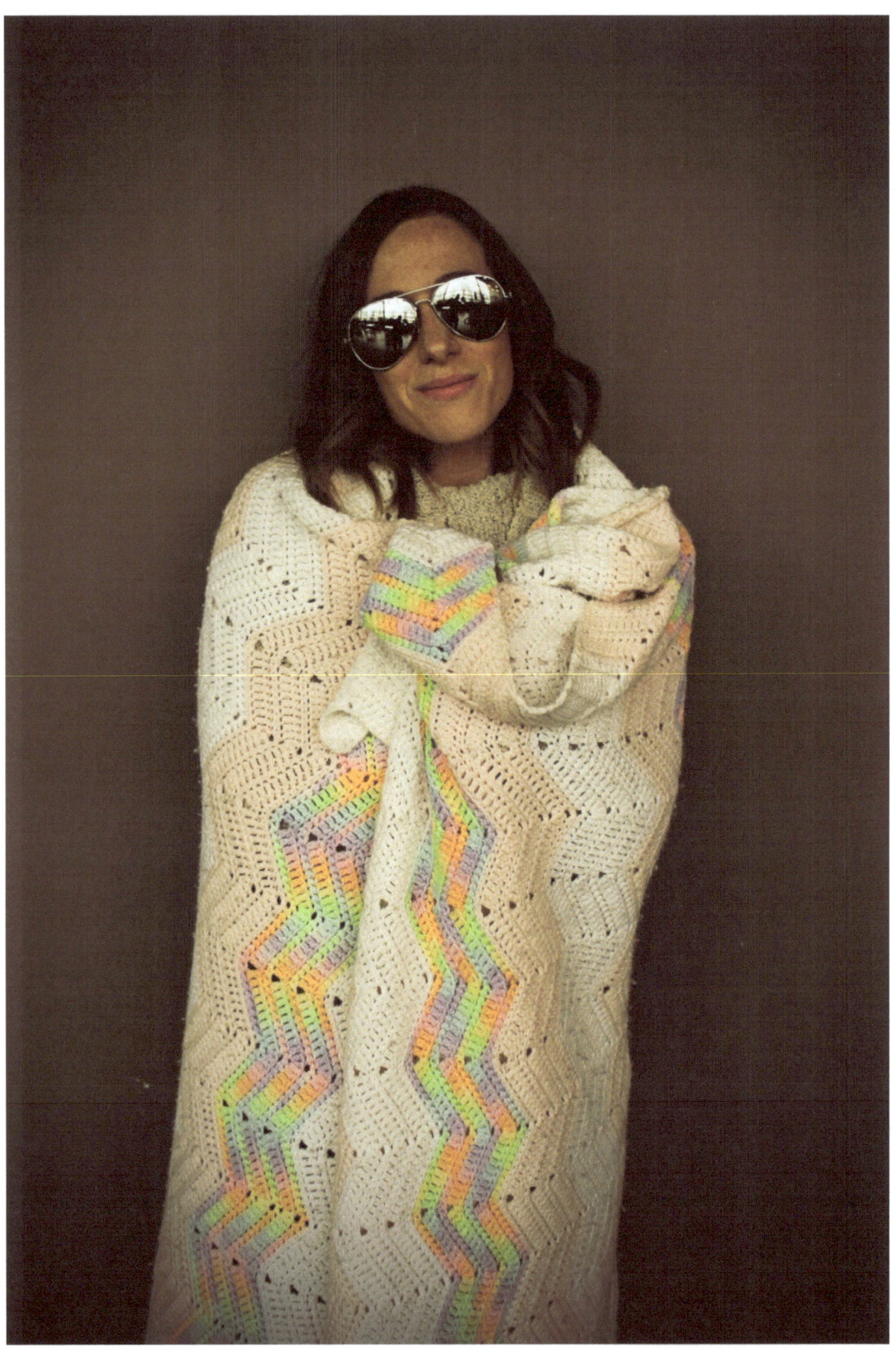

OBJECT:

BLANKET

WHY IS IT IMPORTANT TO HER?

"I BROUGHT A BLANKET THAT MY AUNT, ON MY DAD'S SIDE, KNIT FOR ME WHILE MY MOM WAS PREGNANT WITH ME. SHE GAVE IT TO ME WHEN I WAS BORN AND I'VE HAD IT EVER SINCE. I MEAN IT'S A HUGE BLANKET. LIKE A QUEEN-SIZED, BED-SIZED BLANKET! I BROUGHT THAT ONE BECAUSE FAMILY REALLY MEANS A LOT TO ME. AND BEING AWAY FROM HOME RIGHT NOW, EVEN THOUGH I'M IN PURSUIT OF MY CAREER, IT'S STILL HARD TO NOT BE THERE WITH THEM AND FEEL LIKE I'M MISSING OUT ON THINGS. SO THAT BLANKET REPRESENTS KEEPING THEM CLOSE TO ME.

ALSO, WHEN YOU THINK OF BLANKETS, YOU THINK OF COMFORT. SO, I REALLY LOVE PROVIDING COMFORT FOR OTHER PEOPLE. AND SO I LOVE BEING THE PERSON THAT MY FRIENDS CAN GO TO WHEN THEY NEED A SAFE PLACE OR WHEN THEY NEED ADVICE OR JUST SOMEONE TO LISTEN AND TALK TO. I LOVE BEING ABLE TO HELP PEOPLE THROUGH CROSSFIT AND CHIROPRACTIC. AND IT JUST EMBODIES MY WHOLE LIFE AND BEING SOMEONE THAT OTHER PEOPLE CAN RELY ON AND CAN BE THERE OWN BLANKET IN TIMES OF NEED. WHETHER THAT BE PERSONAL, FITNESS, CAREER WISE. WHATEVER THEY NEED, I LIKE BEING THAT PERSON TO WRAP THEM UP AND BE THERE FOR THEM."

QUINTON

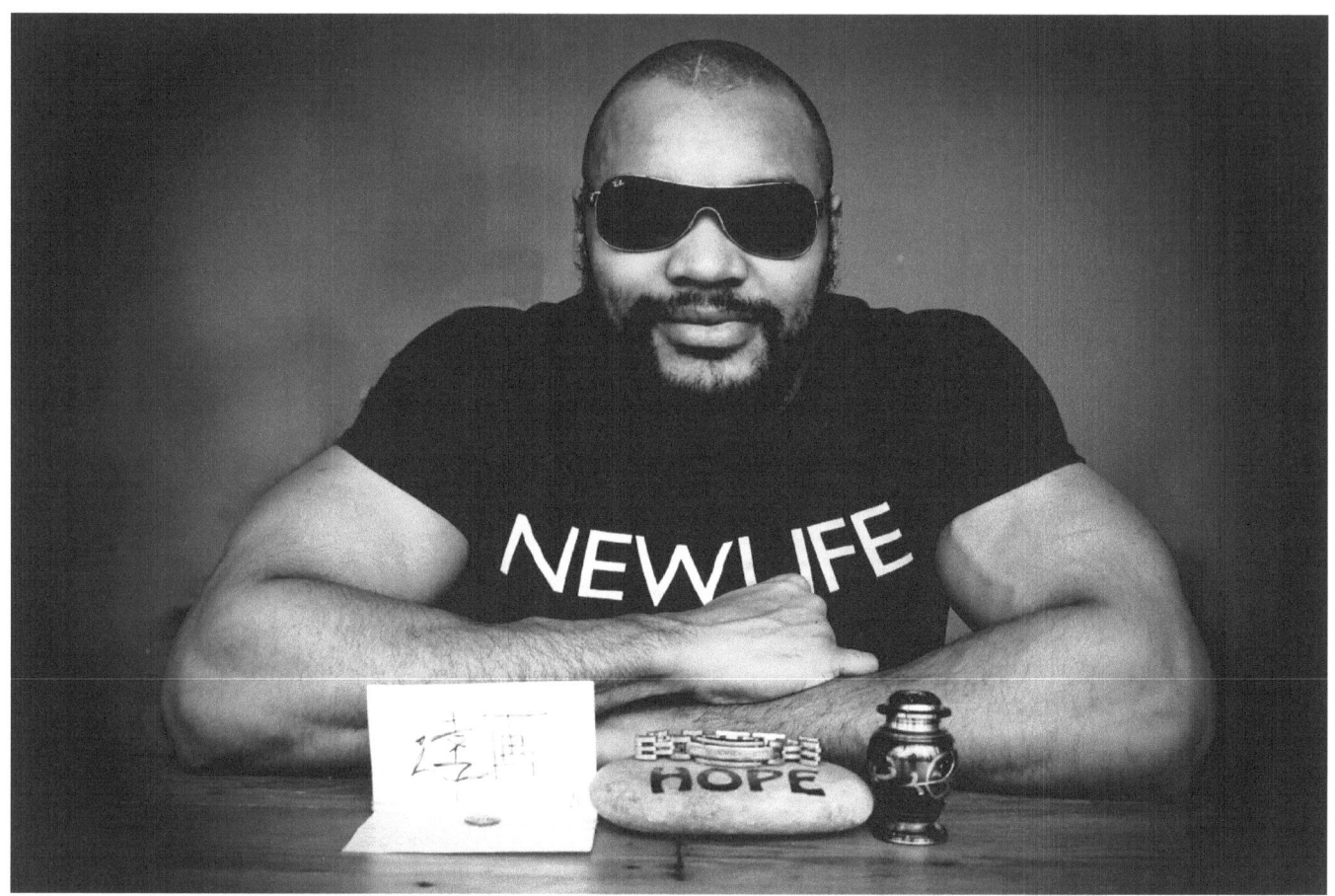

OBJECT:

FAMILY MEMORABILIA

WHY IS IT IMPORTANT TO HIM?

"I BROUGHT A ROCK OF HOPE BECAUSE MY UNCLE DIED OF CANCER AND HE ALWAYS HAD HOPE THAT HE WOULD GET BETTER. HE SPREAD THAT HOPE TO ME THROUGH JESUS CHRIST, MY LORD AND SAVIOR.

I ALSO BROUGHT MY DAD'S BRACELET THAT I BOUGHT HIM FOR FATHER'S DAY. IT SAYS "DAD" ON IT. IT HURTS RIGHT NOW THAT HE'S DEAD AND GONE. I ENVY PEOPLE WHO HAVE DADS RIGHT NOW AND FATHER FIGURES.

I ALSO BROUGHT MY GRANDMA'S ASHES. SHE IS EVERYTHING THAT MADE ME NOW. MY GRANDMA WAS THE MOST AWESOME, CARING, FUNNY, LOVING, SUPPORTIVE PERSON THAT I COULD EVER WISH TO HAVE. SHE WAS THE BEST GRANDMA EVER. I WAS WITH HER IN HER LAST DAYS. THERE WAS SO MUCH LOVE AND PEACE THAT SHE SPREAD TO ME AND THE FAMILY AND SO MUCH FORGIVENESS. I MISS HER A LOT. I LOVE HER.

I ALSO BROUGHT A FIVE-CENT YEN COIN FROM MY COUSIN. SHE'S MY FAVORITE COUSIN. I LOVE HER A LOT. ME AND HER GREW UP TOGETHER."

MEG

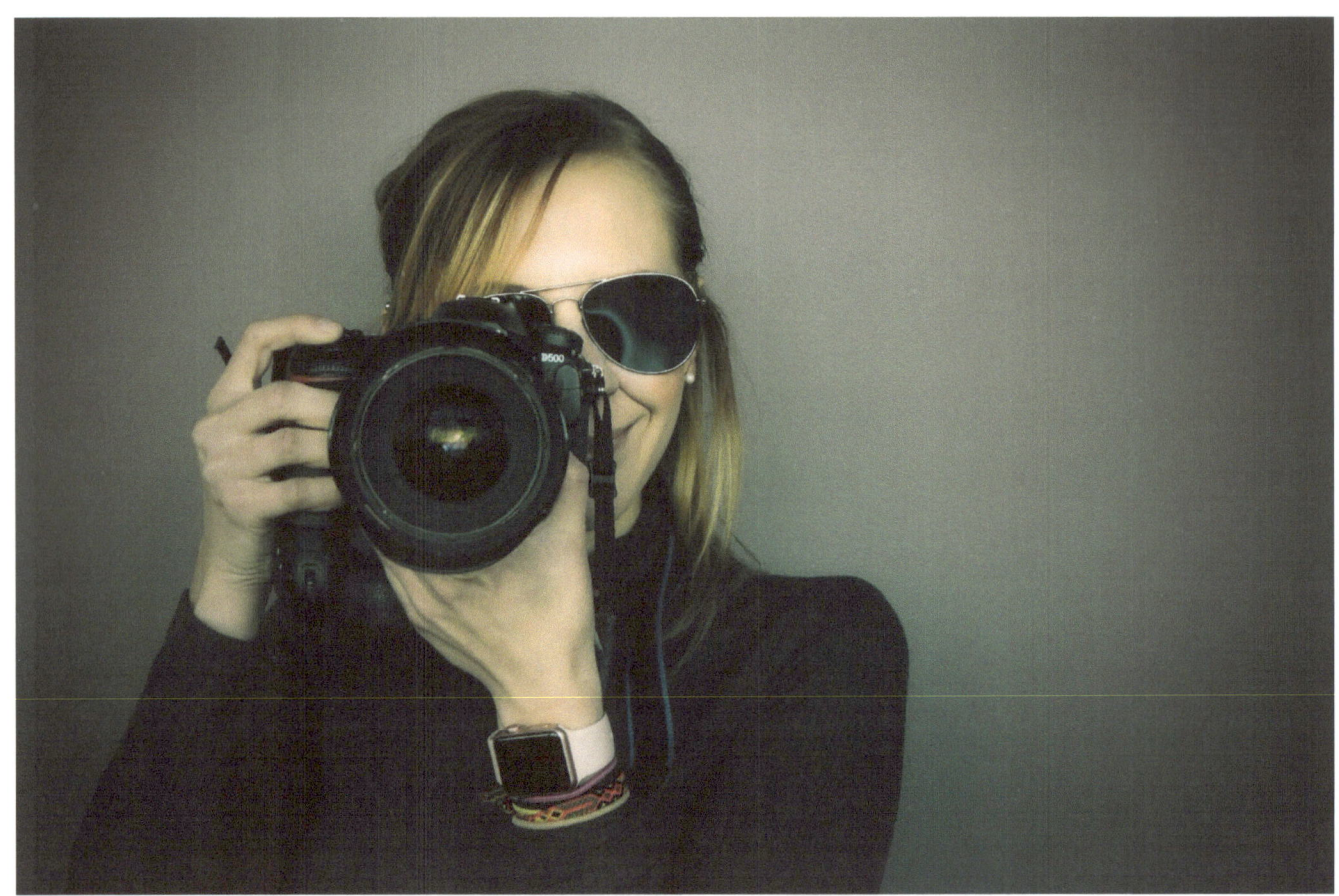

OBJECT:

CAMERA

WHY IS IT IMPORTANT TO HER?

"MY CAMERA IS THE MOST IMPORTANT OBJECT THAT I HAVE BECAUSE IT'S THE FIRST TIME I BOUGHT SOMETHING SO EXPENSIVE ON MY OWN AND I PAID FOR IT WITH MONEY THAT I WORKED FOR. SO IT'S THE FIRST COUPLE THOUSAND-DOLLAR OBJECT THAT I'VE EVER BEEN ABLE TO BUY ON MY OWN AND I WAS REALLY PROUD OF THAT.

ANOTHER REASON WHY IT'S SO IMPORTANT TO ME IS BECAUSE I BELIEVE IT'S MY TICKET TO LIFE. I THINK IT'S AN OBJECT THAT ALLOWS ME TO RECORD OTHER PEOPLES LIVES. I CAN SPOTLIGHT PEOPLE'S PERSONALITIES WITH A SINGLE IMAGE. I THINK I CAN CHANGE THE WORLD TRULY IF GIVEN THE RIGHT OPPORTUNITY AND I TAKE THE RIGHT PICTURE. THAT'S WHY THIS CAMERA IS SO IMPORTANT TO ME BECAUSE I THINK THAT I CAN REALLY MAKE A DIFFERENCE WITH IT."

JOE

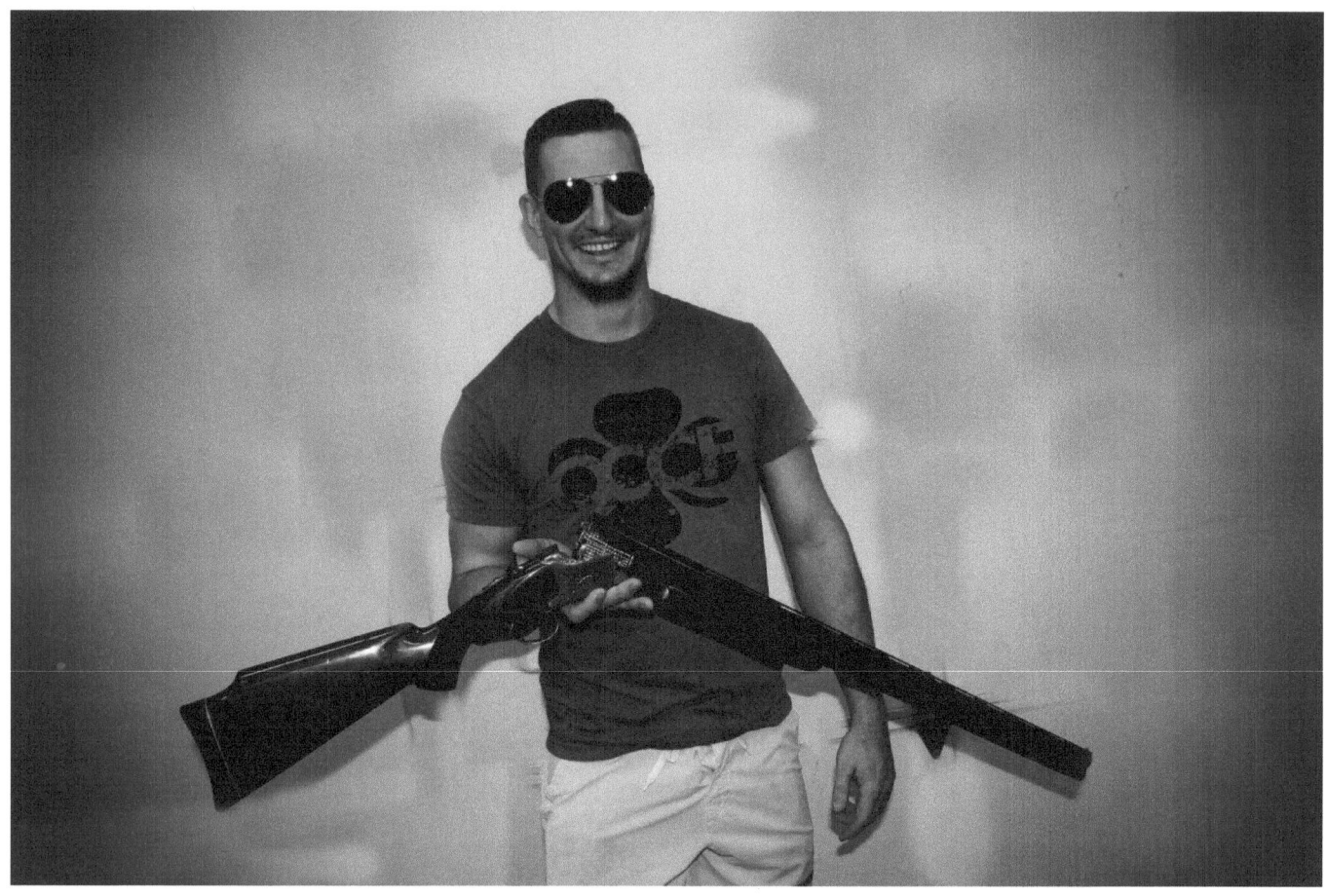

OBJECT:

SHOTGUN

WHY IS IT IMPORTANT TO HIM?

"This is the shotgun that I won Grand Nationals with in 2002 and I was 15 years old. It's a Winchester 101 Pigeon Grade. I've been trap shooting since I was around eight years old and been doing it ever since!"

HOLLY

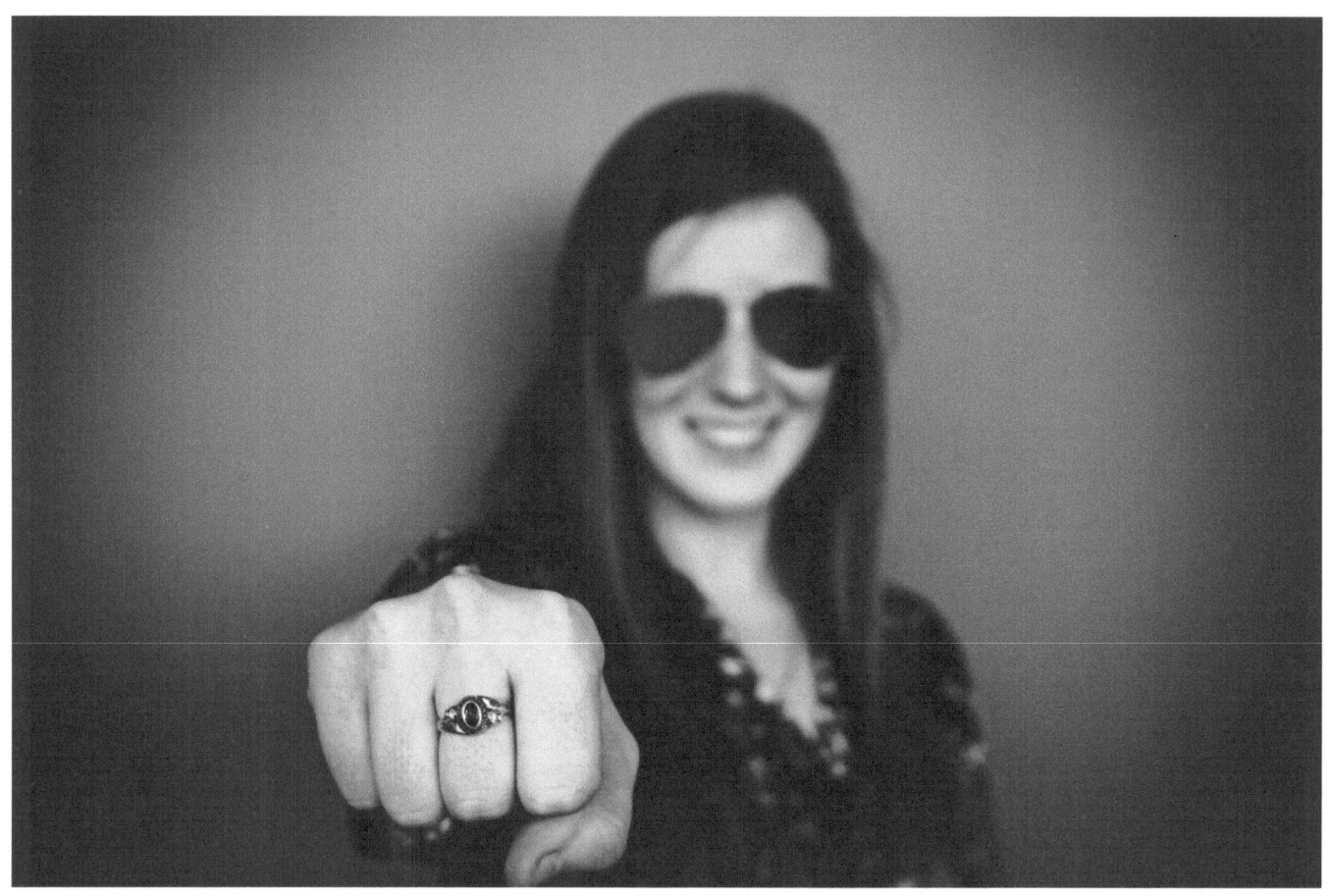

OBJECT:

UNIVERSITY RING

WHY IS IT IMPORTANT TO HER?

"MY PARENTS GOT IT FOR ME FOR GRADUATION. IT SAYS 'UNIVERSITY OF WESTERN ONTARIO' AROUND THE TOP AND IT'S PURPLE BECAUSE THAT WAS OUR SCHOOL COLOR... AND THEN (POINTS TO INSCRIPTIONS ON RING) 'KINESIOLOGY' AND THEN '2015'... AND THEN IT JUST SAYS 'LOVE MOM AND DAD.'

I ALMOST NEVER TAKE IT OFF. IT'S ACTUALLY BROKEN RIGHT NOW AND I HAVEN'T TAKEN IT OFF ONCE LONG ENOUGH TO FIX IT. SO I JUST WEAR IT ALL THE TIME. IT'S A REMINDER, BECAUSE I GO TO PALMER RIGHT NOW, OF WHERE I CAME FROM AND HOW FAR I'VE COME AND JUST TO KEEP PUSHING AND IT'LL ALL BE WORTH IT."

SAM

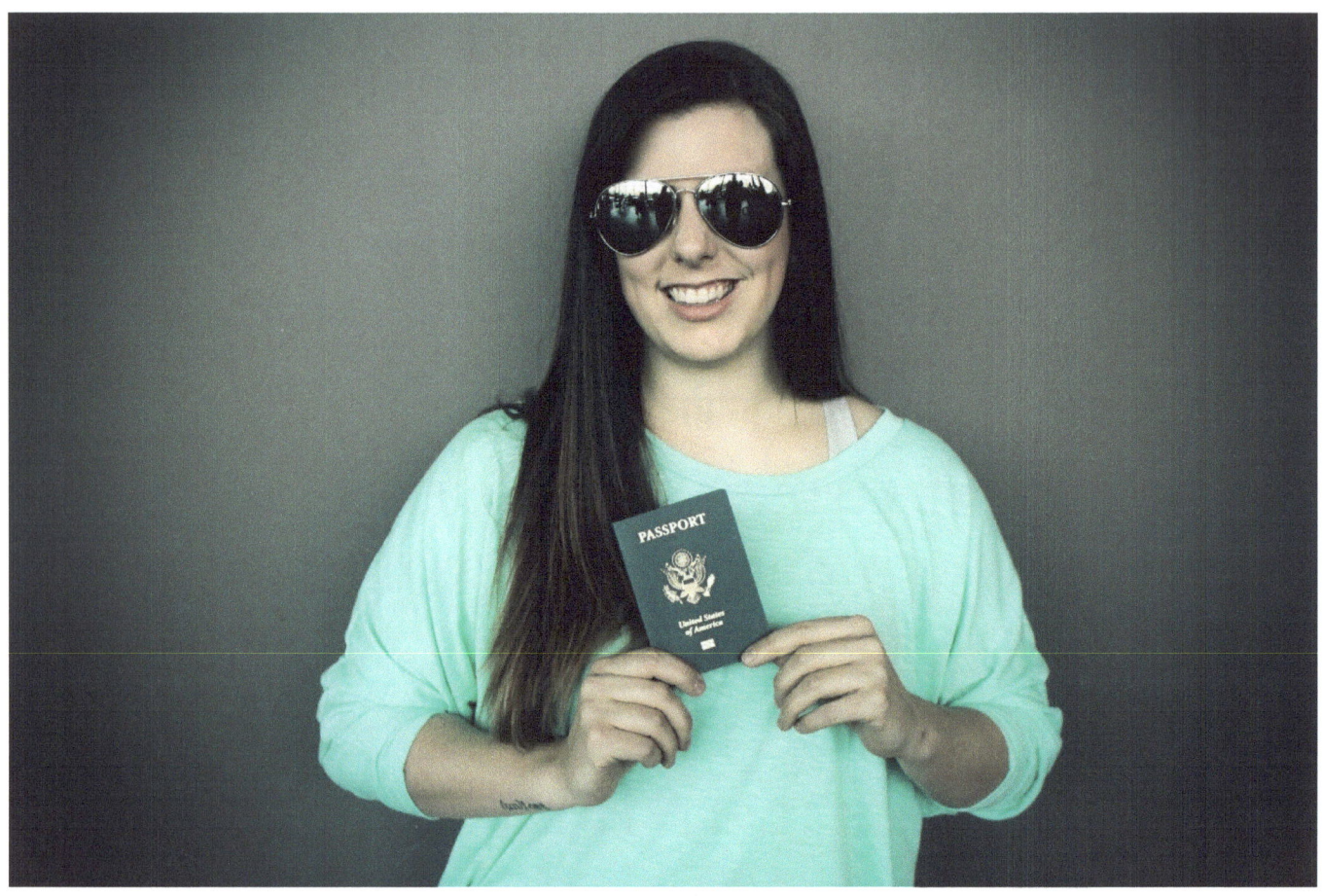

OBJECT:

Passport

WHY IS IT IMPORTANT TO HER?

"I've only had it for the last two years. So not super long, and I've only been to a couple places. I took myself to Paris. That was the first place I went, and I took myself to London.

Initially leaving the country, it's kind of a shock. Especially when you go to somewhere else that doesn't speak English, but I think once you get past that shock, you realize that no matter where people are, or what's going on, they're all doing the same thing as you.

They're all going to work. They're all coming home to their families. They're all going to see friends and going out to eat and whatever they may be doing, it's the same everywhere and people are people and we have more in common than we have different.

I think it's really important to get out of our bubble that we can get stuck in if we don't go anywhere and get to know other people. Get to know other kinds of people. Just to be more accepting, open minded, and welcoming."

RAMON

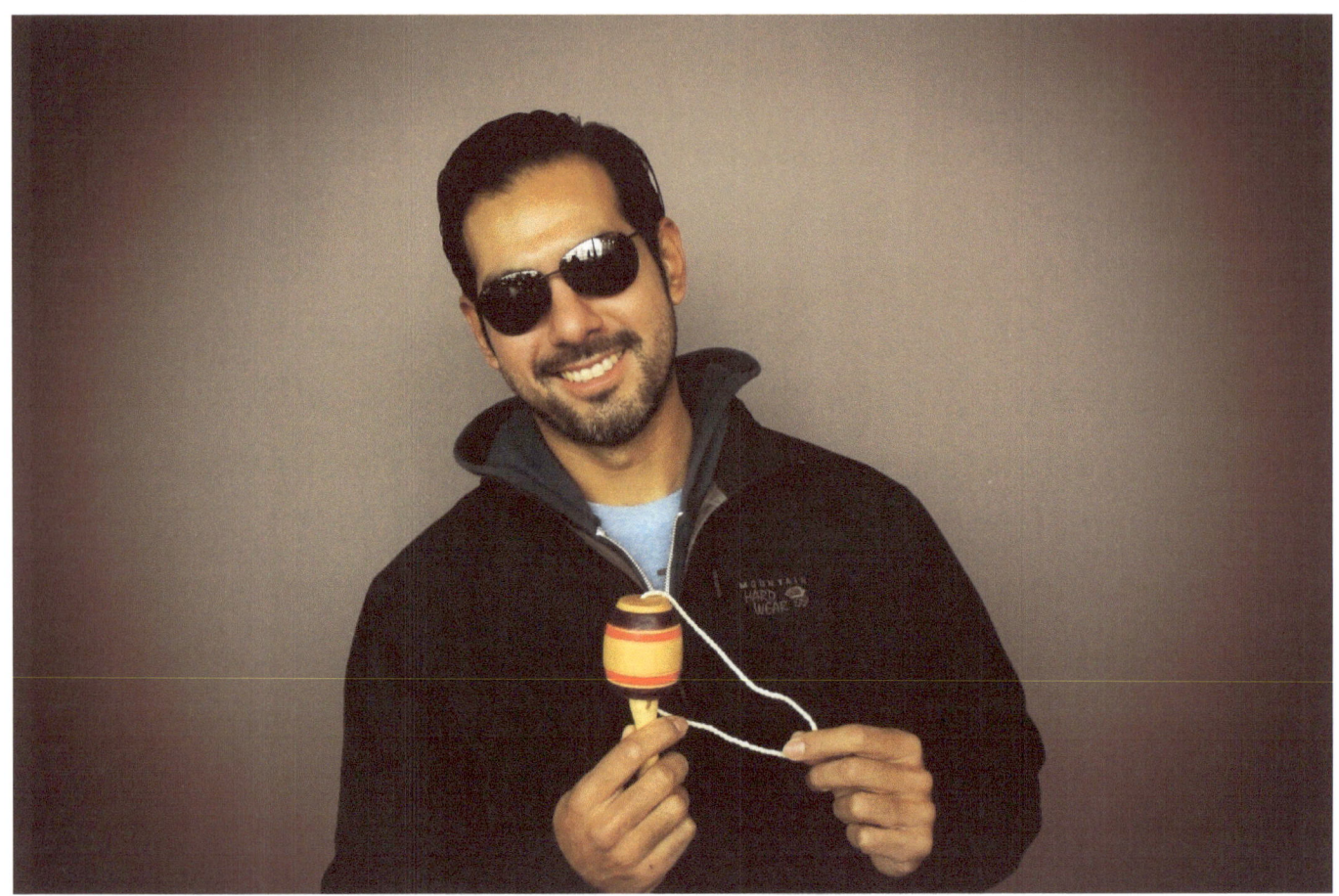

Object:

Traditional Mexican Toy – Valero

Why is it important to him?

"My dad gave it to me. He passed away three years ago. So every time I look at it, it reminds me about my dad and everything he taught me. How cool he was. It also in a way reminds me where I'm coming from. Don't forget my roots. Nobody plays this anymore, so my dad used to play it. He was super good at it. So every time he would show me how to do it, I was impressed.

You're supposed to flip this (the top) and it's supposed to go 360 and you're supposed to catch it with this thing (the bottom handle). You can do several tricks with it. It reminds me a little bit of a yo-yo. You can do a lot of tricks with those. So this one is a little different. It's hard!

It's an identity thing. Reminds me where I'm coming from and reminds me of my dad and my family back in Mexico."

SCOTT

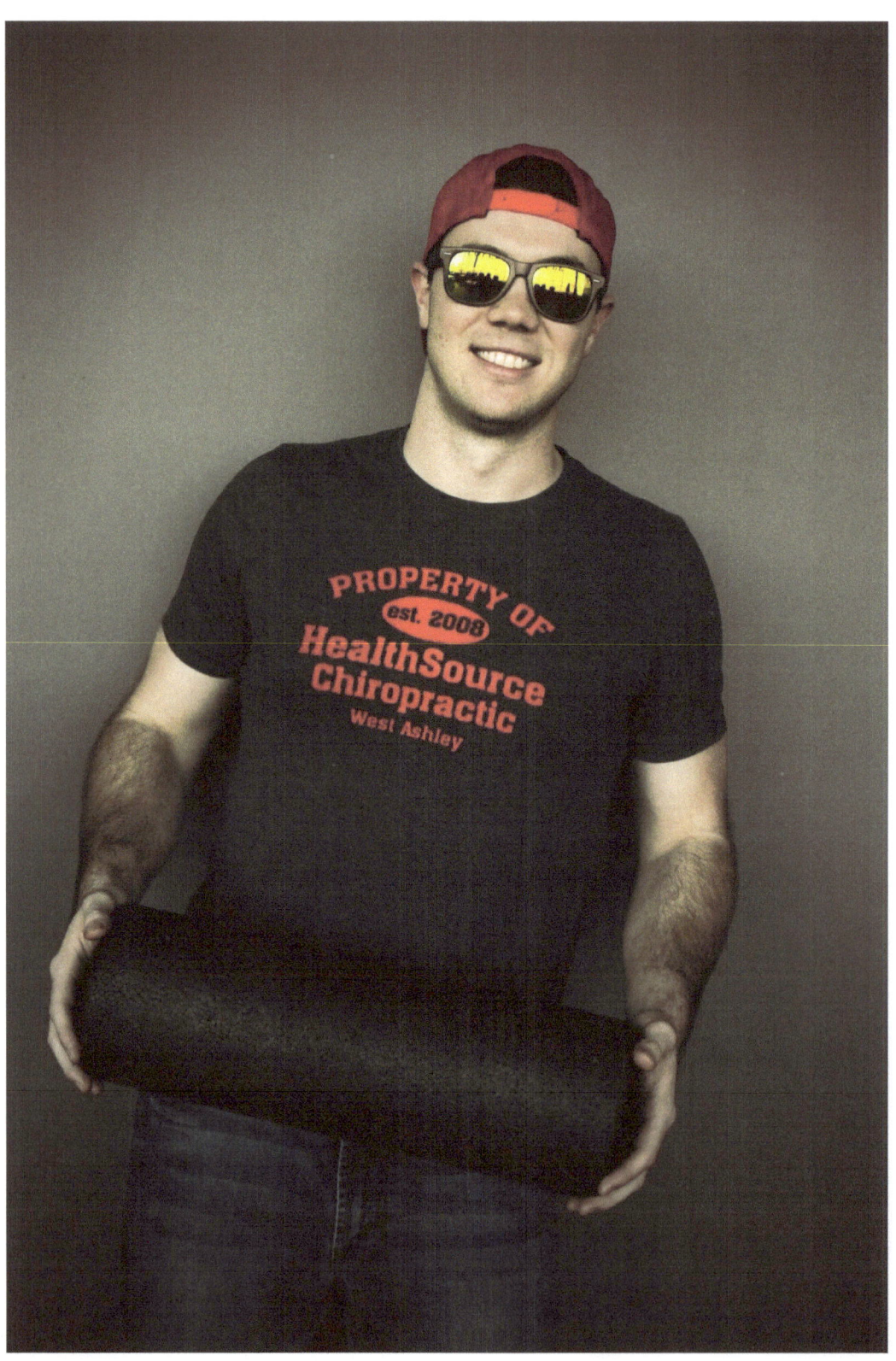

OBJECT:

FOAM ROLLER

WHY IS IT IMPORTANT TO HIM?

"I PUT A LOT OF VALUE IN GOOD POSTURE. I GO TO CHIROPRACTIC SCHOOL AT PALMER SO I'M REALLY INTERESTED IN HOW THE BODY WORKS AND TRYING TO MAKE IT WORK AS EFFICIENTLY AS POSSIBLE. NOW, THE FOAM ROLLER IS GOING TO ALLOW YOU TO MAKE SURE THAT YOU HAVE GOOD MOBILITY IN YOUR MOVEMENTS. MAKE SURE YOUR MUSCLES ARE FUNCTIONING PROPERLY. THAT THEY HAVE GOOD PROPRIOCEPTION AND VASCULARITY. SO IT'S BASICALLY WHAT MY WHOLE LIFE IS. I'M EITHER AT THE GYM OR AT SCHOOL LEARNING CHIROPRACTIC AND HOW THE BODY WORKS. SO, I FEEL IT'S UNIQUE ABOUT ME BECAUSE WHAT I WILL BE DOING FOR A LIVING.
I PERSONALLY HAVE REALLY GOOD MOBILITY AND I HAVE REALLY GOOD FORM IN ALL OF MY LIFTS. I FOAM ROLL EVERY SINGLE NIGHT AND IT REALLY HELPS ME IN EVERYTHING I DO. BOTH AT THE GYM, IT KEEPS ME HEALTHY. I RECENTLY GOT MY X-RAYS OF MY SPINE AND I'M DOING PRETTY WELL. I HAVE REALLY GOOD DISC SPACE SO IT'S ALL REALLY GOOD!"

KRISTEN

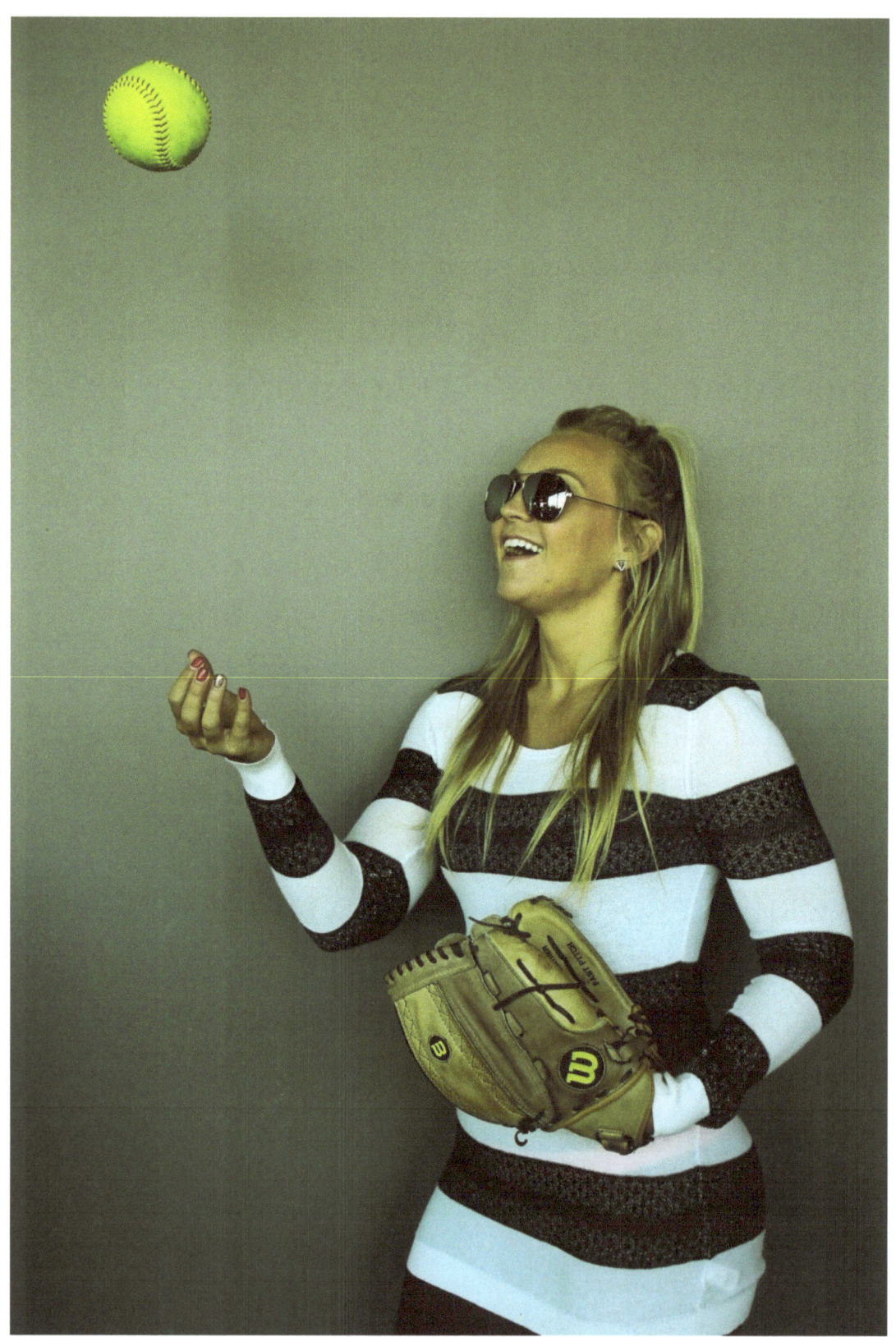

OBJECT:

SOFTBALL AND GLOVE

WHY IS IT IMPORTANT TO HER?

"SINCE I WAS A LITTLE KID, I HAVE ALWAYS BEEN INTO SPORTS. I STARTED PLAYING SOFTBALL WHEN I WAS ABOUT FOUR YEARS OLD. IN KINDERGARTEN I ACTUALLY HAD MY FIRST HOME RUN! SO, I DON'T KNOW IF IT REALLY COUNTS AS A HOME RUN, BUT I HIT IT OVER EVERYONE'S HEAD AND MADE IT HOME! FOR WHATEVER REASON SINCE THEN IT JUST STUCK WITH ME.

GROWING UP WITH SOFTBALL, IT WAS ALWAYS HARD BECAUSE I HAD COACHES SOMETIMES DIDN'T REALLY BELIEVE IN ME, OR THEY WOULDN'T PLAY ME BECAUSE THEIR DAUGHTER MAY HAVE BEEN ON THE TEAM AS WELL. SO, THERE WAS A PERIOD OF TIME WHERE I WAS ON THE BENCH AS A TEN YEAR OLD. I REMEMBER FEELING UPSET, BUT YOU'RE A KID SO YOU STILL HAVE FUN AND YOU HAVE FRIENDS AND YOU PLAY. I STILL STUCK WITH IT. I LOVED IT SO MUCH THAT IT DIDN'T BOTHER ME AT THE TIME.

BY THE TIME I WAS IN MIDDLE SCHOOL, I WAS ON THREE DIFFERENT SOFTBALL TEAMS FOR TWO OR THREE YEARS. MAYBE EVEN FOUR YEARS. SOMETIMES I HAD COACHES WHO LOVED ME AND I ALWAYS PLAYED, AND THERE WERE OTHER COACHES THAT NEVER PLAYED ME. STILL, I LOVED IT SO MUCH. I KEPT PRACTICING. I KEPT PLAYING. I JUST DID ANYTHING I COULD TO PLAY SOFTBALL.
TO THIS DAY I THINK BECAUSE OF SOFTBALL I HAVE THAT DRIVE AND DETERMINATION AND THAT WORK ETHIC TO JUST BE BETTER.

BY THE TIME I WAS IN HIGH SCHOOL I HAD THIS COACH RIGHT AWAY WHO BELIEVED IN ME AND DID EVERYTHING HE COULD TO HELP ME AND MAKE ME BETTER. BY THEN I WAS ALWAYS, ALWAYS PLAYING AND I LOVED IT. I JUST HAD CONFIDENCE. I WAS ALWAYS HITTING THE BALL HARD, AND AGAIN IT WAS STILL JUST SO MUCH FUN.

SO, BECAUSE OF HIGH SCHOOL, I ENDED UP PLAYING SOFTBALL IN COLLEGE. I WENT TO INDIAN HILLS COMMUNITY COLLEGE AND PLAYED SOFTBALL THERE. WE WENT TO NATIONALS MY FIRST YEAR. THE SECOND YEAR WAS A LITTLE BIT HARDER FOR ME JUST BECAUSE THERE WAS COMPETITIVENESS INVOLVED MORE IN COLLEGE THAN IN HIGH SCHOOL. AND I STILL THINK TO THIS DAY THAT DRIVE AND THAT WORK ETHIC, I BROUGHT IT WITH ME FOREVER AND I'LL HAVE THAT WITH ME FOREVER. IT WAS BECAUSE OF SOFTBALL THAT I AM SUCH A HARD WORKER AND THAT I MAKE MYSELF BETTER EVERY SINGLE DAY.

BY THE TIME I WENT TO ST. AMBROSE FOR MY JUNIOR AND SENIOR YEAR, I STILL PLAYED SOFTBALL AND MY SENIOR YEAR WAS PROBABLY THE BEST YEAR OF MY LIFE! IT WAS ALL BECAUSE OF THE HARD WORK GROWING UP SINCE I WAS FOUR YEARS OLD THAT BROUGHT ME TO THAT MOMENT. I HAD RECORDS IN THE AMBROSE RECORD BOOK. I HAD 12 HOME RUNS THAT YEAR. I MADE ALL TEAM, ALL CONFERENCE, FIRST TEAM ALL MIDWEST REGION. SO, KNOW I WAS ONE OF THE BEST IN THE MIDWEST WAS JUST SUCH AN ACCOMPLISHMENT. I LOOK BACK AND I FEEL SO PROUD OF MYSELF BECAUSE I WORKED SO HARD TO BE JUST A GOOD PLAYER AND I FINALLY DID IT. SO THAT'S WHY IT'S SO CLOSE TO MY HEART."

ERIKA

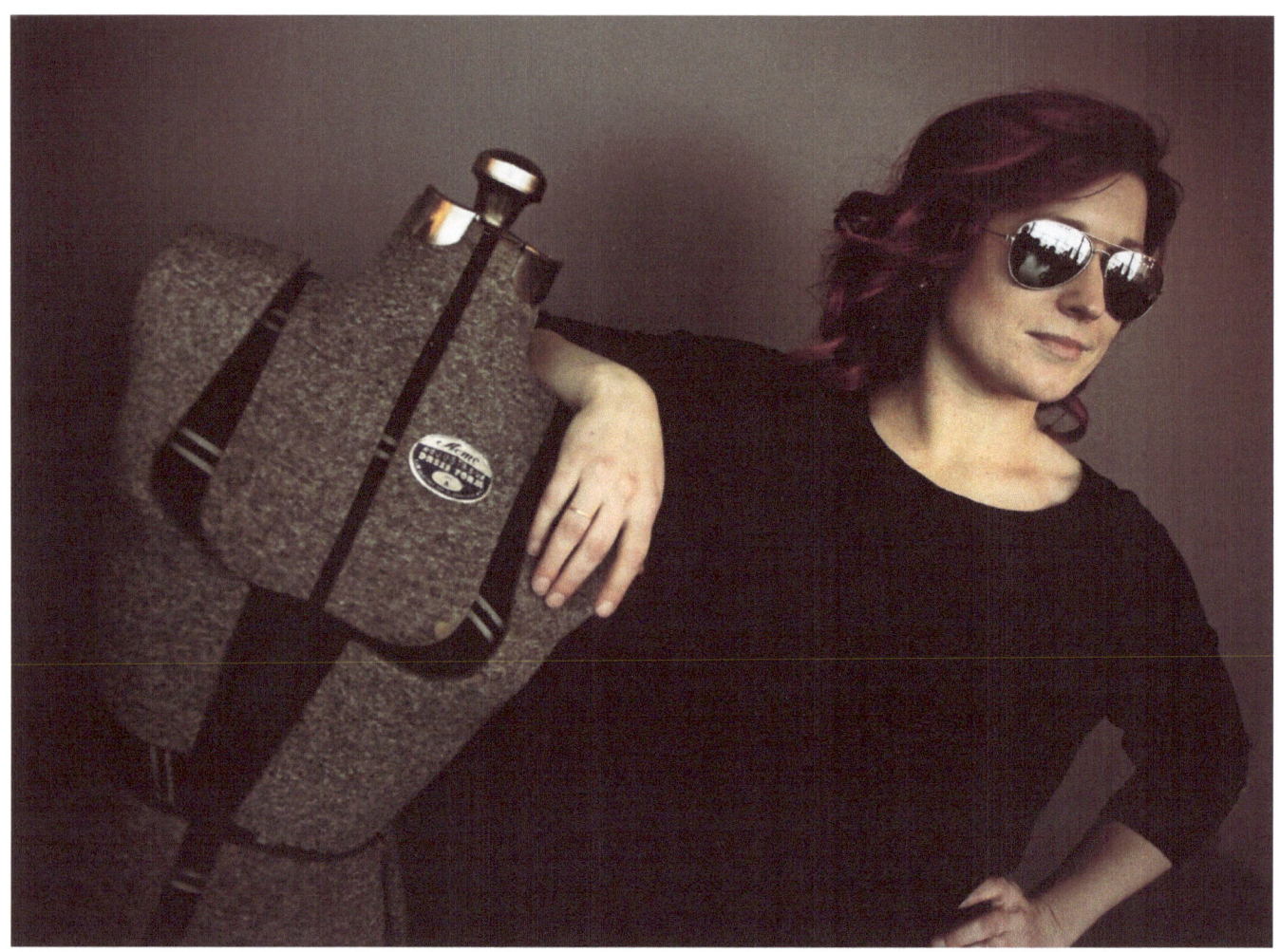

OBJECT:

DRESS FORM

WHY IS IT IMPORTANT TO HER?

"IT IS WHAT I CONSIDER TO BE MY BLANK CANVAS IN LIFE. I HAVEN'T HAD IT THAT LONG, BUT I'VE ALWAYS BEEN INTO THE ARTS AND CREATING THINGS. SO I CONSIDER MYSELF A BLANK CANVAS, AND THIS I THINK IS MORE REPRESENTATIVE OF ME AS A PERSON BECAUSE IT IS ADAPTABLE AND CAN TAKE ON ANY FORM AND NEW IDEAS AT THE DROP OF A HAT. I'VE CREATED MULTIPLE COSTUMES ON IT. HALLOWEEN COSTUMES OBVIOUSLY. THEY'RE A THING OF MINE. A HOBBY OF MINE.

I LOVE CREATING AND WHETHER IT BE ON THE DRESS FORM, ON CANVAS, ON MY HAIR, IN MY HOME, WHATEVER. I LIKE TO ALWAYS BE AWARE AND TAKING IN NEW IDEAS. SO, LIKE MYSELF, THE DRESS FORM IS A BLANK CANVAS. WHEN I LOOK AT THE DRESS FORM, I THINK OF SOMETHING NEW AND SOMETHING I HAVE YET TO DISCOVER!"

JONI

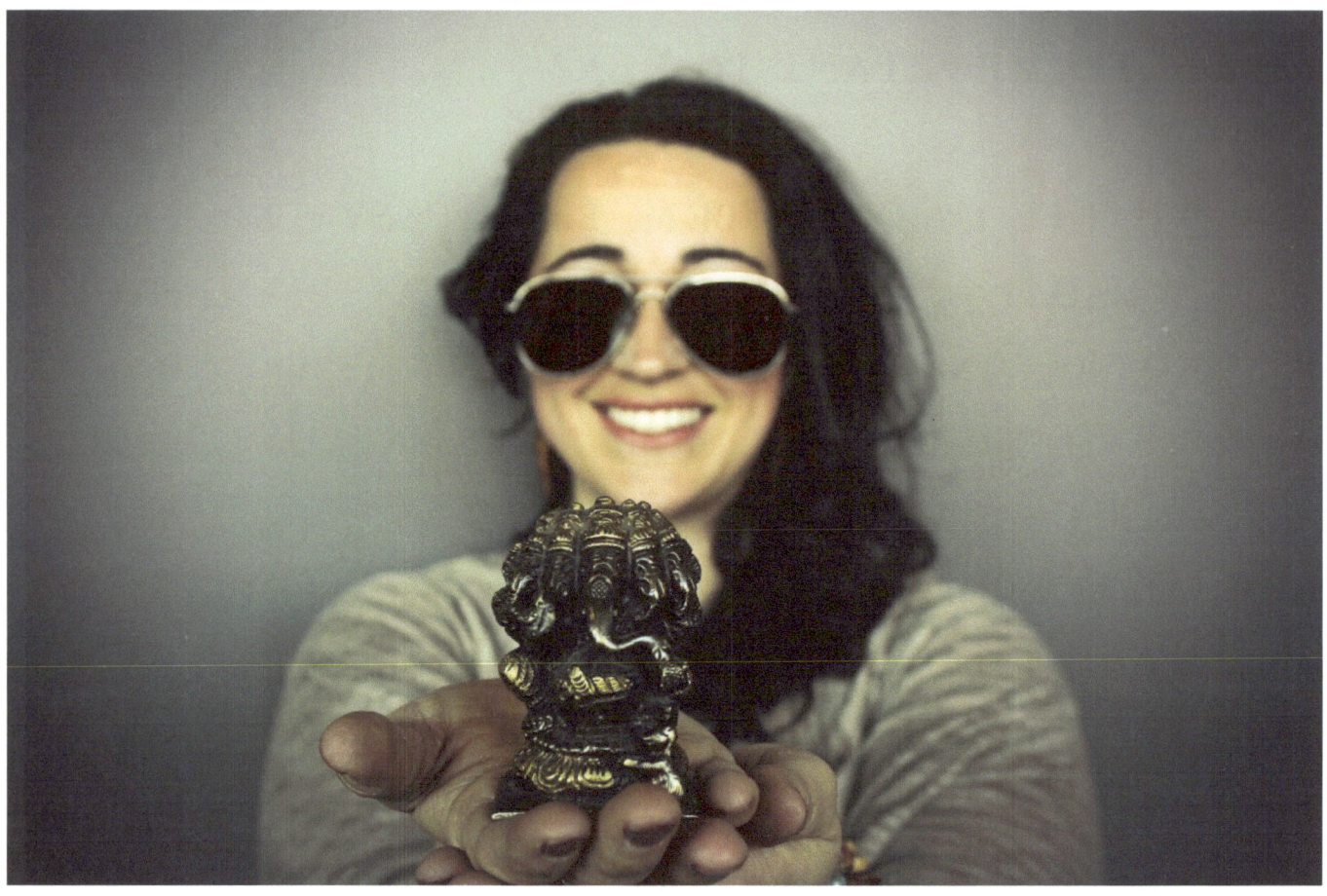

OBJECT:

GANESHA

WHY IS IT IMPORTANT TO HER?

"IT'S ACTUALLY A HINDU GOD. EVEN THOUGH I MYSELF AM NOT HINDU, I FIND CULTURE AND RELIGIONS OF THE WORLD ABSOLUTELY FASCINATING! IT REMINDS ME TO KEEP AN OPEN MIND. IT REMINDS ME TO KEEP A DIFFERENT PERSPECTIVE ON LIFE AND IT HELPS ME UNDERSTAND THAT WE ARE THE MYTHICAL STORYTELLING SPECIES THAT WE ARE! WE ARE A STORY TELLING PEOPLE AND WE HAVE BEEN SINCE THE BEGINNING OF TIME. SO, IT REALLY TACKLED SOME OF MY INTELLECT WITH STUDYING TRIBAL CULTURES AND RELIGIONS OF THE WORLD.

THIS GANESHA WAS GIVEN TO ME BY A VERY GOOD FRIEND WHO HAD SUFFERED LOSS IN HIS LIFE. HE SUFFERED IMMENSE CHILDHOOD PAIN AND TRAUMA AND WHEN HIS BEST FRIEND AND PARTNER DIED, THIS WAS A GIFT THAT SHE HAD ACTUALLY GIVEN TO HIM. IT'S BEEN PASSED ON TO ME AS A REMOVER OF OBSTACLES. THAT'S WHAT THIS GANESHA MEANS. IT MEANS 'A REMOVER OF OBSTACLES.' A PATRON OF THE ARTS AND SCIENCES. IT HELPED DURING CREATIVE WRITING. SO IT WAS GIVEN TO ME ON A SENTIMENTAL LEVEL, BUT ALSO I CONTINUE TO BE FASCINATED THE MORE I LEARN ABOUT IT!"

MARA

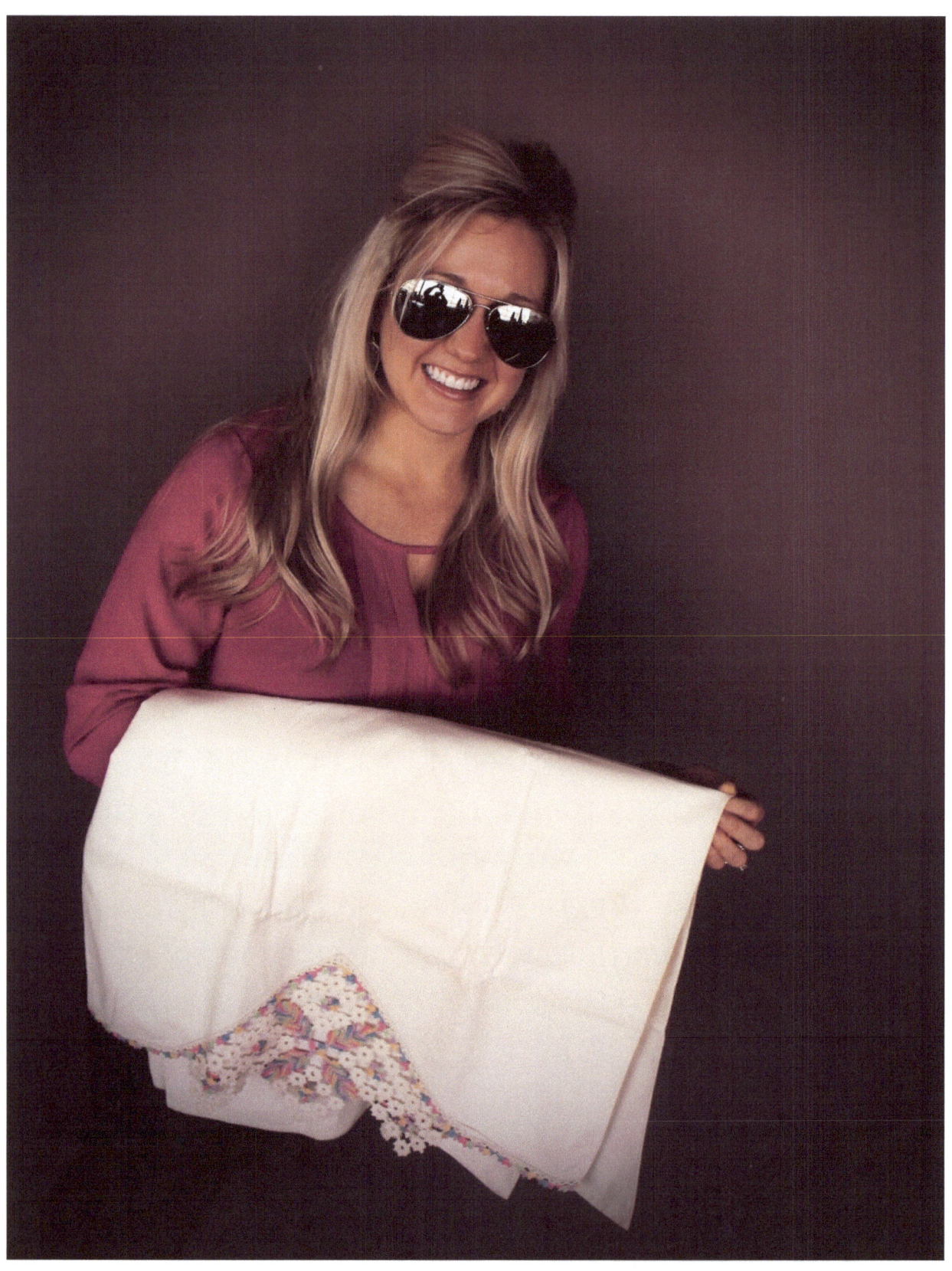

OBJECT:

PILLOW CASES

WHY IS IT IMPORTANT TO HER?

"THE ITEM I BROUGHT TODAY IS A PILLOW CASE THAT WAS GIVEN TO ME BY MY GRANDMA. IT'S ALL HAND STITCHED AROUND THE EDGING AND SHE GOT IT ABOUT 63 YEARS AGO AS A WEDDING GIFT AND SHE'S KEPT IT THAT WHOLE TIME AND SHE GAVE IT ME RIGHT AFTER I GOT MARRIED. SO IT'S SOMETHING THAT'S VERY SPECIAL TO ME AND HAS A LOT OF MEANING AND I HOPE TO HOLD ONTO IT FOR A LONG TIME AS WELL. I DON'T THINK I'LL EVER USE THEM FOR DISPLAY OR SET THEM OUT BECAUSE I DON'T WANT ANYTHING TO HAPPEN TO THEM. SO FOR NOW I JUST KEEP THEM IN A SAFE SPOT AND JUST LOOK AT IT EVERY ONCE IN A WHILE."

CHRISTIE

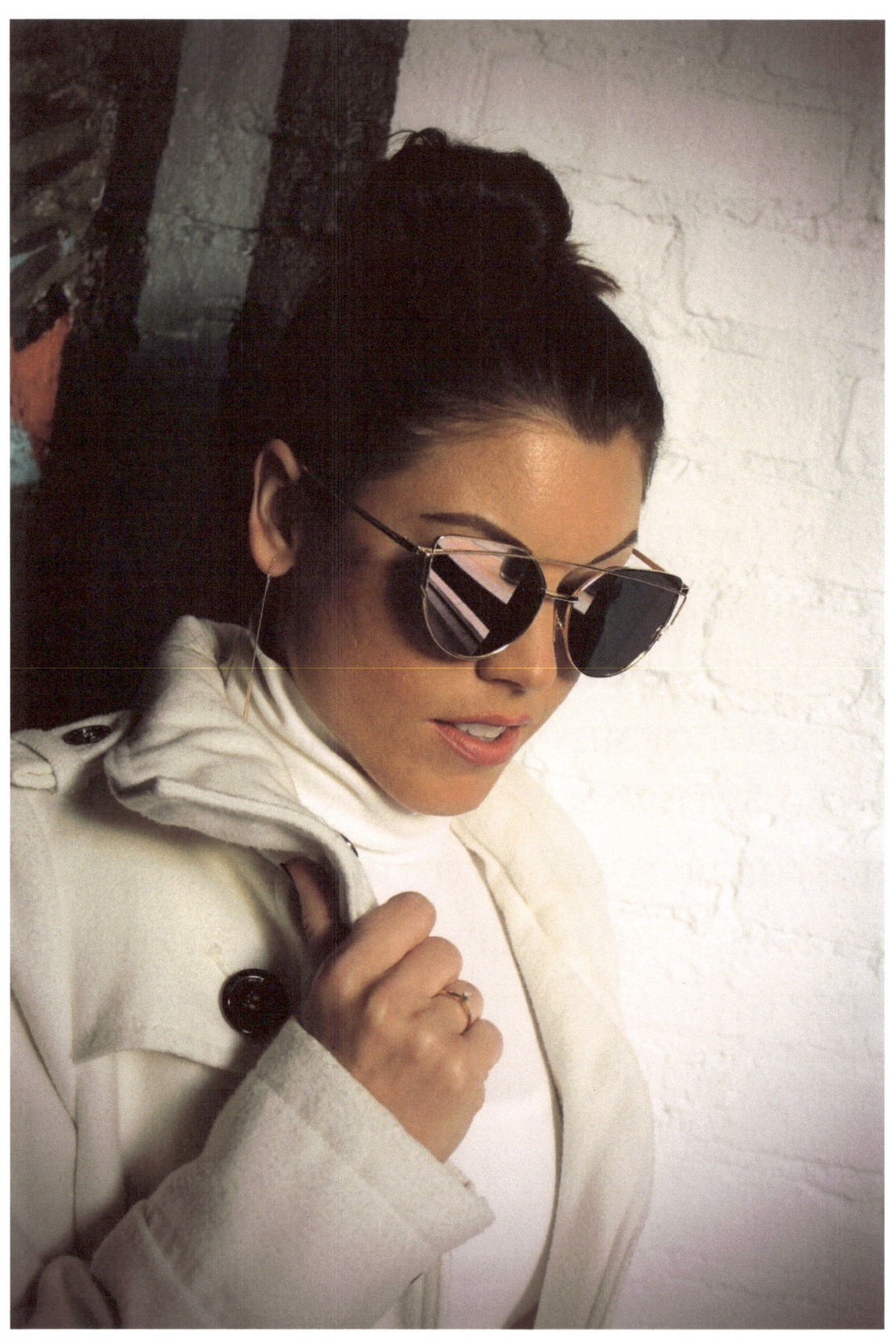

OBJECT:

Ring given to her by her mother

WHY IS IT IMPORTANT TO HER?

"I had always asked her if I could have one of her rings because she always wore so much jewelry. She always said that I couldn't have one because she didn't think I was responsible enough. That I would lose it. So, eventually one day just out of nowhere, she gave me the ring and she said, 'You can keep this and this is a promise ring. That I'll always be there for you.'

Since then, it has not come off my finger. So it's something that I always look at as the one consistent thing in my life, which is my mother. And it show to me that things, people, and experiences change day by day, but I know looking at this ring that I have this one constant thing. That I can always count on my mother to be there for me."

HECTOR

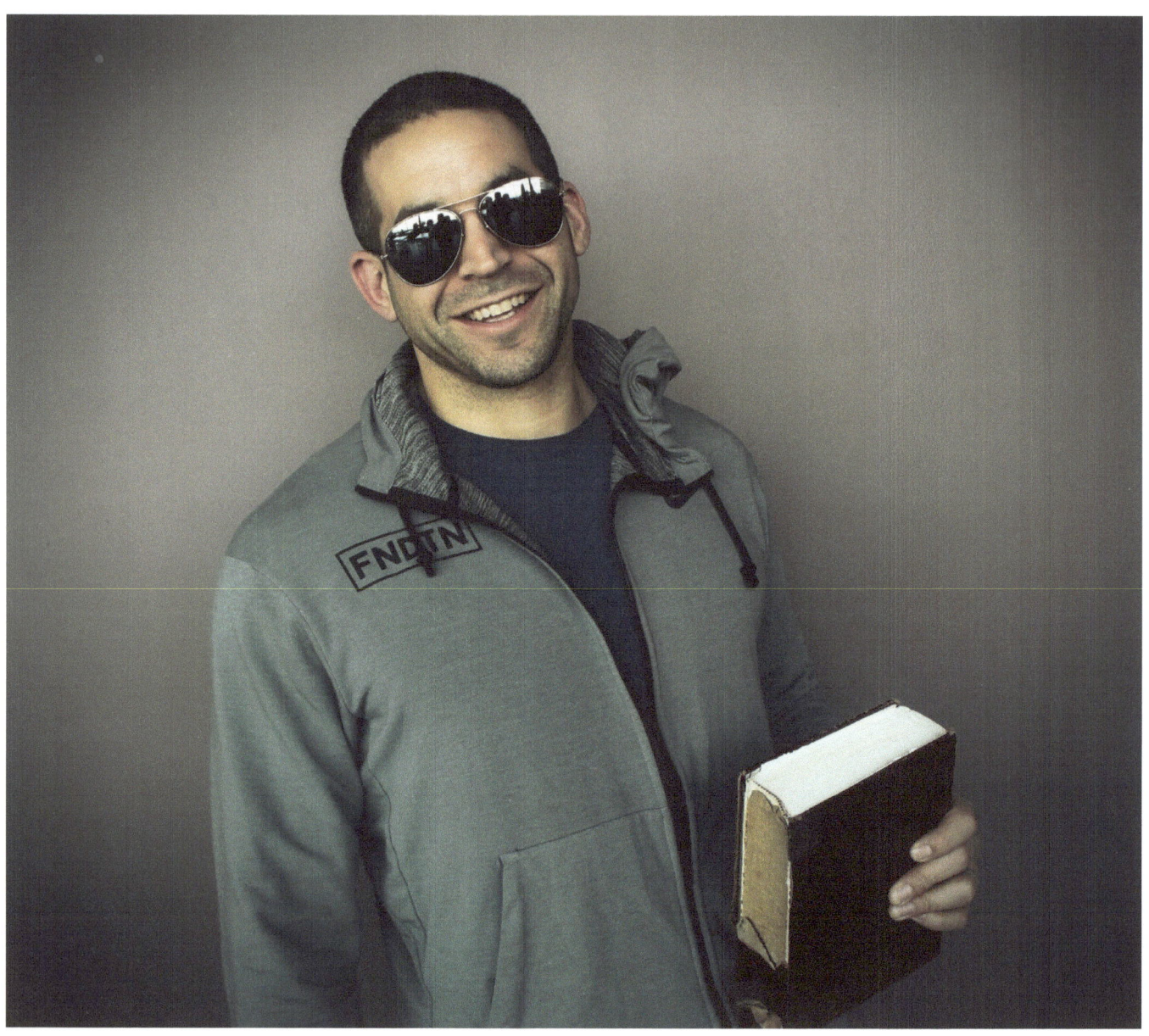

OBJECT:

BIBLE

WHY IS IT IMPORTANT TO HIM?

"IT WAS MY FATHER'S BIBLE ACTUALLY. THE REASON WHY IT'S
IMPORTANT TO ME WHEN IS BECAUSE IT SYMBOLIZES TWO THINGS. IT'S A
SPANISH/ENGLISH BIBLE. IT SYMBOLIZES MY CULTURE, AND IT COULD BE
THIS BIBLE. IT COULD BE ANOTHER ONE. THIS ONE JUST HAPPENS TO BE MY
FATHER'S BIBLE. THE REASON WHY IT'S IMPORTANT TO ME IS BECAUSE OF
THE VALUE THAT IT'S INSTILLED IN MY LIFE.

I THINK I'VE MADE A LOT OF DIFFERENT DECISIONS AND THERE'S BEEN A
LOT OF OUTCOMES IN MY LIFE THAT ARE CONTRIBUTED TO THIS BIBLE OR
THE WORD OF GOD. SO IT'S REPRESENTATIVE OF THE VALUES THAT HAVE
BEEN INSTILLED IN ME THROUGH MY CULTURE. I'M HISPANIC. I'M
MEXICAN. MY PARENTS ARE MEXICAN. SO, THE FACT THAT IT'S AN
ENGLISH/SPANISH BIBLE IS REPRESENTATIVE OF MY CULTURE. ESPECIALLY
MY LATINO CULTURE THAT I'M NOT ONLY MEXICAN, BUT I'M ALSO
AMERICAN. SO I'M MEXICAN, AMERICAN, AND LATINO.

IT HAS SHAPED ME IN MY LIFE. IT HAS PUT MY LIFE INTO PERSPECTIVE IN A
LOT OF DIFFERENT WAYS. SO THAT'S WHY IT'S IMPORTANT TO ME."

KATE

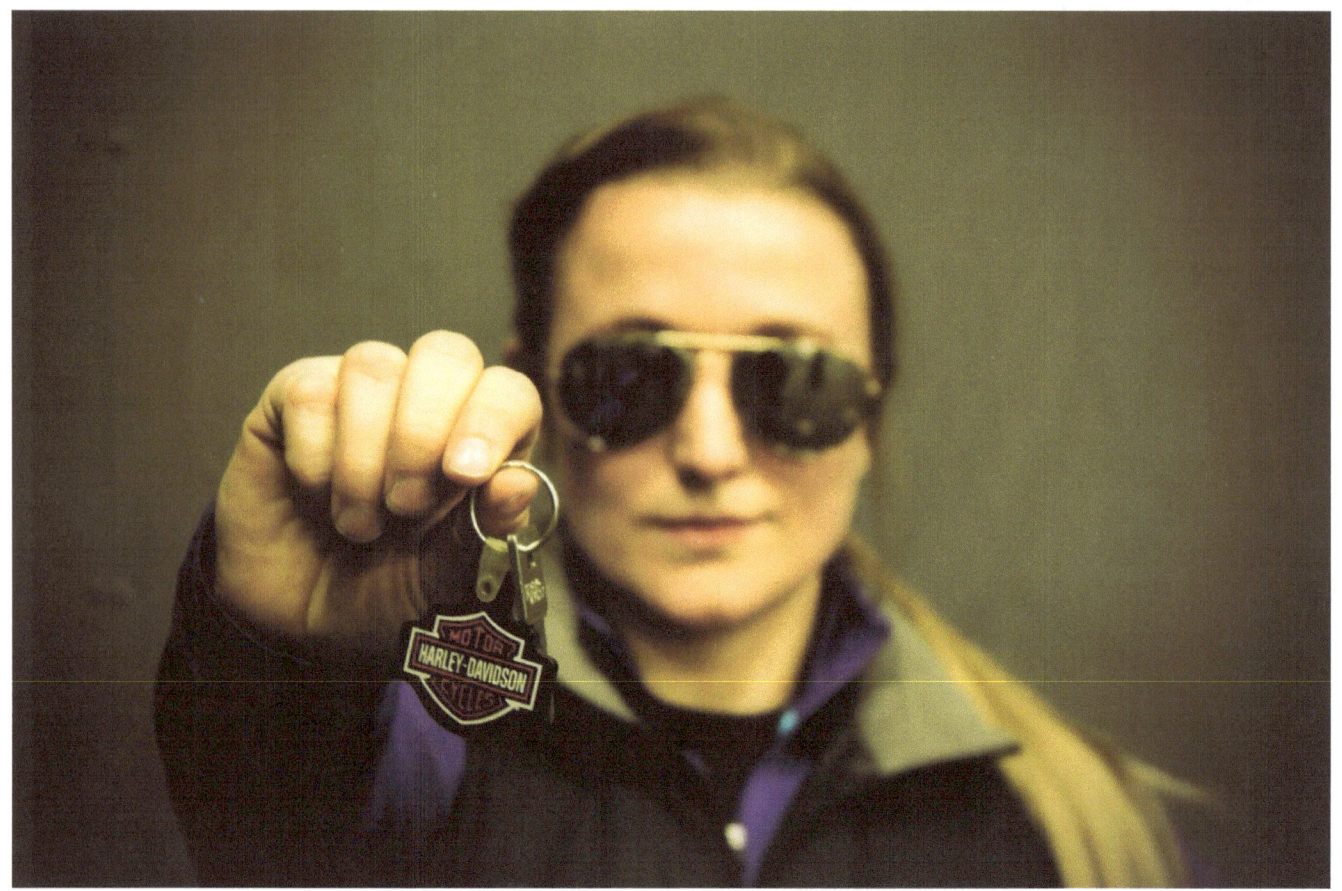

OBJECT:

MOTORCYCLE KEY

WHY IS IT IMPORTANT TO HER?

"TO ME IT'S A SYMBOL OF ME FINDING MY INDEPENDENCE. I HAD JUST GRADUATED FROM COLLEGE AND I WAS KIND OF LOST AT WHO I WAS AND WHERE I WAS GOING. ALL I KNEW IS THAT I REALLY LIKE TO RIDE MOTORCYCLES AND I WAS ALWAYS WAITING ON SOMEONE ELSE TO GIVE ME A RIDE AS A FEMALE.

SO AT THE END OF THE SUMMER I DECIDED I WASN'T GOING TO WAIT ANY MORE. I JUST WENT AND SCHEDULED TO TAKE A CLASS TO LEARN HOW TO RIDE AND I SET A GOAL TO BUY A HARLEY BY THE END OF THE MONTH, AND I GOT IT DONE!

I SPENT MY SUMMER RIDING AROUND THE MID-WEST FINDING MYSELF AND GAINING MY FREEDOM AND STRENGTH. SO I EVOLVED INTO A STRONG INDEPENDENT WOMAN BECAUSE OF MY BIKE, WHICH I FEEL LIKE HAS JUST OPENED UP SO MANY OTHER DOORS FOR ME!"

GYASI

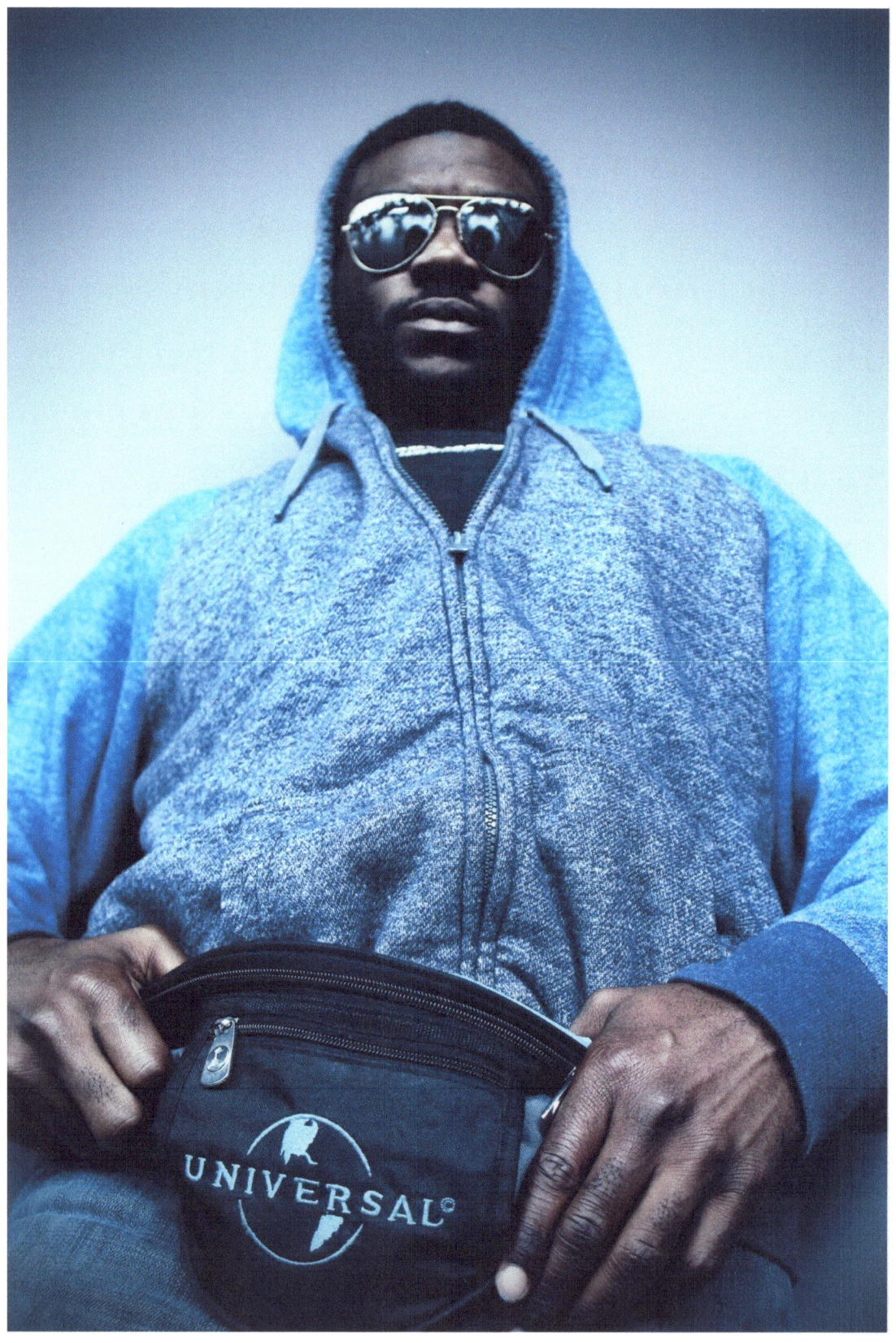

OBJECT:

FANNY PACK

WHY IS IT IMPORTANT TO HIM?

"I HAVE WITH ME MY 'UNIVERSAL STUDIOS' FANNY PACK THAT WAS GIVEN TO ME BY A VERY AWESOME PERSON THAT I HAVE MET IN MY LIFE, MR. JACKSON KELLY. STRAIGHT OUT OF AUSTRALIA. ABOUT A MONTH AGO HE MOVED BACK TO AUSTRALIA AND DID THIS REALLY COOL THING WHERE HE LEFT EACH ONE OF THE GUYS FROM THE HOUSE (THEY ALL USED TO LIVE TOGETHER) SOMETHING SPECIAL TO HIM. ONE OF OUR FRIENDS GOT A WRESTLEMANIA COWBOY HAT. SOMEBODY GOT A BOTTLE OPENER OR A POSTER OR WHATEVER. HE LEFT ME A 'UNIVERSAL STUDIOS' FANNY PACK THAT I HAVE NOW MADE A TREND ALL OVER THE GLOBE! IT IS THE GREATEST THING IN THE WORLD!"

LINDSAY

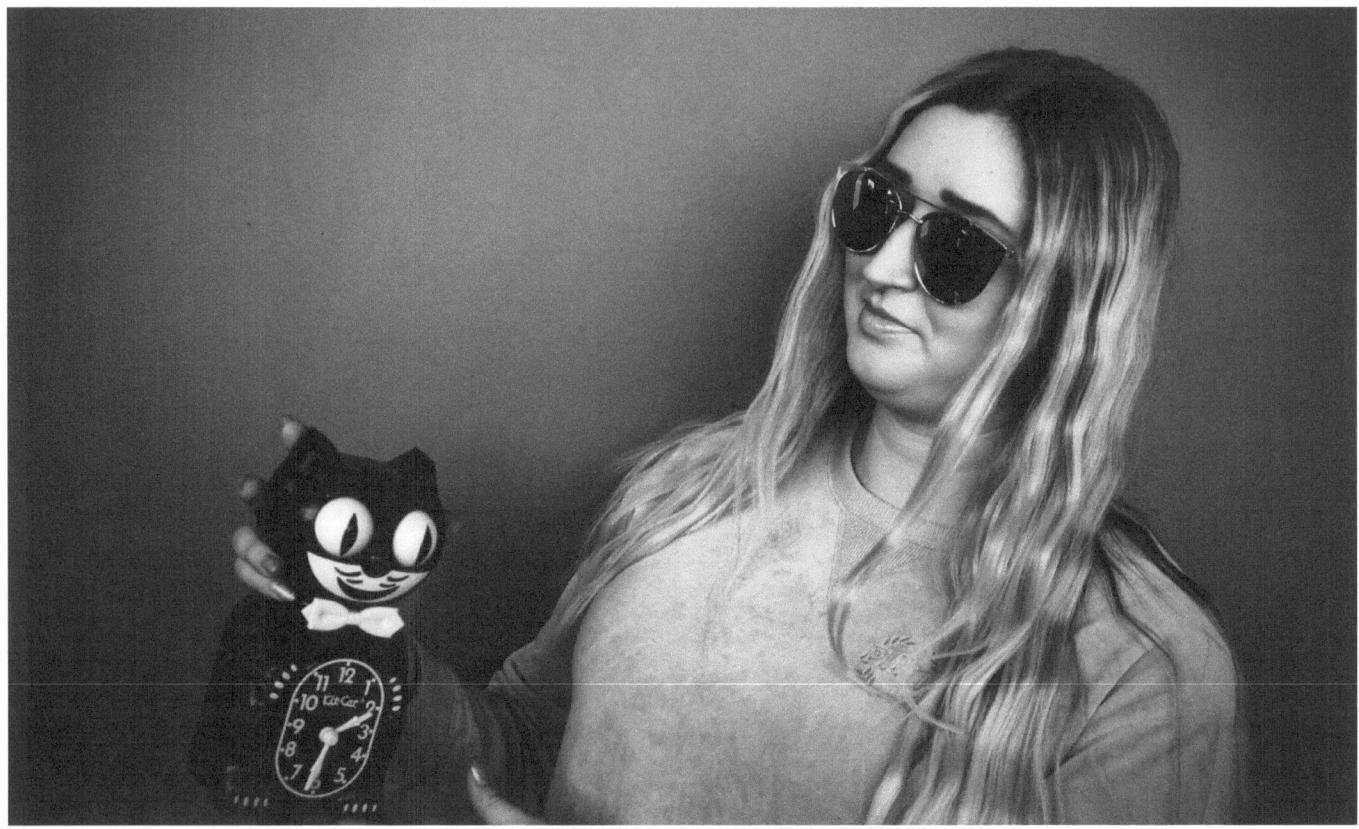

OBJECT:

KIT CAT CLOCK

WHY IS IT IMPORTANT TO HER?

"1. BECAUSE IT'S A CAT AND CATS ARE PRETTY AWESOME. I LIKE ANIMALS A LOT.

2. I GOT IT ABOUT A YEAR, OR YEAR AND A HALF AGO WHEN I WAS GOING THROUGH SOME REALLY BIG CHANGES IN MY LIFE. SOME GOOD CHANGES, BUT IT WAS KIND OF A SCARY TIME, SO IT KIND OF MAKES ME THINK OF HOW FAR I'VE COME.

THE 3RD REASON IS BECAUSE IT'S A CLOCK. I KIND OF THINK DEEPLY INTO THINGS. PROBABLY A FEW TIMES A DAY. I THINK PEOPLE MINDLESSLY LOOK AT CLOCKS AND WISH THEIR TIME AWAY DURING THE DAY, AND I THINK THAT TIME MEANS MORE THAN WHAT PEOPLE GIVE IT CREDIT FOR SOMETIMES. I THINK THAT EVERY MOMENT THAT YOU'RE GIVEN IS A GIFT AND I TAKE TIME TO REFLECT UPON MY LIFE AND IF I'M LIVING IT HOW I'D LIKE TO LIVE IT. TRYING TO MAKE SURE THAT I'M FOLLOWING THROUGH WITH MY DREAMS.

I JUST THINK THAT IT'S IMPORTANT TO REALIZE THAT LIFE'S A GIFT, AND THAT SINCE YOU'RE NOT GIVEN GUARANTEED AMOUNT OFF TIME, THAT YOU TELL YOUR LOVED ONES THAT YOU LOVE THEM EVERYDAY AND JUST REALLY TRY TO FOCUS ON FOLLOWING THROUGH WITH YOUR DREAMS."

ZACH

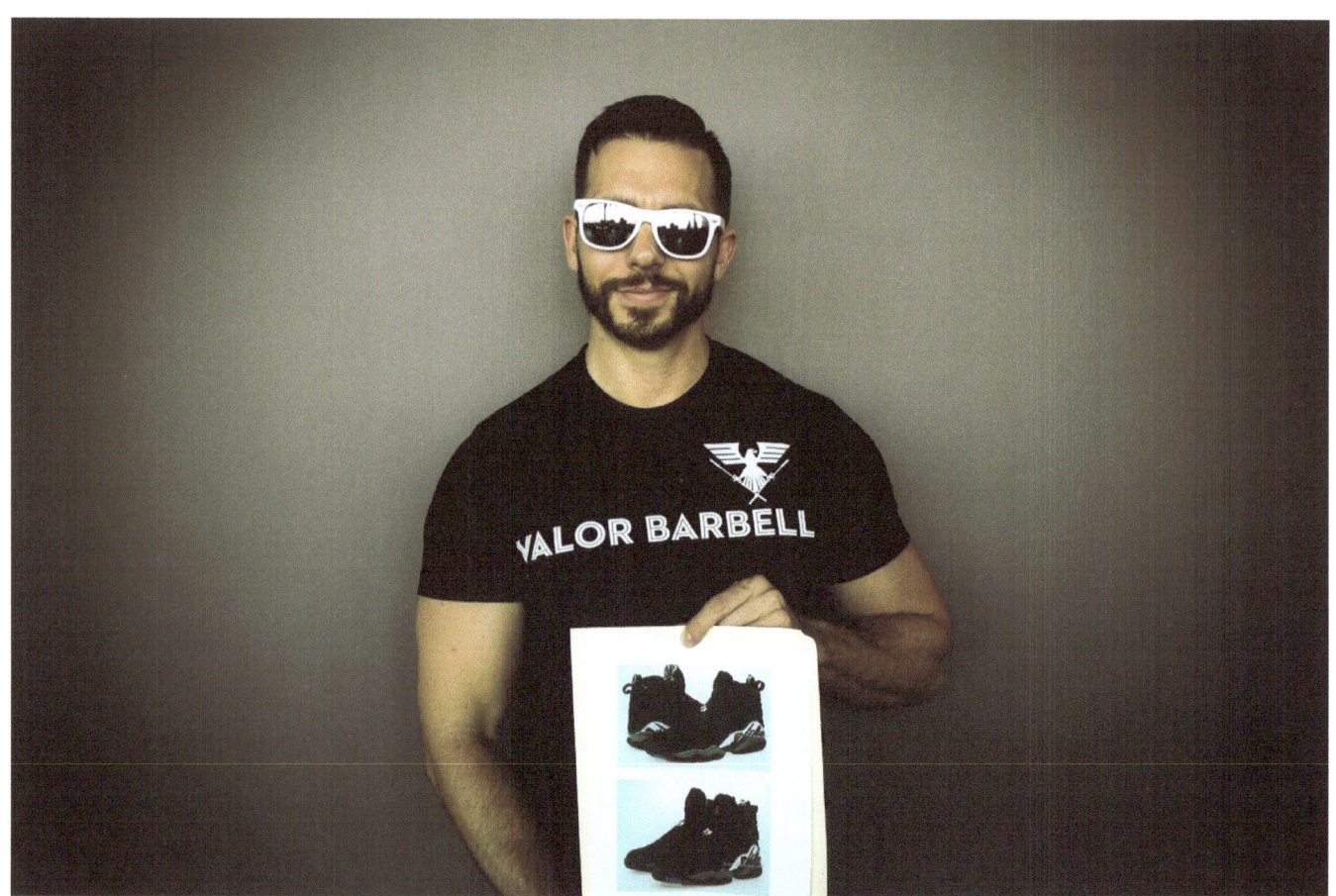

OBJECT:

JORDAN 8 SHOES

WHY ARE THEY IMPORTANT TO HIM?

"A lot of people do not realize that I grew up fairly poor. Shortly after my parents divorced, my Mom decided to go back to college and did not work at the time. We lived in low income housing and lived on a tight budget. I did not have name brand clothes or shoes growing up. The kids at school would pick on me or make fun of me frequently for not having name brand cloths or shoes.

One day I was able to convince my Dad to buy me the 1993 Air Jordan's. I'm not sure what the occasion was for buying them, but I could not wait to wear the coolest shoe on the market to school. When I went to school the next day, the kids noticed the new shoes. I still remember a kid saying, 'It's about time you got a decent pair of shoes.' Not only was I poor, but was also the smallest kid in class so I was often bullied. The 93 Air Jordan was the first name brand shoe I had that I can remember and represented one less thing for kids to pick on me about.

Unfortunately kids can be very materialistic. I don't know if you could ever truly stop bullying, but I encourage everyone to donate their old cloths or shoes. They may go a long way for some kid out there and mean more to them than you may think."

CRYSTAL

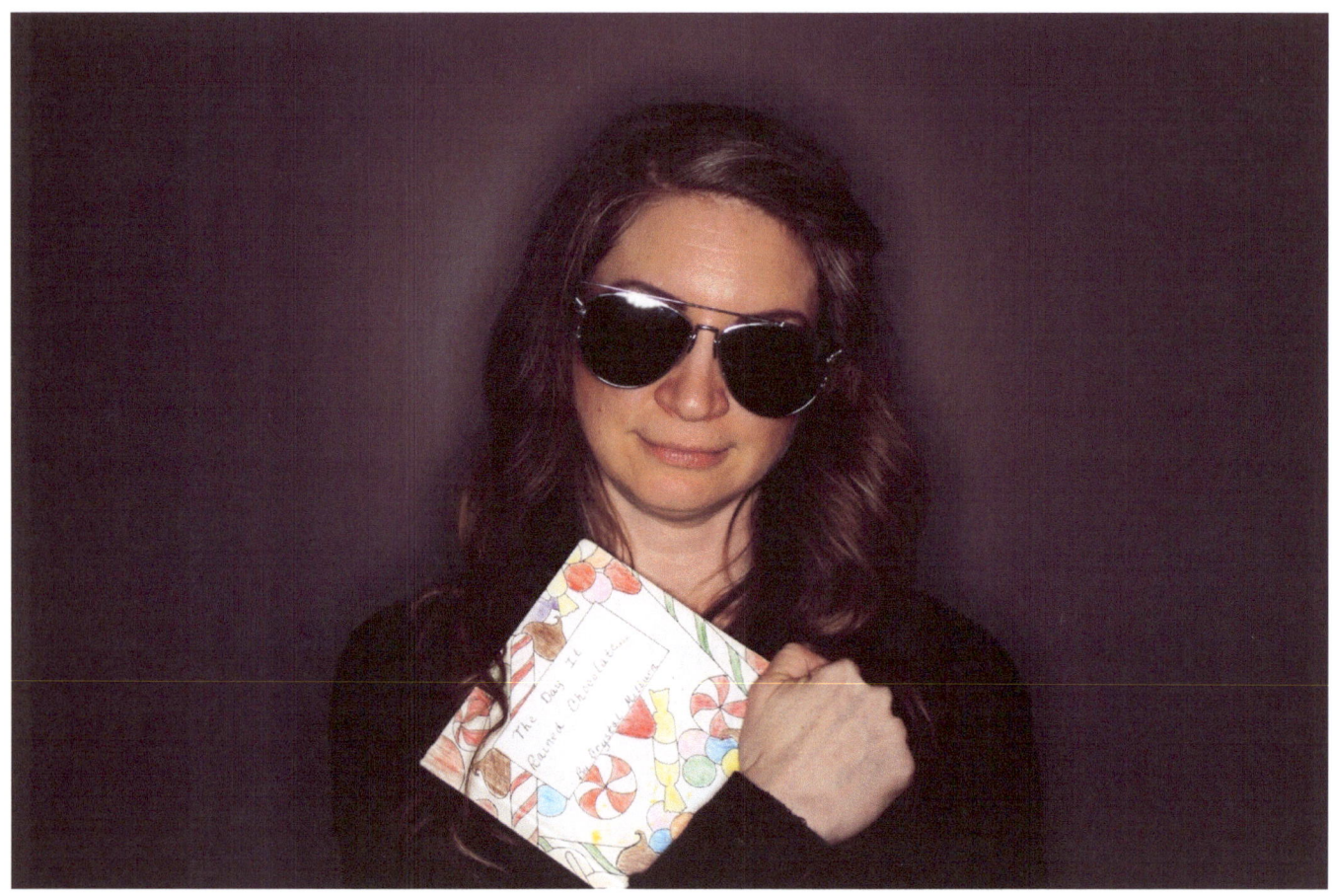

OBJECT:

Her first book

WHY IS IT IMPORTANT TO HER?

This is for the gendered and the non-gendered. The parents and the non-parents. The marrieds and the singles. The baby boomers and the millennials. The artsy folks and the left brained folks. This is for everyone.

I entered a book writing contest in in 3rd grade and made it to the next level of competition. I don't recall how far I got or what small prize I won because the moral of the story has less to do with the contest and more to do with learning a life lesson...or 12.

There's something special about firsts, and there's something uninhibited about being a kid. This book reminds me of a time I had no fear and was unfiltered. When I wasn't trying to fit a mold or expectation. When I just put it all out there with zero regard for judgment or failure.
I haven't written a book since. I didn't even realize that I wanted to be a writer until about 30 years later. My first thought about writing a book now? Oh gosh, me? Maybe someday but certainly not now. How could I do that now?! I'm not an AUTHOR!

And then this book reminds me that I am - I am whatever I want to be - and I already got the first one out of the way! Initial hurdle cleared.

A few things I think humankind could use more of are: Big Magic, Untethered Soul(s), Love Warrior(s) and lots of Rising Strong (some of my favorite books but also great sentiments, dontchathink?). The more we can untether from who we thought we were supposed to be and just be; the more we can lift each other up, starting with ourselves; the more we can love fearlessly and keep our hearts open; the more we can rise strong...the more content I think we will be. Content with ourselves, which is super important so that we can then be content with others. With..."outsiders."
Yup, inner and world peace. Because, why not?

Who else wants in (or out, where applicable)? Here's to channeling our fearless, youthful selves and being BIG rather than making ourselves small. Our gifts - your gifts - are needed and wanted and only we can give them. Don't keep your true self – your whole-soul-self - from this world because this world needs you. All of you. Don't hold back but instead rise STRONG, warriors!

P.S. There really is no such things as outsiders! We (humans) totally made that up.

MIGUEL

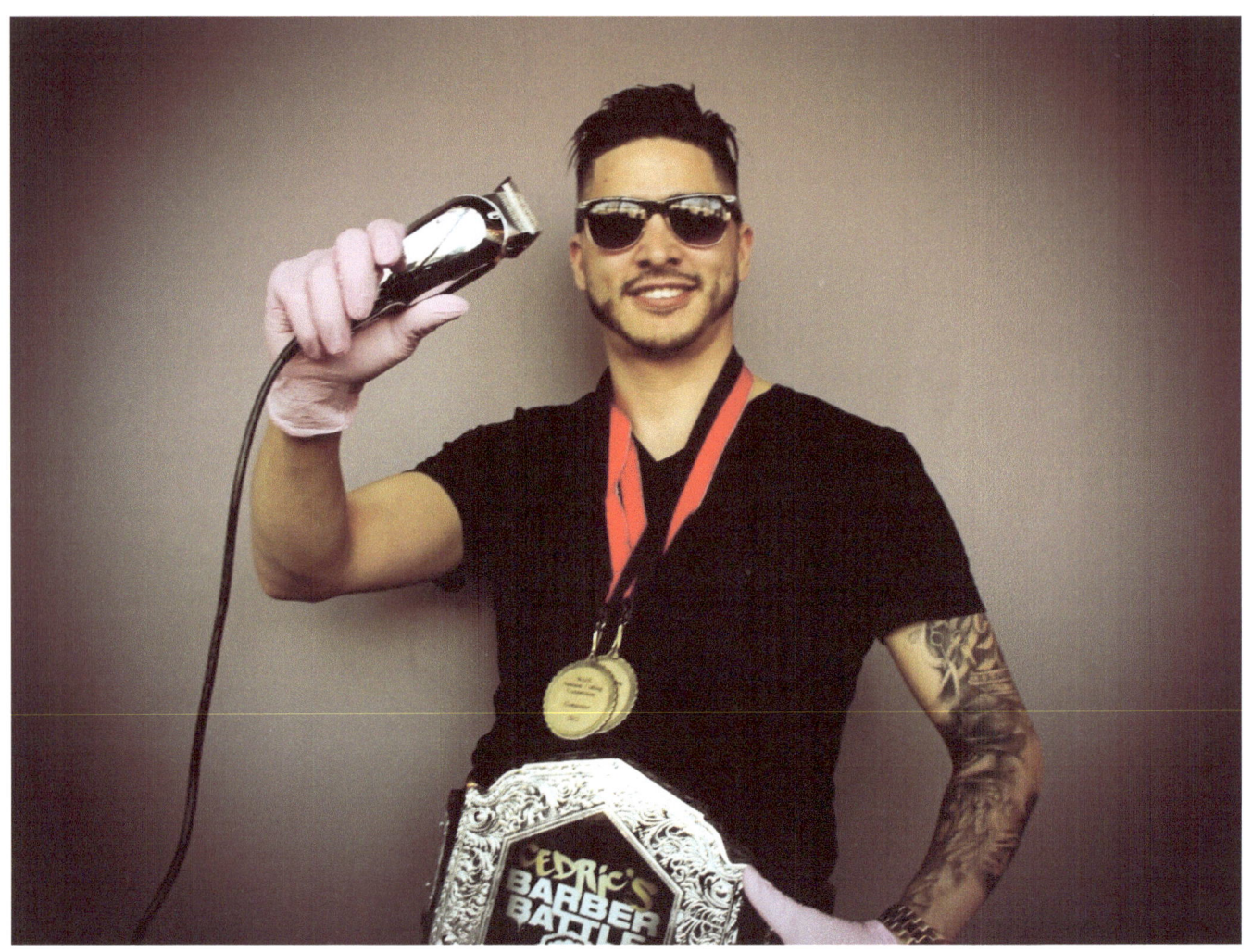

OBJECT:

Clippers and hair cutting awards

WHY ARE THEY IMPORTANT TO HIM?

"I do a lot of hair designs and I used to compete. I don't compete any more, but that was one of the things that inspired me. I started going to barber shows and I started seeing these barber battles. So I decided I wanted to enter them, because you could win trophies and also you're the best of the best if you're winning. So I wanted to be the best.

I started attending barber shows in 2011 and ever since I started competing up until probably two years ago (was when I stopped), I competed in over a dozen hair shows...and I've won 26-27 trophies since then!

What I have with me today? One of them is a medal from 2012 for a 'Wahl National Haircut Cutting Competition.' One of them was from 2011, which was the first one I ever attended. In the first one I ever attended, I actually got 3rd place in.

I brought my favorite pair of clippers, which are the Whal Sterling Reflections, and it's pretty much the clippers that I use on almost all the haircuts that I do.

I brought, it looks like a championship wrestling belt or boxing belt, fighting belt, UFC belt. It's a belt that I won attending a TV show with Cedric the Entertainer. It was a barber battle reality TV show. Each episode had one winner, and the episode that I was on, I won! So each winner won a belt and $15,000!"

ADARA

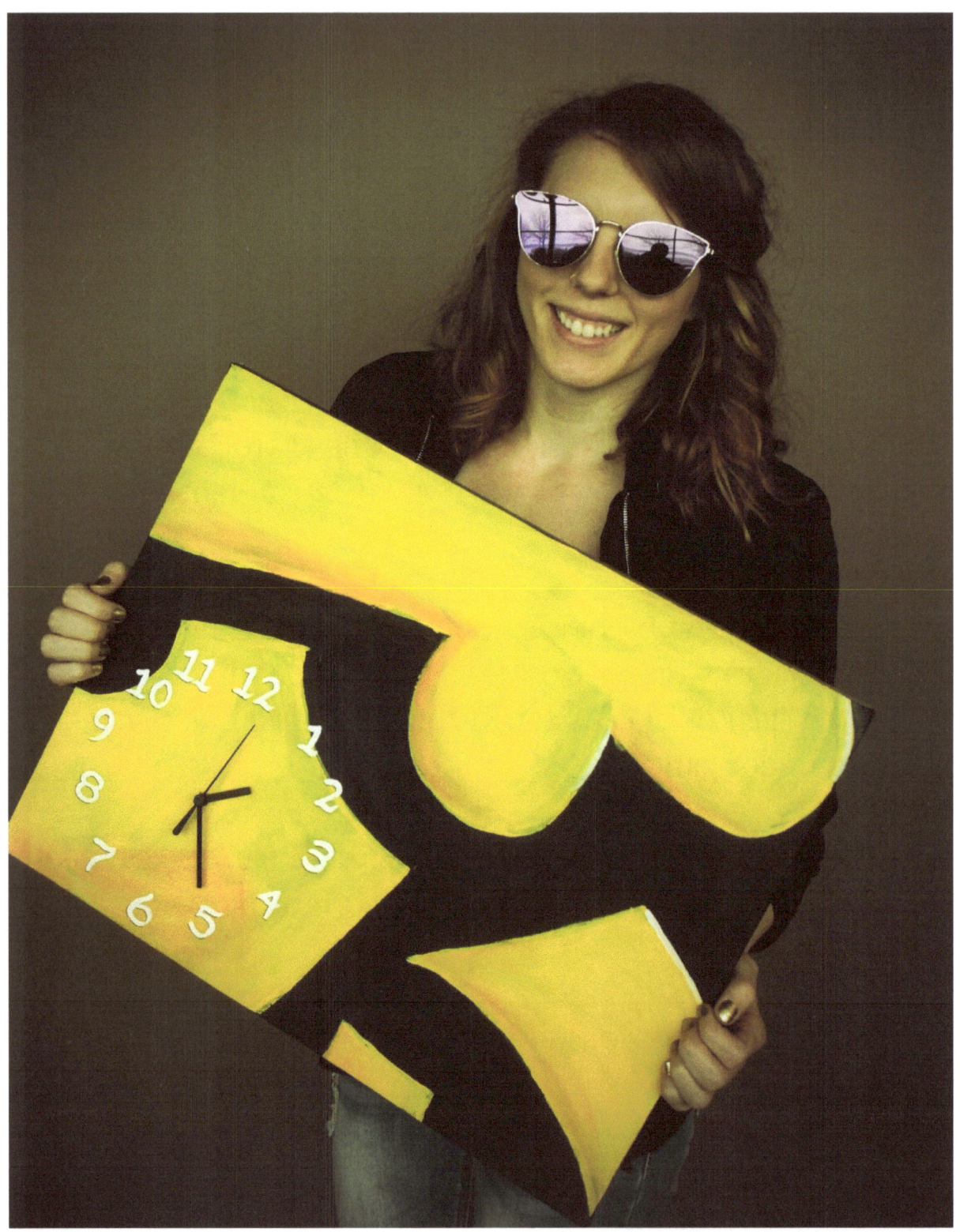

OBJECT:

Hawkeye Clock

WHY IS IT IMPORTANT TO HER?

"My brother actually painted this. He's a good artist and for the longest time I always wanted him to paint me something. I went away to Iowa (University of Iowa) my freshman year and he asked me that summer what motivated me. It took me a couple days to finally get back to him, but I finally said, time motivated me to pursue the things I love. Especially because I was on the gymnastics team at the time there, so that's what I was pursuing at the time and that's what my passion was.

So that December for Christmas, he actually painted me a Hawkeye that was on a canvas with a clock in the corner, because time motivates me. That was actually the first gift that I've ever gotten for Christmas or from anyone that actually made me cry!"

JOHNNIE

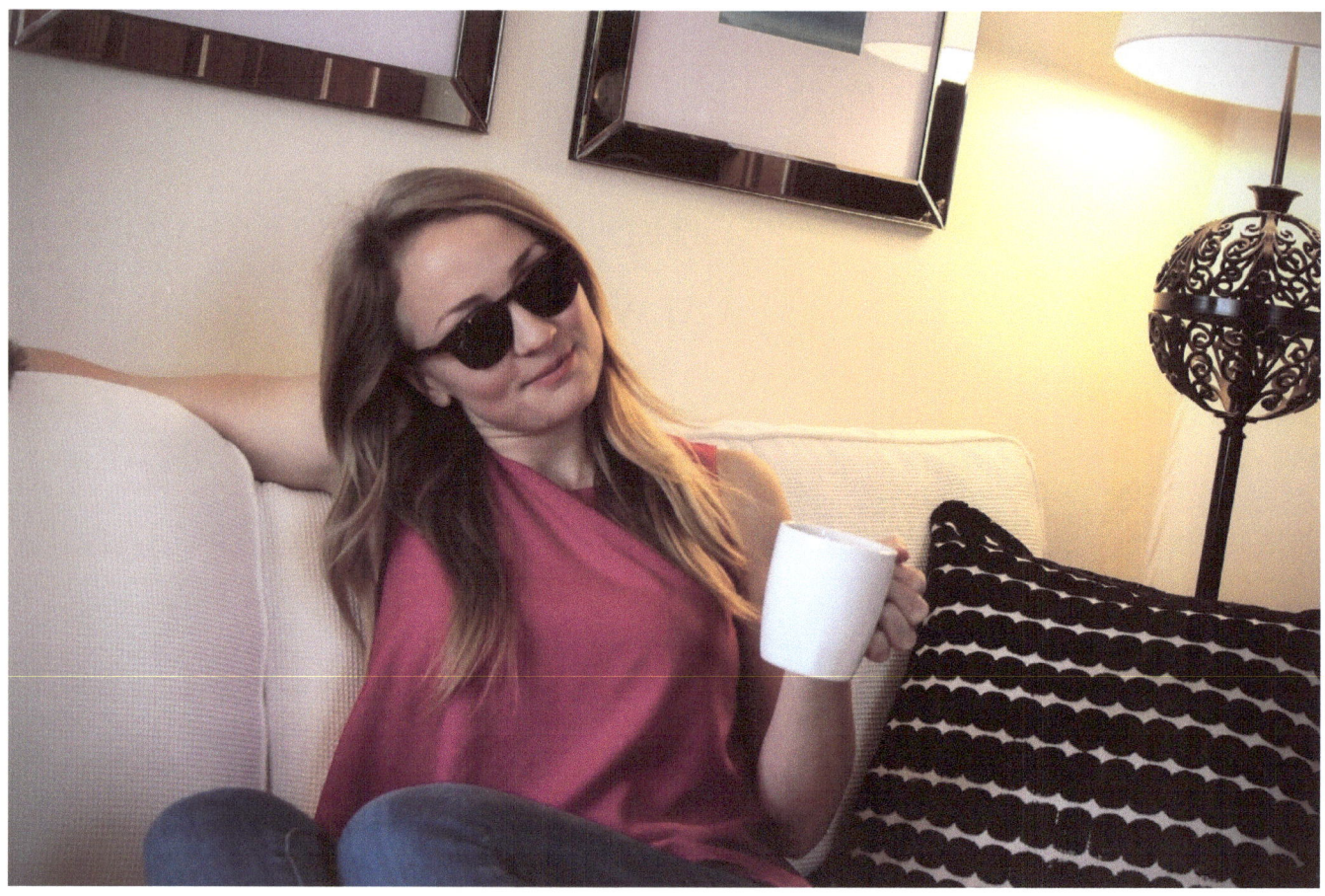

OBJECT:

COFFEE CUP

WHY IS IT IMPORTANT TO HER?

"FAMILY IS #1 TO ME. WE ARE SPREAD OUT ACROSS THE COUNTRY. CALIFORNIA TO ALABAMA TO IOWA - SO WHEN WE ARE ALL TOGETHER, I AM HAPPY! I CHOSE A CUP OF COFFEE FOR MY 100 SHADES DEBUT BECAUSE EVEN MORE THAN FABULOUS BACKYARD GRILL OUTS OR SHOPPING TRIPS OR ANY OTHER FAMILY ACTIVITY DURING OUR TIME TOGETHER - MY FAVORITE IS COFFEE KLATCH. COFFEE KLATCH IS WHEN EVERYONE ROLLS OUT OF BED, COMES DOWN THE STAIRS, GATHERS AROUND THE KITCHEN AND DRINKS OUR FIRST CUP OF COFFEE. COFFEE KLATCH IS ALWAYS ON THE ITINERARY. WE TALK ABOUT THE NIGHT BEFORE AND PLANS WHICH LIE AHEAD, BUT MOST OF ALL, WE'RE JUST TOGETHER."

RENEE

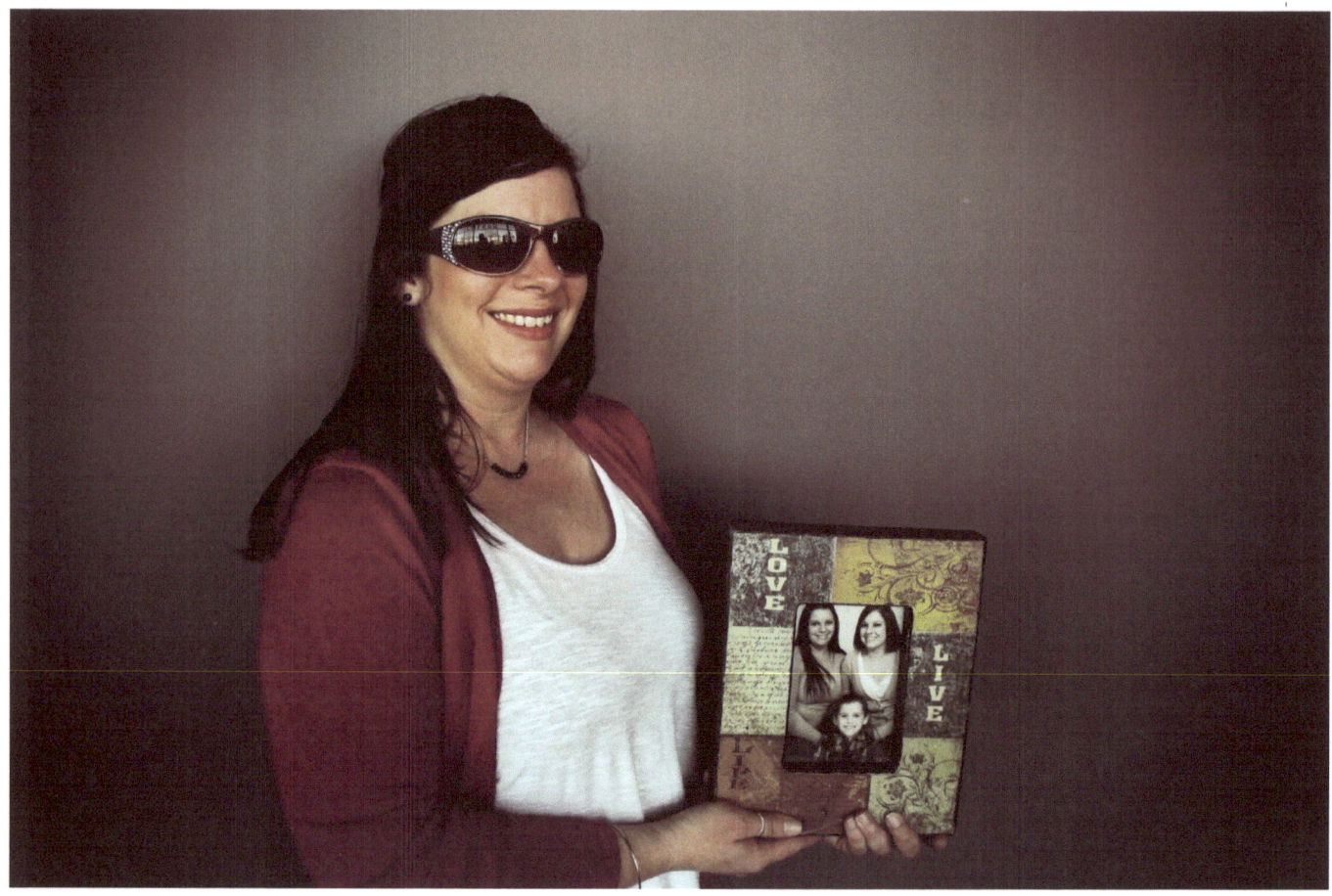

OBJECT:

Photo of sister and son

WHY IS IT IMPORTANT TO HER?

"They mean everything to me. They have been the ones that have pushed me and inspired me to continue to work hard everyday and provide for them, and become the woman I've become. They're my everything. They're my family. They've kept me in my faith. They've gotten me my faith. Without those two, I don't even know where I would be. I'm very proud of my sister for doing what she has done and just having her in my life has been a blessing to have her as my best friend, my sister, and for her and my son to be so close to each other.

The bond that we have is something that I have never seen anyone have, as far as siblings and it means everything to me. For her to be gone (she recently moved out of the state) is very hard, but it's also very good for us to separate and do our lives separately and grow."

BEETO

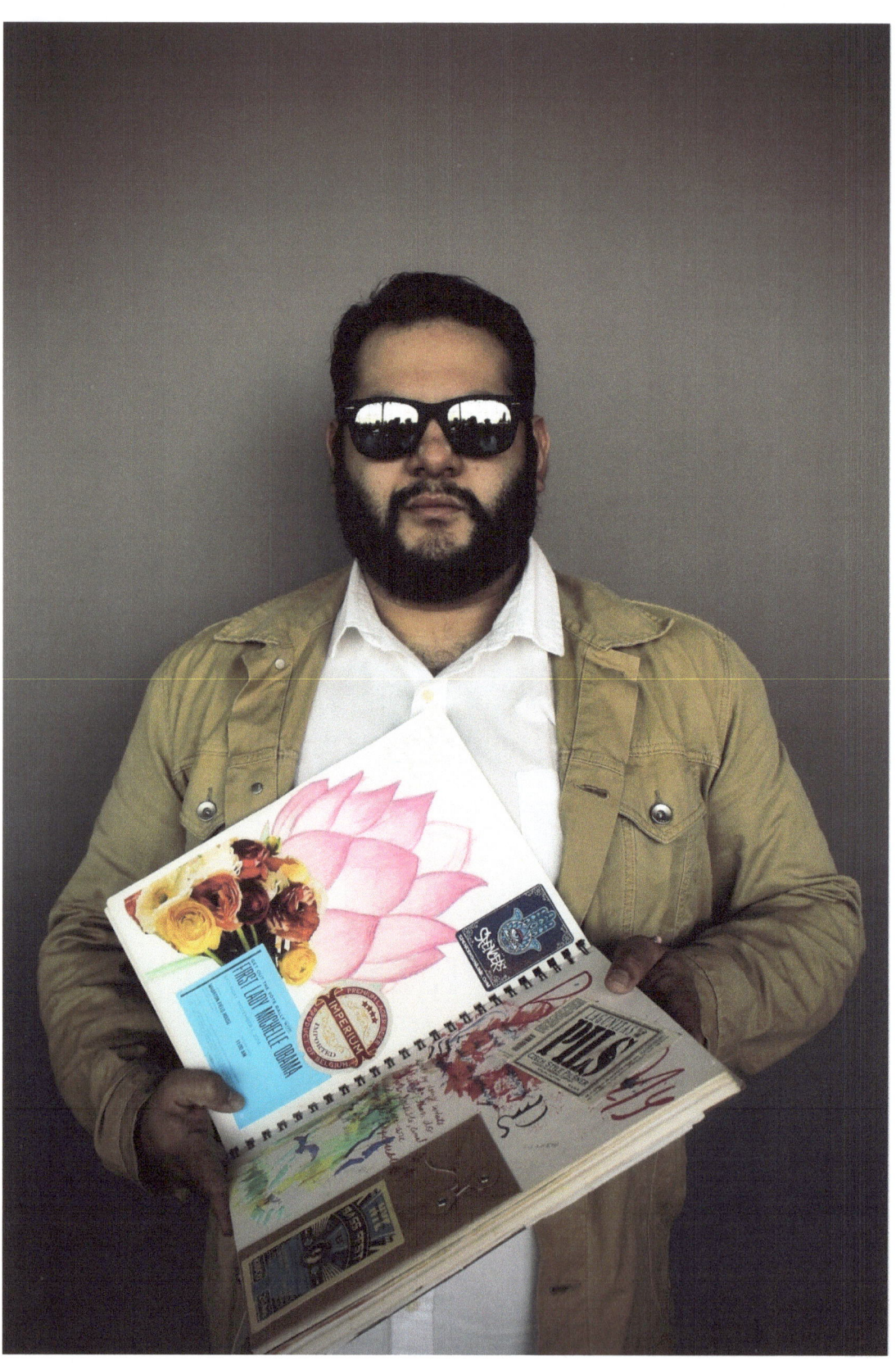

OBJECT:

SKETCH PAD

WHY IS IT IMPORTANT TO HIM?

"It's full of stuff. When I get random thoughts, I just put it in there. Sometimes I need release or things are on my mind and I just need to list it out, write about it, and then I get everything in order...whatever I need. Thoughts, ideas, imagination.

I wanted to go to art school and I was really, really good at school, but everything was more aimed towards math and science, so art was one of those things that got pushed back and out... and I had to focus on other things.

With math and science, I was alright in it, but my mind was always more this. More creative. More creation versus following. So this is a way to still let that out. Now I'm teaching my self instead of going to professional classes. So that's why I like it. This is my thing! This is mine! This is me!"

HEATHER

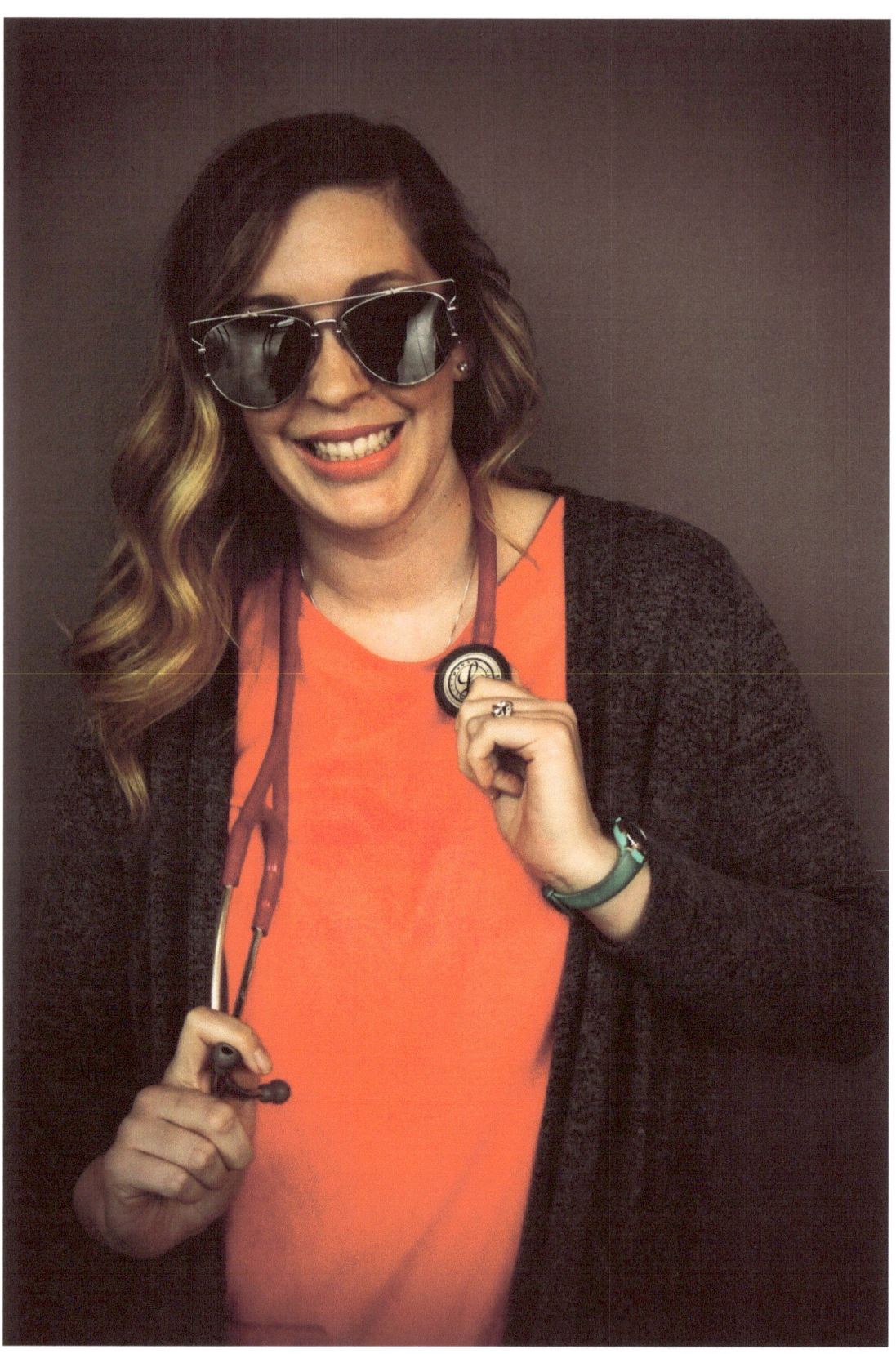

OBJECT:

STETHOSCOPE

WHY IS IT IMPORTANT TO HER?

"I BECAME A NURSE BECAUSE I CARED FOR PEOPLE AND THAT'S WHO I'VE BEEN GROWING UP. MY FAMILY HAD A LOT OF ILLNESS AND I FOUND OUT REALLY YOUNG THAT MY PASSION WAS FOR CARING FOR PEOPLE. SO IT'S WHO I AM. NOT ONLY AS MY JOB, BUT AS WHO I AM AS A PERSON FROM THE GET GO!"

CHRISTINA

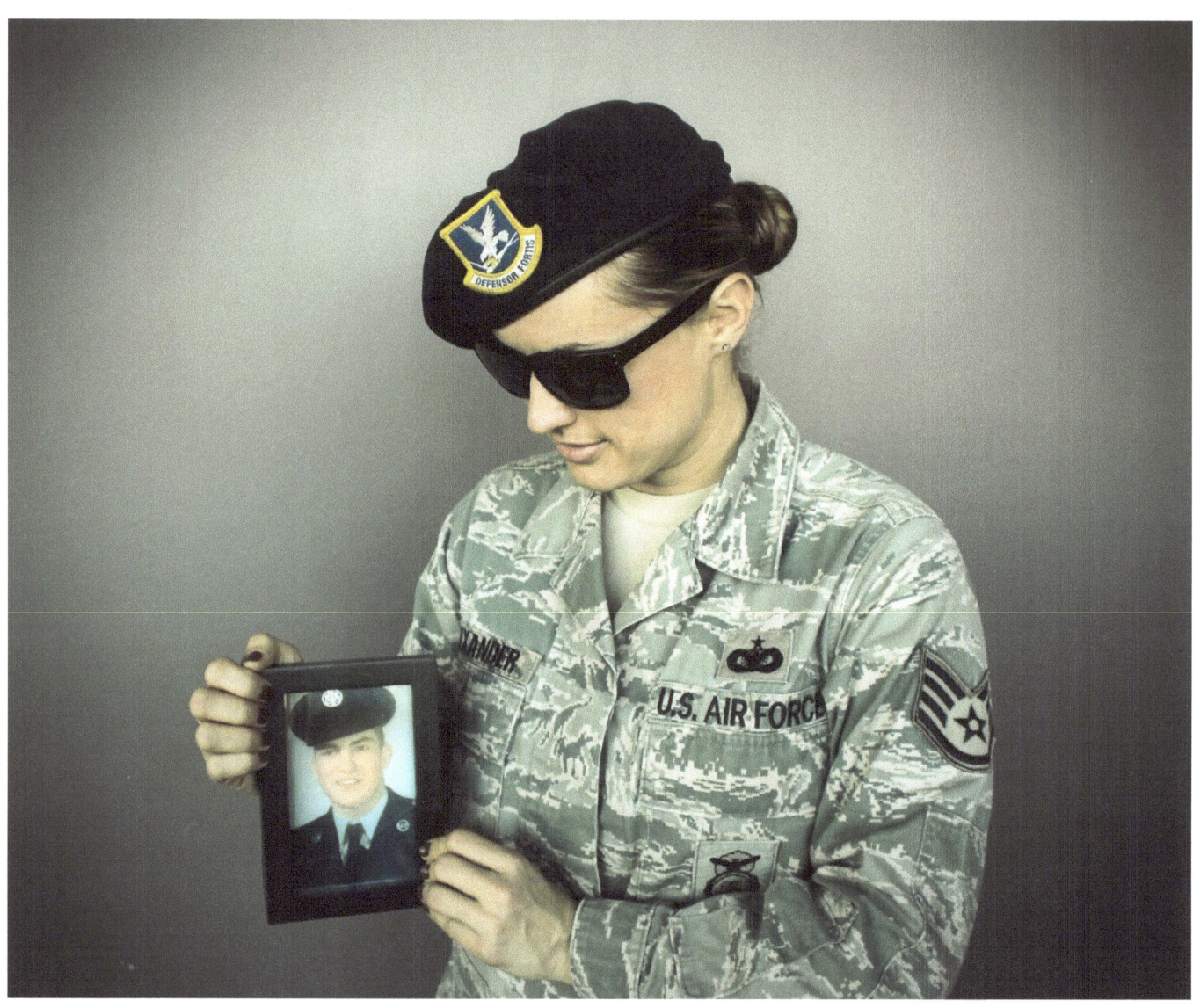

OBJECT:

PHOTO OF HER GRANDFATHER WHO SERVED AND RETIRED FROM THE UNITED STATES AIR FORCE.

WHY IS IT IMPORTANT TO HER?

"GROWING UP I ALWAYS KNEW I WANTED TO DO SOMETHING IN LIFE THAT REQUIRED ME TO LIVE AN ACTIVE LIFESTYLE. BUT I KEPT FINDING MYSELF RUNNING IN CIRCLES. I WAS GOING TO COLLEGE AND KEPT CHANGING MY MIND AS TO WHAT I WANTED MAJOR IN. I WAS SLOWLY GIVING UP AND FEELING LOST AS TO WHAT I WAS GOING TO DO. THAT'S WHEN MY GRANDFATHER'S LONG TALKS STARTING REPLAYING IN MY MIND. I FACTORED IN ALL THE POSSIBILITIES. ESPECIALLY AFTER 9/11 TOOK PLACE I KNEW I WANTED TO DO MY PART TO SERVE SO I DECIDED I WOULD SERVE FOR AT LEAST 4 YEARS AND THEN GET OUT. WITH THE SUPPORT OF MY PARENTS, I TOOK THE PLUNGE AND MY GRANDFATHER WALKED ME INTO THE AIR FORCE RECRUITING OFFICE AND AT THAT POINT MY LIFE CHANGED FOR THE BETTER. THAT'S WHEN I BECAME A COP FOR THE UNITED STATES AIR FORCE. FAST-FORWARD 10 YEARS AND I AM STILL SERVING.

IN THAT TIME I HAVE SEEN THE WORLD, DEPLOYED, COMPLETED COLLEGE, AND HAD A BEAUTIFUL DAUGHTER ALONG THE WAY AND I OWE IT TO HIM FOR SETTING THE PATH OF MY CAREER. NOW I'M AN AIR FORCE RECRUITER HELPING PEOPLE TAKE THAT SAME STEP I DID 10 YEARS AGO. IT'S A VERY HUMBLING FEELING FOR ME AND I COULDN'T BE HAPPIER. I DIDN'T REALIZE IT AT THE TIME BUT THE IMPACT MY GRANDFATHER HAS MADE ON MY LIFE AND CAREER AS AN AIRMAN, MOTHER, AND AS A PERSON HAS BEEN MORE THAN I COULD IMAGINE. I OWE A LOT TO HIM AND MY FAMILY FOR THE GUIDANCE AND DIRECTION THAT HAVE LEAD ME TO WHERE I AM TODAY."

HARSHAD

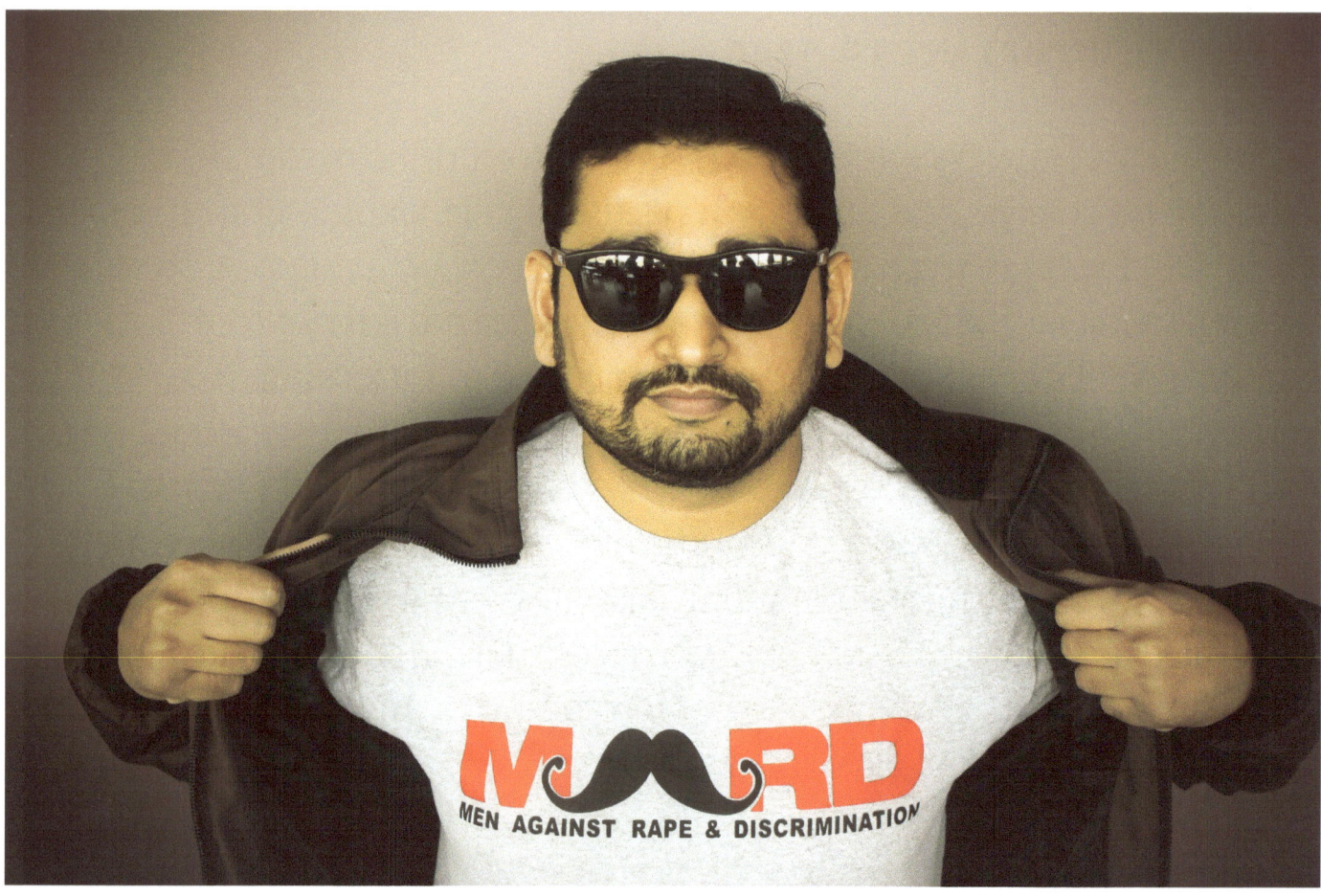

OBJECT:

MARD

WHY IS IT IMPORTANT TO HIM?

"MARD: (Hindi: मर्द) - THE ENGLISH TRANSLATION IS MAN. THE FULL FORM OF MARD IS MEN AGAINST RAPE AND DISCRIMINATION. THIS IS A SOCIAL CAMPAIGN STARTED BY INDIAN ACTOR/DIRECTOR FARHAN AKHTAR. THE CAMPAIGN AIMS TO RAISE SOCIAL AWARENESS AGAINST RAPE AND DISCRIMINATION OF WOMEN.

THE RISE IN RAPE, HUMAN TRAFFICKING, HARASSMENT AND DISCRIMINATION SHOWS THAT WE ARE FAILING AS MEN. EVEN AFTER SO MANY YEARS WE HAVE NOT BEEN ABLE TO PROVIDE THEM UTTER INDEPENDENCE. THEY HAVE TO FACE THE DISCRIMINATION AGAINST THEIR MALE COUNTERPARTS AT EACH AND EVERY POINT OF THEIR LIFE. WE SEE ALL THE NEWS FILLED WITH NEWS OF FEMALE FOETICIDE, RAPE CASES, EVE-TEASING AND SO ON.

BESIDES SEXUAL ASSAULTS WOMEN HAVE TO DEAL WITH SEXUAL HARASSMENT AND SEXUAL ABUSE ON A DAILY BASIS. IN THIS DISMAL SCENARIO FARHAN AKHTAR'S ORGANIZATION IS RAY OF HOPE. EACH MAN FROM ALL OVER THE WORLD SHOULD COME AHEAD AND SUPPORT AN ORGANIZATION LIKE THIS. EACH BOY HAS TO GROW UP TO BE A GENTLEMAN, WHO IN THOUGHT, WORD AND ACTION WILL ALWAYS RESPECT WOMEN. A WOMAN SHOULD FEEL SAFE IN HIS COMPANY. HE SHOULD STAND FOR WOMAN RIGHTS AND ACCEPT HER AS AN EQUALLY IMPORTANT PART OF THIS SOCIETY. HE SHOULD RESPECT WOMAN IRRESPECTIVE OF HER AGE, CASTE, CREED AND COLOR. HE SHOULD TRY TO BE HER REAL FRIEND, COMPANION AND CONFIDANT. HE SHOULD VENERATE WOMEN FOR HER MIND, BODY AND SOUL AND ENSURE THAT HER DIGNITY WILL NEVER BE COMPROMISED. IT'S HIGH TIME WE SHOULD ADOPT "ZERO TOLERANCE" AGAINST WOMEN CRIMES AND DISCRIMINATION AND CONDEMN ALL TYPES OF VIOLENCE AGAINST THEM. MEN OF THIS WORLD SHOULD UNDERSTAND THAT WOMEN ARE ALSO HUMAN AND THEY ALSO HAVE SAME ASPIRATIONS, GOALS AND EMOTIONS LIKE MEN. WHEN THEY ARE HAPPY THEY RADIATE THEIR HAPPINESS WHICH FILLS THEIR FAMILIES AND SOCIETY WITH LOVE, WARMTH AND OPTIMISM. I HOPE ALL THE MEN TAKE A PLEDGE TO RESPECT THE WOMEN AND MAKE THIS WORLD A BETTER PLACE TO LIVE IN FOR THEIR MOTHERS, SISTERS AND DAUGHTERS.

AT LAST I WOULD LIKE TO MENTION 2 THINGS:

A TWEET FROM FARHAN AKHTAR: "IF YOU ARE A MAN WHO RESPECTS WOMEN... HER RIGHTS, HER DIGNITY, HER INDEPENDENCE, HER MIND, HER BODY, HER LIFE... YOU ARE A #MARD.

THE ESSENCE OF MARD- (THOUGH IT IS INTERPRETED INNUMERABLE WAYS, BELOW ARE A FEW OF THEM)
HE, WHOSE EYES SPARKLE WITH HONESTY
WHOSE MANNER IS IMPECCABLE,
WHOSE DEMEANOR IS GENTLE
WHOSE WORDS ARE TRUTHFUL YET POLITE
WHOSE HEART HOLDS RESPECT, WHOSE DEEDS DISPLAY HONOR.
HE. WHO VENERATES WOMEN FOR THEIR MIND, BODY AND SOUL
WHO ENSURES THAT THEIR DIGNITY WILL NEVER BE COMPROMISED
WHO NEVER EVER FORGETS THAT LIKE HIM, SHE IS AN INDIVIDUAL
HE, WHO HAS CHARACTER
WHO HAS STRENGTH AND AN INDOMITABLE SPIRIT
HE, WHO IS A COMPANION, A FRIEND, A CONFIDANT
HE IS A MAN."

Leah

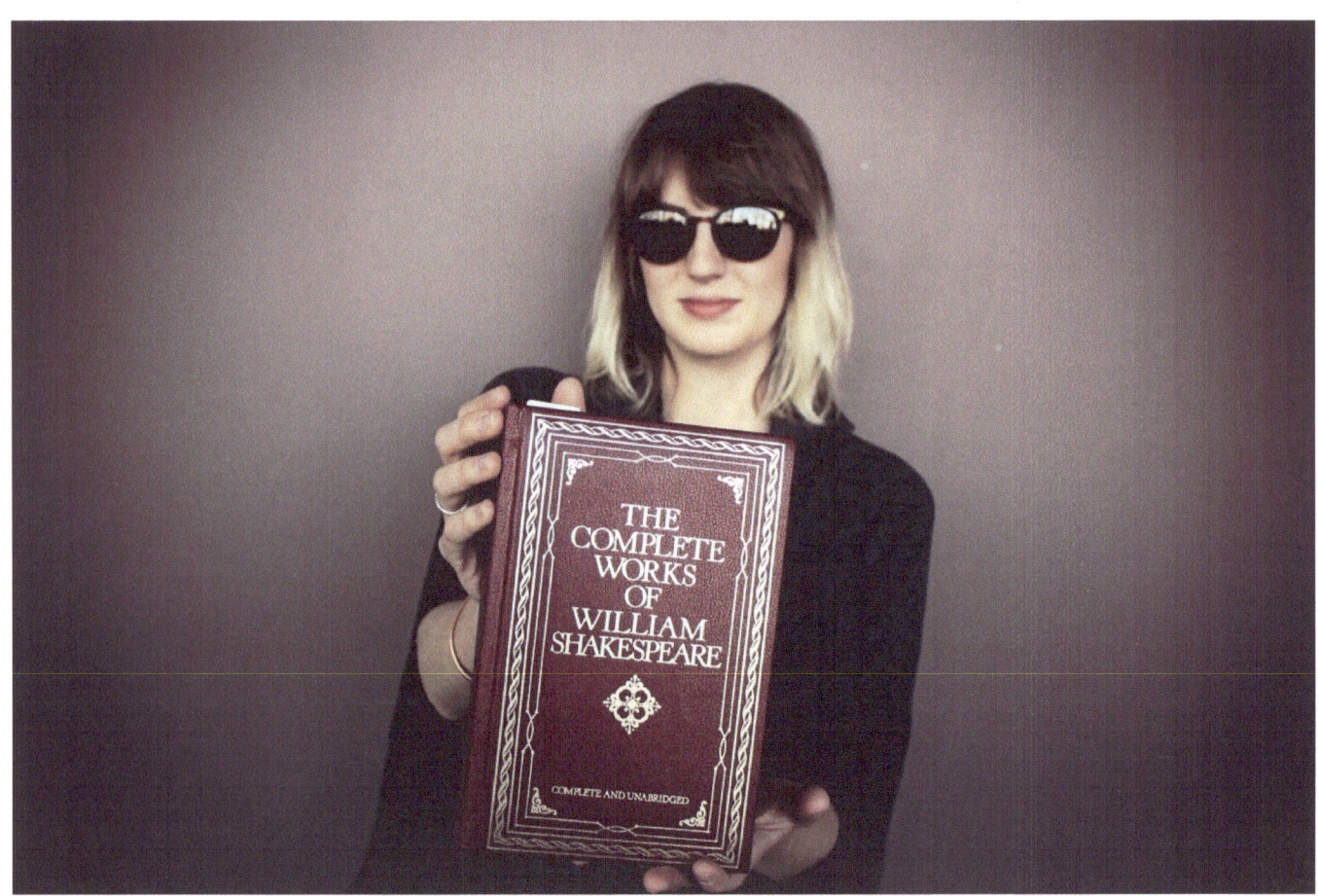

OBJECT:

THE COMPLETE WORKS OF WILLIAM SHAKESPEARE

WHY IS IT IMPORTANT TO HER?

"IT'S A GIANT BOOK THAT USED TO BE MY GRANDFATHER'S. HIS NAME WAS ROBERT BARKER, BOB BARKER. NOT RELATED TO THE GAME SHOW HOST! IT'S GOT SOME OF HIS WRITING ON IT AND THAT'S SPECIAL TO ME BECAUSE HE'S GONE NOW.

MAYBE BY THE TIME I'M 70 OR SO I'LL GET THROUGH THIS WHOLE BOOK AND READ IT. I THINK IT'S COOL THAT IT'S SOMETHING THAT HE REALLY LIKED. HE WAS VERY SMART AND PRACTICALLY KNEW THE ANSWER TO ALL JEOPARDY QUESTIONS AND WE JUST THOUGHT HE WAS THE COOLEST GRANDPA EVER. HE WAS REALLY A STUDENT OF LITERATURE AND I DON'T THINK HE GRADUATED PAST 8TH GRADE, BUT HE READ ALL THE TIME AND HE WAS SO SMART.

I JUST THINK THAT'S SO COOL THAT HE CAN PASS THAT ON TO ME AND HOPEFULLY MY KIDS WILL ENJOY SOME OF THE SAME BOOKS AND THINGS THAT HE LIKED."

JEREMY

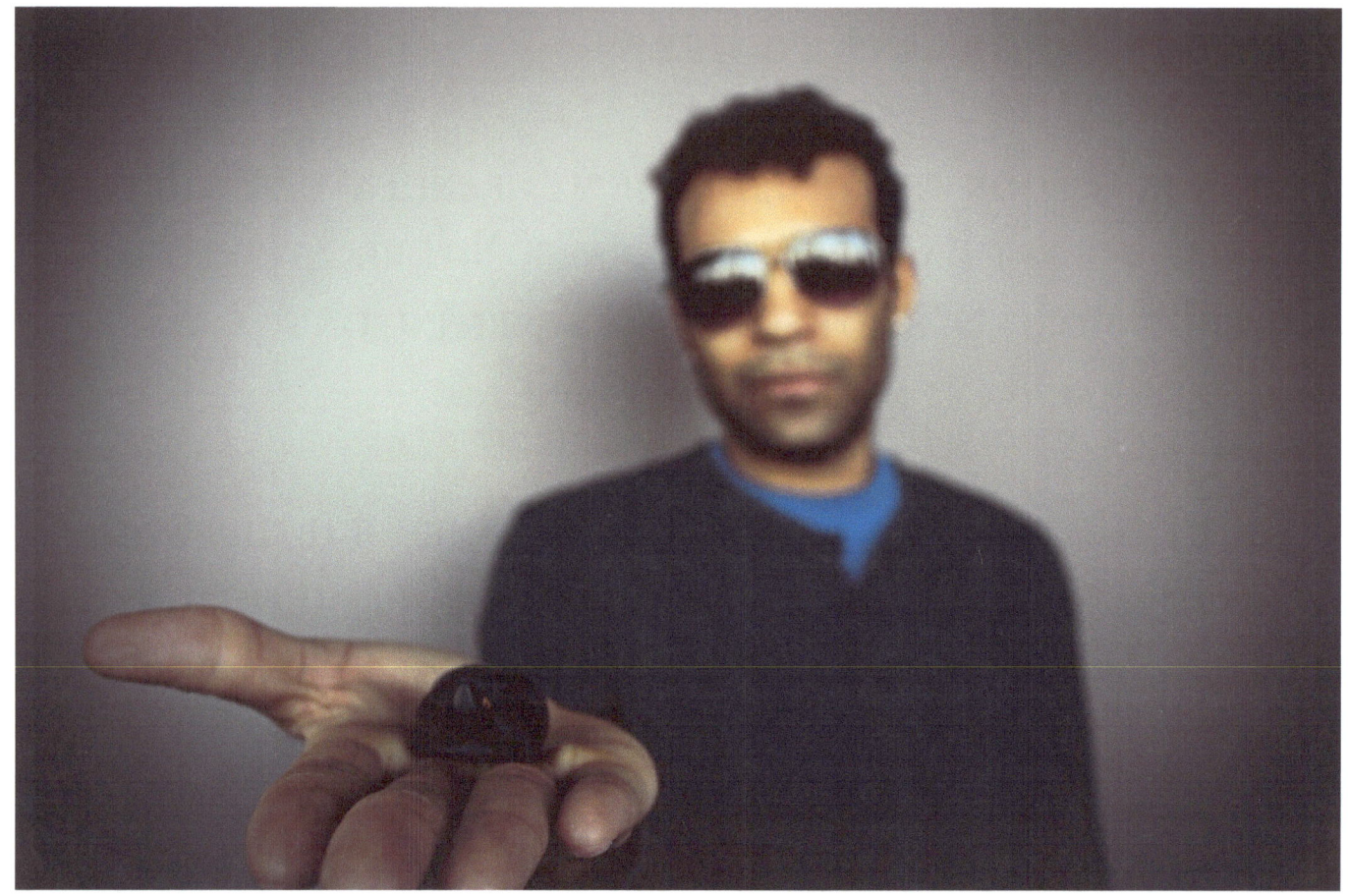

OBJECT:

WOODEN TURTLE

WHY IS IT IMPORTANT TO HIM?

"I went to Mercado on 5th and I wasn't looking for anything in particular, and then I found a vendor. These three ladies from Ghana had many different items. They were hand crafted by a gentleman that still lives in Ghana. There were many items. Most of them were very big and there was a small little tortoise that actually stood out amongst the other ones that were similar as well. So I decided to go ahead and buy that.

The relationship I have with that item needs some context. So I wrote, probably about three or four years ago, a story about a little boy and a turtle. I won't get into depth about the whole story, but it's an allegorical story. It's about three things...

1.) My relationship with something and 2.) this something that I pursue, and also 3.)what I am as a storyteller. So that three part is what the tortoise represents for me. So it's always at my bed side. Sometimes I take it with me. It's not an idol, but it is a symbol.

What I pursue? It's very difficult for me to explain, but it's both tangible and intelligible at the same time. You can compare it to a tree, both the trunk and the roots. Some people use words, maybe like 'spirituality.' Other people maybe pursue it through religion and use the word God. I do not consider myself religious, but I do consider myself in the simple pursuit and this turtle definitely a part of that and my relationship to it. So it's a relationship, not a religion for me."

KELSEY

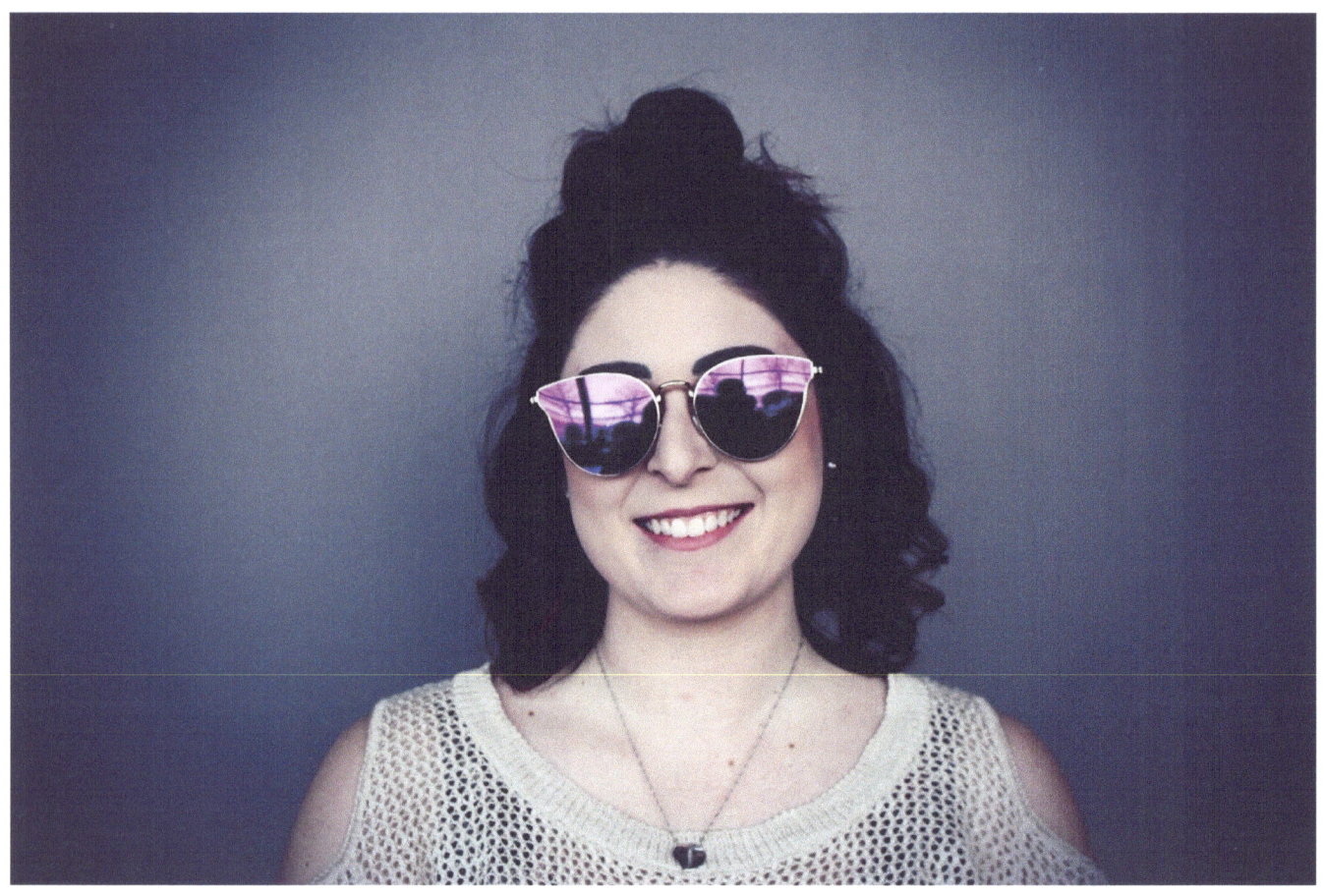

OBJECT:

NECKLACE

WHY IS IT IMPORTANT TO HER?

"I got this necklace from my grandparents for my high school graduation…and my grandpa passed away in September. So a couple months ago. Since then it's meant a lot to me. I wear it everyday. I never take it off. It's kind of like a closure type thing. Like if I'm in a situation that I don't feel comfortable in, I grab it and think about my grandpa and my grandma.

On the back is says, 'Precious granddaughter. I love you today, tomorrow, and always.' So it's a constant reminder that I always have my grandparents with me."

AMELIA

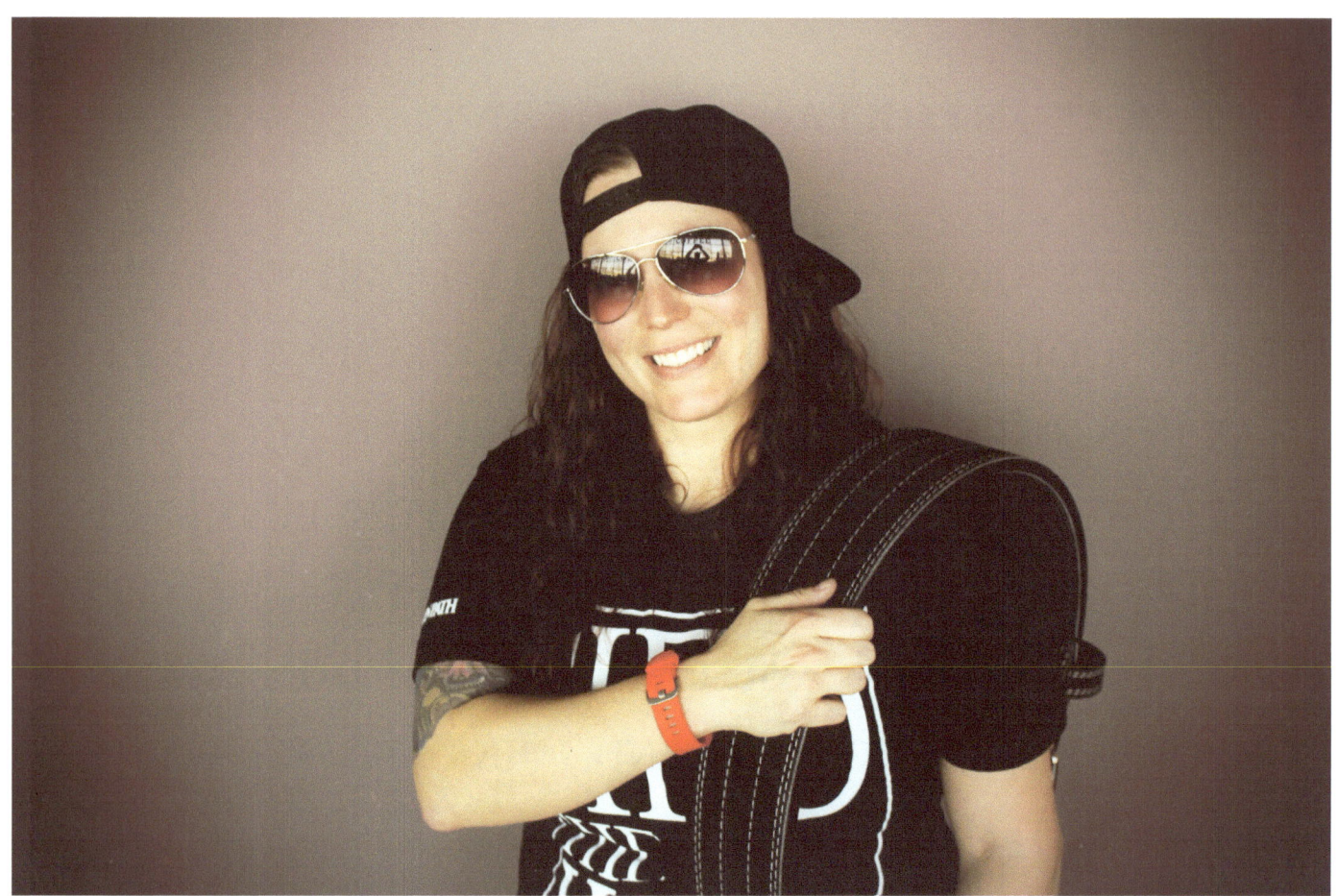

OBJECT:

POWERLIFTING BELT

WHY IS IT IMPORTANT TO HER?

"My trainer said that when you get a belt, it's your belt for life. So I can look at this and not only does it represent where I'm at as far as with my weightlifting goals, but it also represents the future and the goals that I want to get and hit. Not only is it my stability and support, it keeps me optimistic to think, 'OK. in the future, I want to set these goals and use it for that.

The powerlifting belt was my first serious purchase for powerlifting and so it represents my commitment to powerlifting and serves as a reminder of my dedication and desire to have no excuses. I can take it to any gym and get in there and push my limits and lift heavy. I love everything fitness, but powerlifting stole my heart. From the first day I started training, I just fell in love with the grind. It's an outlet for me, I can have the best day and lifting heavy just betters it. Or I could be having the worst day and channel that into my lifts and after, I always walk away feeling positive and happy and more driven."

CHRIS

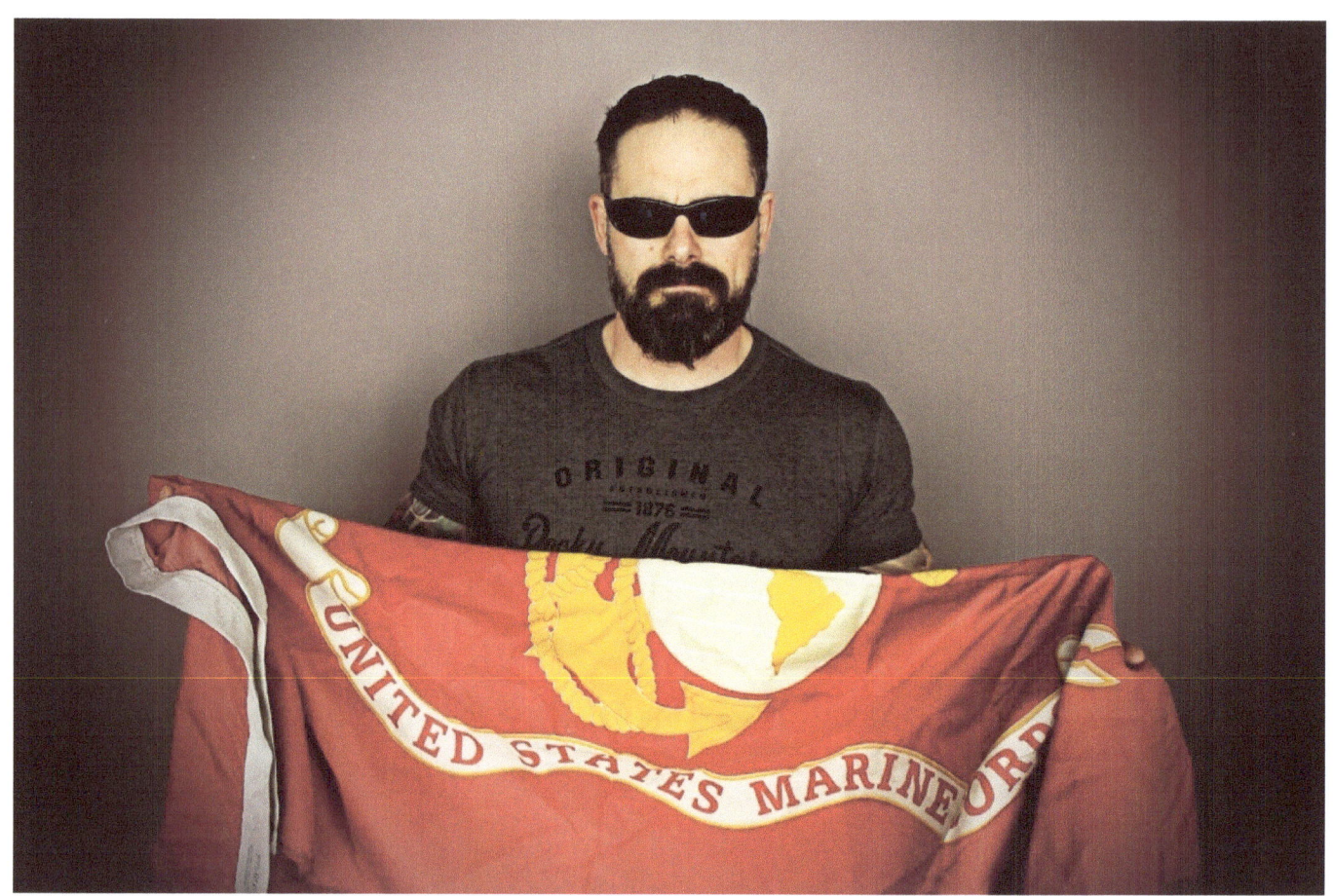

OBJECT:

UNITED STATES MARINE CORPS FLAG

WHY IT'S IMPORTANT TO HIM?

"I GOT IT IN 2001. THE FIRST TIME I TOOK IT ANYWHERE WAS TO NICARAGUA. WE WENT DOWN TO NICARAGUA TO BUILD SOME SCHOOLS AND DO SOME HELP WITH THE INNER PART OF THE COUNTRY. SO WE FLEW INTO THE CAPITAL AND OUT TO THE MOUNTAINS AND BUILT SOME SCHOOLS FOR KIDS. THEN I TOOK THIS WITH ME TO IRAQ AND I FLEW IT EVERY TIME I WENT AND I WENT TWICE.

IT'S KINDA OLD AND BEAT UP AND TATTERED, BUT I KEEP IT IN A BOX USUALLY. I BROUGHT IT HOME WITH ME AND I TOOK IT BACK AND BROUGHT IT HOME WITH ME. IT'S JUST A REMINDER THAT I WENT THROUGH A LOT. SAW A LOT OF THINGS. GOOD AND BAD EXPERIENCES.

I JUST CAN'T SEE PARTING WITH IT, EVEN THOUGH IT'S TORN AND TATTERED. IT'S JUST BEEN THROUGH A LOT. I REMINDS ME OF A LOT OF THE GOOD TIMES AND SOME OF THE BAD TIMES. IT'S FUNNY... AS YOU GET OLDER, YOU TEND TO FORGET BAD TIMES, SO YOU TEND TO JUST THINK ABOUT THE GOOD TIMES. SO IT REMINDS ME OF SOME GOOD THINGS, BUT THERE'S SOME BAD TIMES ASSOCIATED WITH THIS. THIS LOSS OF SOME FRIENDS. SO IT'S JUST A GOOD REMINDER OF THAT FOR ME. A PIECE OF MEMORABILIA FROM THE TIME THAT I SERVED."

BRITTANY

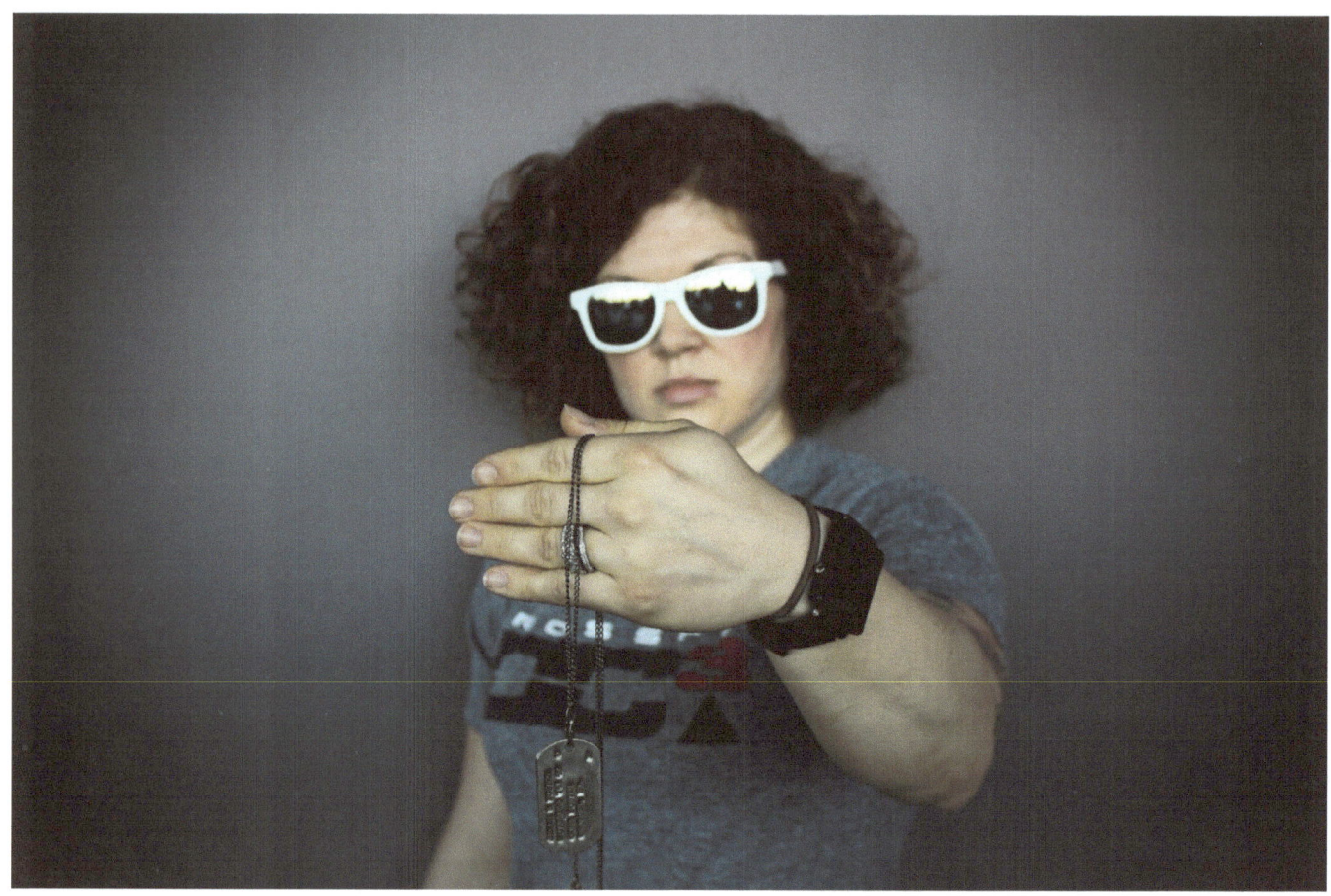

OBJECT:

Her Grandfather's Dog Tags

WHY IS IT IMPORTANT TO HER?

"They were given to me when he passed away. He never talked about being in World War 2 until one day when I was 5 or 6. I don't remember this but my parents do and have told me this story many of times. Grandpa never talked about the war until I asked. Then, he never stopped talking about it.

This led to army reunions with his company, many of which I was lucky to attend. I'm lucky to have a first hand account of World War II and I remember many of the stories well. His dog tags are not just a piece of history, but remind me of how lucky I am to have the freedoms we have.

They also remind me of values that were instilled in me by my grandpa and dad. Courage, integrity, loyalty, strength, and determination. Everyday, I try to live what they taught me, and make them proud even though they are no longer here."

VICTORIA

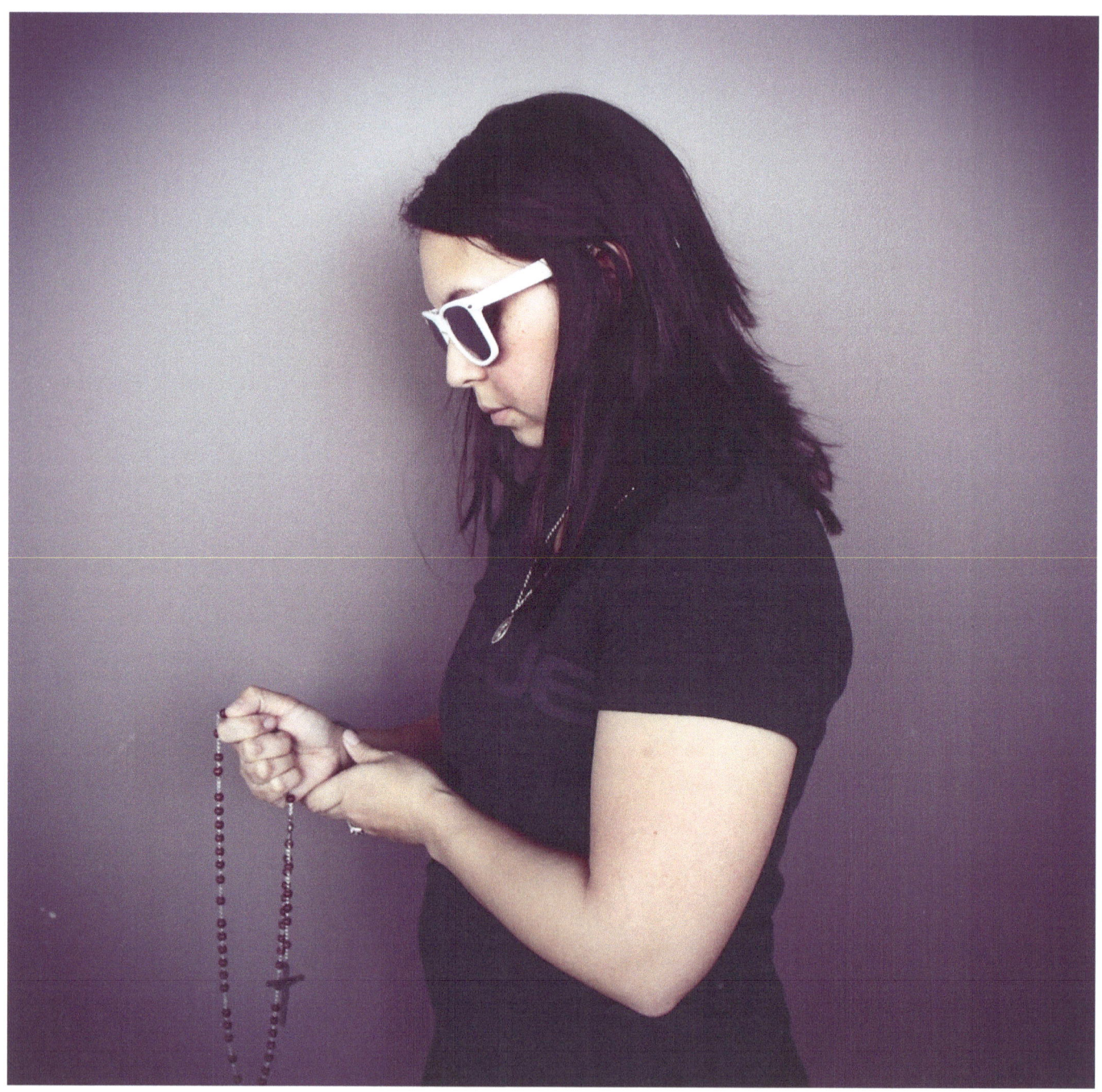

OBJECT:

ROSARY

WHY IS IT IMPORTANT TO HER?

"I brought my rosary that was given to me by my Godfather. It was my Godmother's. She died holding it in her hand. She died February 25th, 2003. She was diagnosed with Thyroid Cancer about a month before. By then it was so advanced, there was nothing they could do except for treat her symptoms and make sure she was pain free. I learned about patience during that time.

My older sister died when I was three and before she had died, she asked my dad to teach her how to pray. So he decided to teach the whole family to pray. I learned the meaning behind the word (pray). I learned how to not just pray with your mouth, but with your heart. this is probably the greatest gift my dad has ever given me. The ability to pray and to know how.

We were going through some rough times when I was in high school and he said, 'You can get through this. We can get all get through this. We survived your sister's death. We can survive this. '

The importance of prayer has become a daily part of my life.

That's why I brought this rosary, because it represents the greatest gift my dad gave me. And the fact that it came from probably the most God fearing, prayerful woman I've ever met in my life, it holds a special meaning for me. I will never leave the house without it. I will forget my phone, my CrossFit shoes...I will forget anything before I forget this."

GERARD

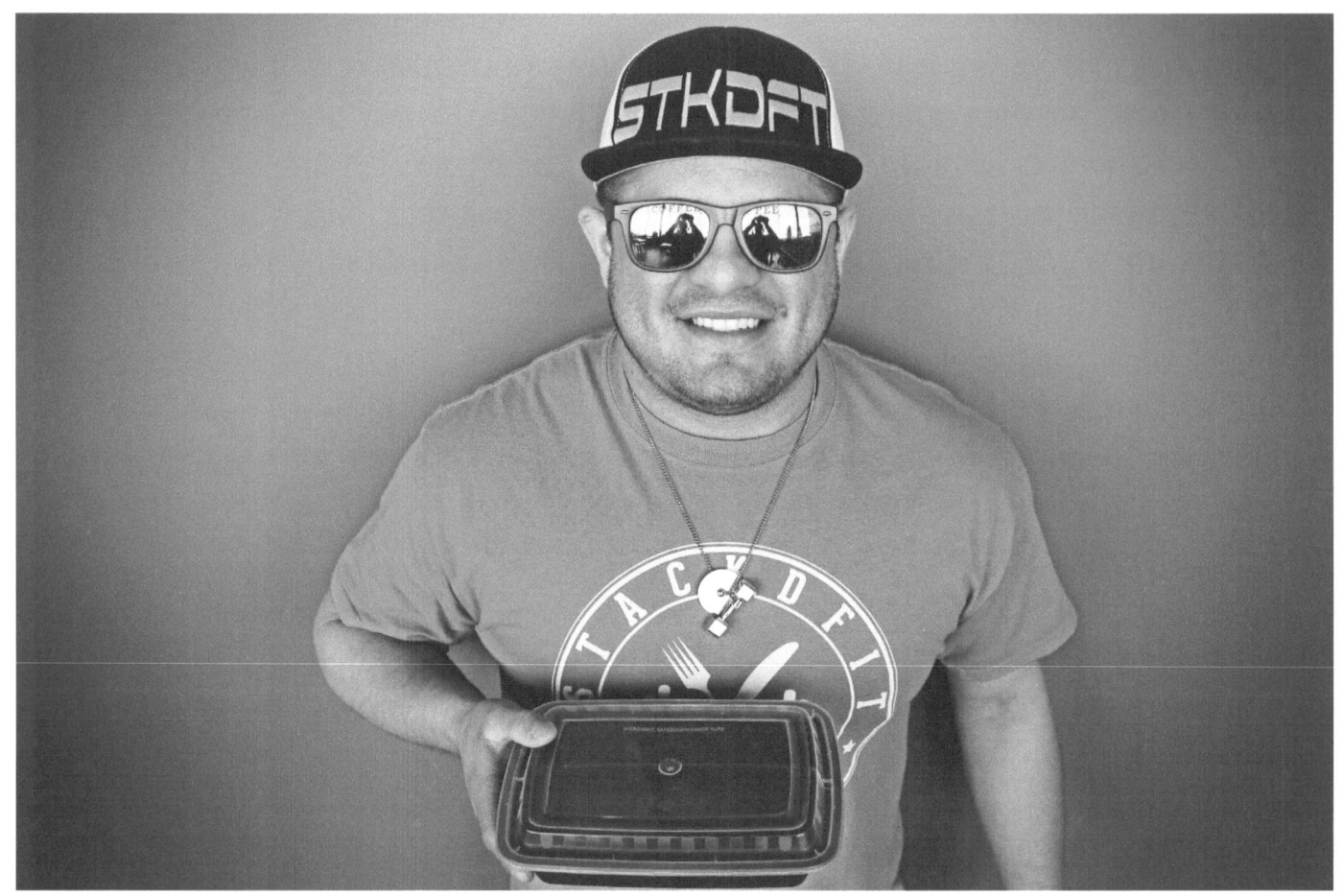

OBJECT:

Meal Prep Container

WHY IS IT IMPORTANT TO HIM?

"StackdFIT Meals has changed me to be a better person physically and mentally. Everyone has a past. Everyone has their own story. It's how we change and tweak it to build a better future.

Now my meals are inside kitchens all through the Quad Cities area including Iowa City, Coralville, Dixon, sterling you name it.

This container may seem like just meal prep to some but for me it represents change and success."

GRACE

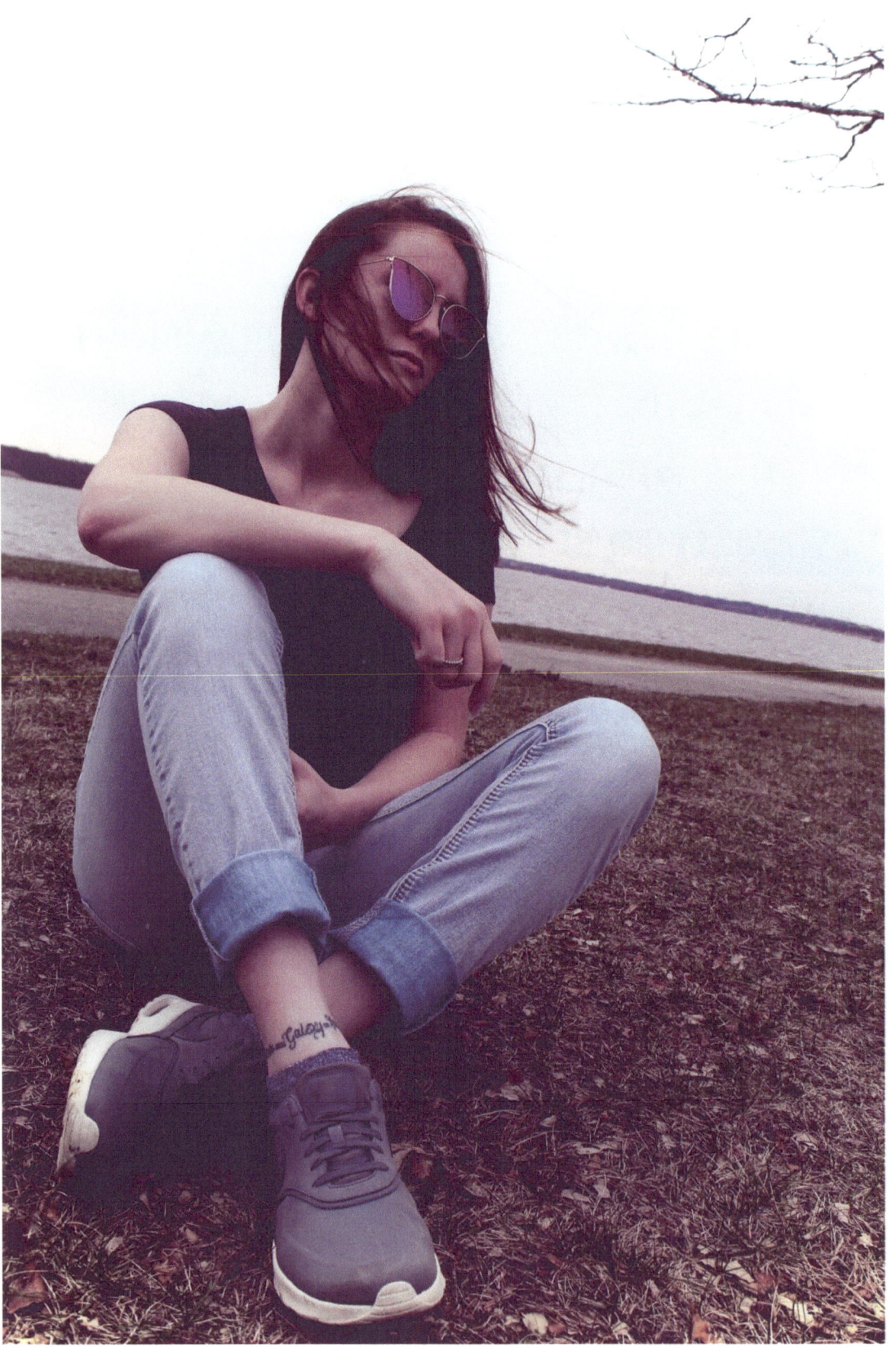

OBJECT:

ANKLE TATTOO

WHY IS IT IMPORTANT TO HER?

"IT HAS MY SIBLING'S NAMES ON IT. I GREW UP IN A HOME WHERE WE WERE ABUSED AS CHILDREN. IT WAS ME AND MY SIBLINGS. I HAVE AN OLDER BROTHER AND A YOUNGER SISTER. WE GREW UP AROUND ALCOHOLISM AND DRUGS AND WE WERE ADOPTED BY OUR BABYSITTER WHEN I WAS IN FIFTH GRADE. I LOOK AT THE TATTOO AS A WAY FOR ME TO SEE STRENGTH BECAUSE THERE'S ALSO OTHER PEOPLE WHO'VE GROWN UP AROUND THAT AND THEY DON'T GET THE CHANCE THAT I GOT.

I HOPE THAT OTHER PEOPLE SEE THAT. SEE THIS POST AS A WAY TO GET OUT OF IT OR TO FIND SOMEBODY FOR IT. I LIKE LOOKING AT IT EVERYDAY TO BE ABLE TO SEE THAT THEY'RE WITH ME."

ELEANOR

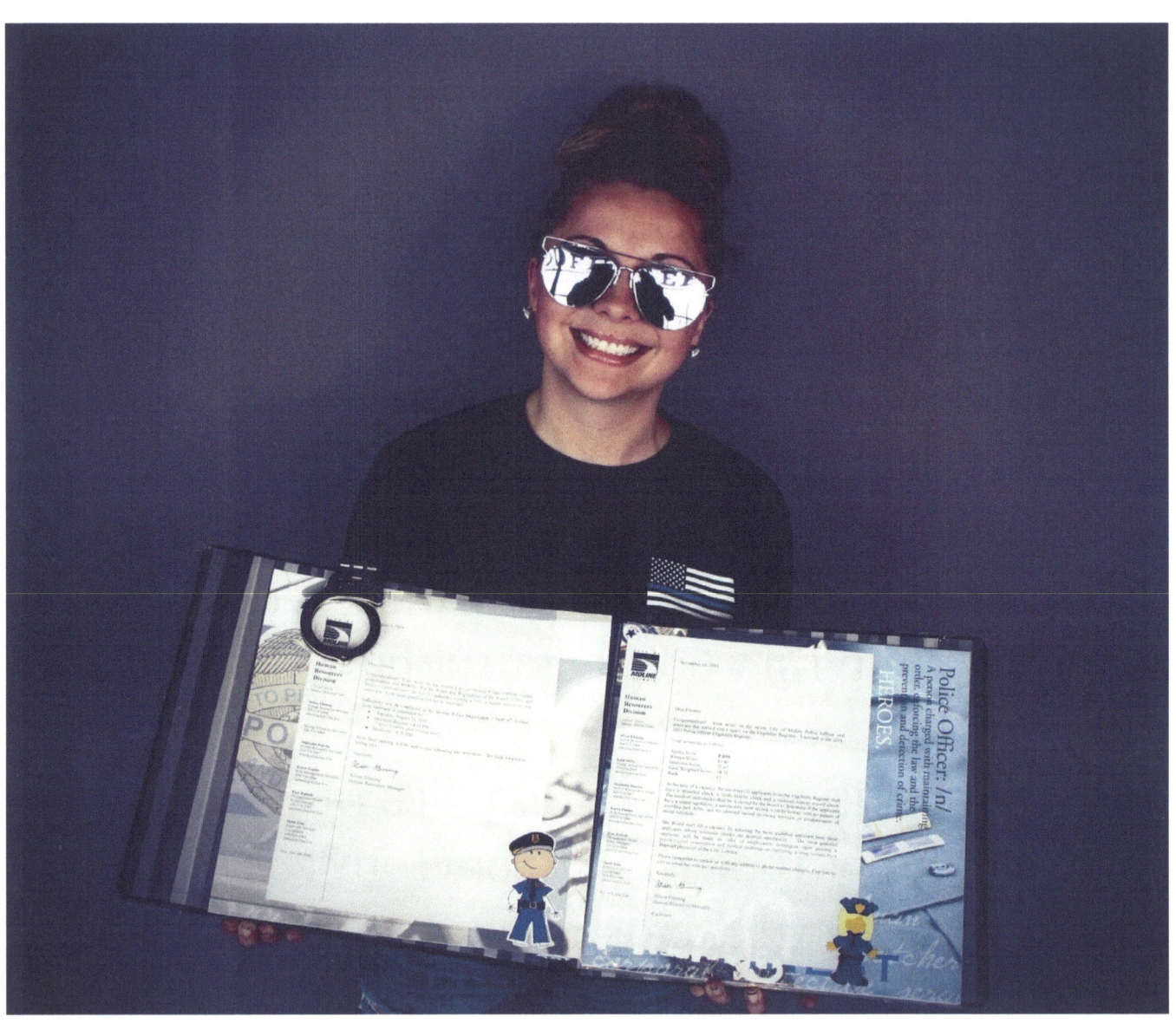

OBJECT:

POLICE LETTERS AND HANDCUFFS

WHY IS IT IMPORTANT TO HER?

"WHAT I BROUGHT TODAY IS A SCRAPBOOK WITH ALL OF MY LETTERS OF MY MAKING POLICE LISTS. IT INCLUDES MOLINE AND MILAN POLICE DEPARTMENTS. THE WHOLE REASON I WANT TO BECOME A POLICE OFFICER IS WHEN I WAS IN SIXTH GRADE, MY AUNT AND UNCLE WERE MURDERED AND I WANTED TO BE ABLE TO BRING CLOSURE TO FAMILIES LIKE WE HAD RECEIVED BACK THEN.

I ALWAYS WANTED TO BE THAT PERSON THAT COULD COMFORT SOMEBODY AND KEEP THEM INFORMED AND MAKE SURE THAT THE VICTIMS OF CRIMES COULD AT LEAST HAVE SOME SORT OF CLOSURE AND COULD UNDERSTAND WHAT WAS GOING ON IN SOCIETY. I'M A STRONG BELIEVER IN JUSTICE AND I THINK THAT EVERYBODY DESERVES SOME SORT OF CLOSURE. SOME SORT OF JUSTICE. EVEN IF THE PERSON WHO COMMITTED THE CRIME CANNON BE FOUND, THEY SHOULD BE ABLE TO HAVE SOME SORT OF CLOSURE AND SOME SORT OF COMFORT KNOWING THAT THEIR COMMUNITY IS STILL SAFE AND THAT THERE ARE PEOPLE OUT THERE THAT ARE WORKING THAT CARE FOR THEM.

I ALSO BROUGHT MY HANDCUFFS BECAUSE I AM A SECURITY OFFICER AT TRINITY IN ROCK ISLAND. MY HANDCUFFS MEAN A LOT TO ME BECAUSE NOT ONLY DO THEY REPRESENT SOME SORT OF RESTRAINT, BUT YOU CAN MAKE GOOD AND BAD DECISIONS, AND HANDCUFFS REPRESENT THE WHOLE TRUTH AND JUSTICE SIDE OF IT. EVERYBODY LOOKS AT THEM AS SOME SORT OF RESTRAINT. THAT YOU'RE GOING TO JAIL. BUT IN ALL HONESTY. THEY REPRESENT SO MUCH MORE. THEY REPRESENT THE FACT THAT PEOPLE ARE ACTUALLY OUT THERE TRYING TO KEEP THE COMMUNITY SAFE."

MATT AKA SILO JIM

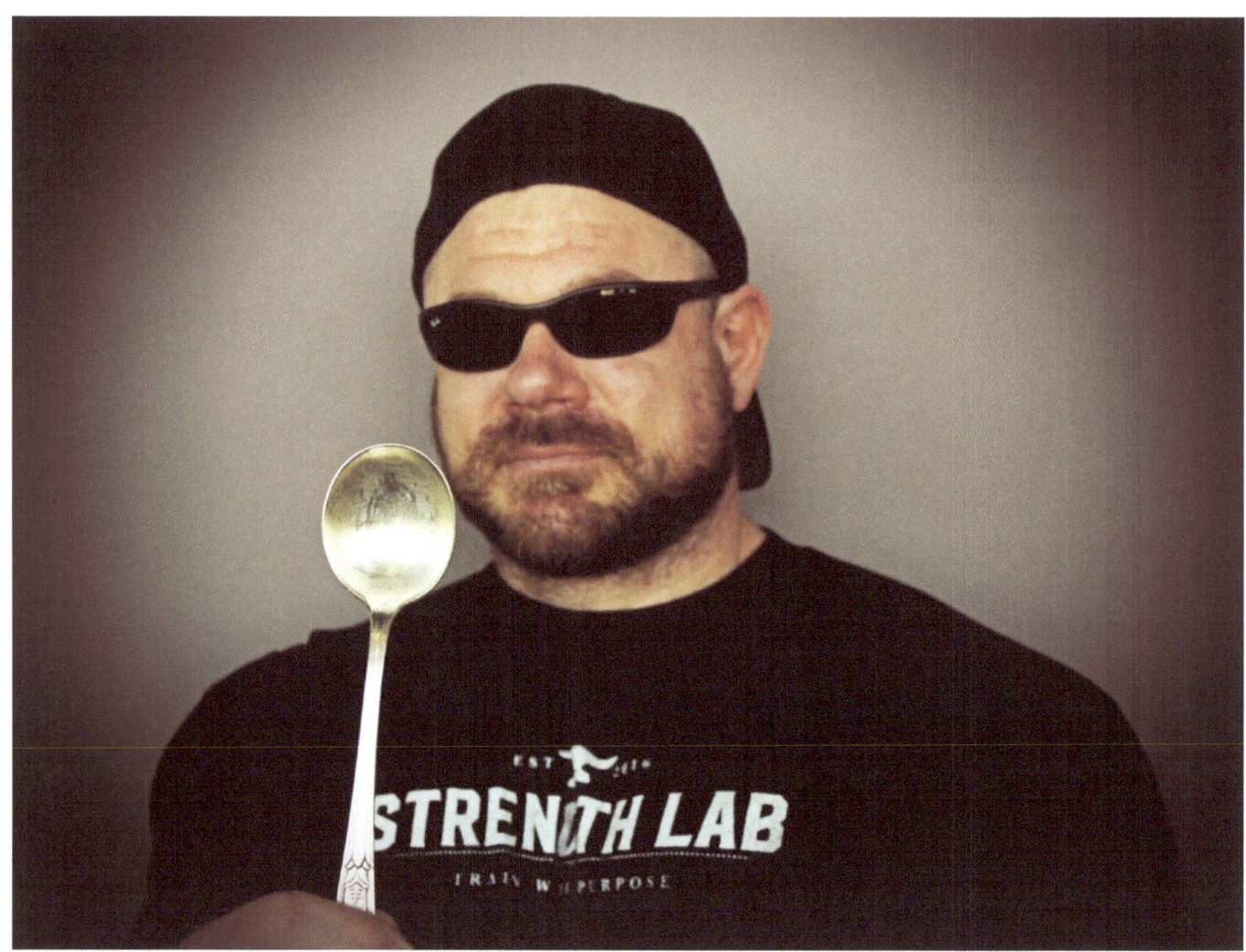

OBJECT:

SPOON

WHY IS IT IMPORTANT TO HIM?

"I FOUND MYSELF AT 23 YEARS OLD. I'M LITERALLY AT MY WITS END WITH EVERYTHING IN MY LIFE. I'VE GOT $110 IN MY POCKET. I'VE GOT THREE CHANGES OF CLOTHES AND ONE PAIR OF BOOTS. AN APARTMENT THAT I HAVE NO IDEA HOW I'M GONNA PAY FOR AND I DON'T CARE WHAT IT TAKES, I'M GONNA REBUILD MY LIFE! I WAS VERY SELECTIVE ABOUT THE PEOPLE I REACHED OUT TO DURING THIS TIME FRAME. ONE PERSON IN PARTICULAR WENT OUT OF THEIR WAY TO DO SPECIAL THINGS.

I ENDED UP WITH AN A.M. JOB WORKING IN A KITCHEN PREPPING FOOD. A P.M. JOB IN A KITCHEN WASHING DISHES AND IN THE DAY GOING TO TRADE SCHOOL. I WAS EATING TWO MEALS A DAY AND THAT WAS IT. WHATEVER I COULD SCRAP TOGETHER. SOME OF THE WAIT STAFF AT THE P.M. JOB, THE WAITRESSES, IF THERE WAS FOOD UNTOUCHED ON A PLATE, THEY WOULD PUT IT IN 'TO GO BOXES' AND THEY WOULD MAKE ME STUFF TO GO HOME WITH. WHAT NOBODY KNEW WAS I DIDN'T HAVE ANY SILVERWARE.

SO ONE OF THE PEOPLE THAT WAS INVOLVED IN MY LIFE, SHE CAME OVER ONE DAY AND SHE WENT TO MY REFRIGERATOR AND SAW THERE WAS NOTHING IN IT, AND THEN STARTED OPENING CUPBOARDS AND REALIZED THAT THIS WAS A KITCHEN, BUT THERE WAS NOTHING IN IT. SO SHE DRUG ME DOWN TO THE SECOND HAND STORE AND BOUGHT ME A SET OF SILVERWARE AND SOME DISHES. IN THAT SILVERWARE SETTING, SHE FOUND THIS SILVER SPOON. IT'S AN ACTUAL REAL SILVER SPOON. AND THE STORY WAS LIKE 'WELL, YOU WEREN'T BORN WITH ONE, BUT NOW YOU GOT ONE. IT'S YOUR MOVE.'

I HAVE EATEN LUNCH WITH THAT SPOON EVERYDAY FOR 23 YEARS. THE PERSON THAT GAVE ME THAT SPOON, IRONICALLY ENOUGH, IS THE PERSON I MOVED TO THE QUAD CITIES TO BE WITH. TWENTY SOMETHING YEARS LATER."

MOLLY

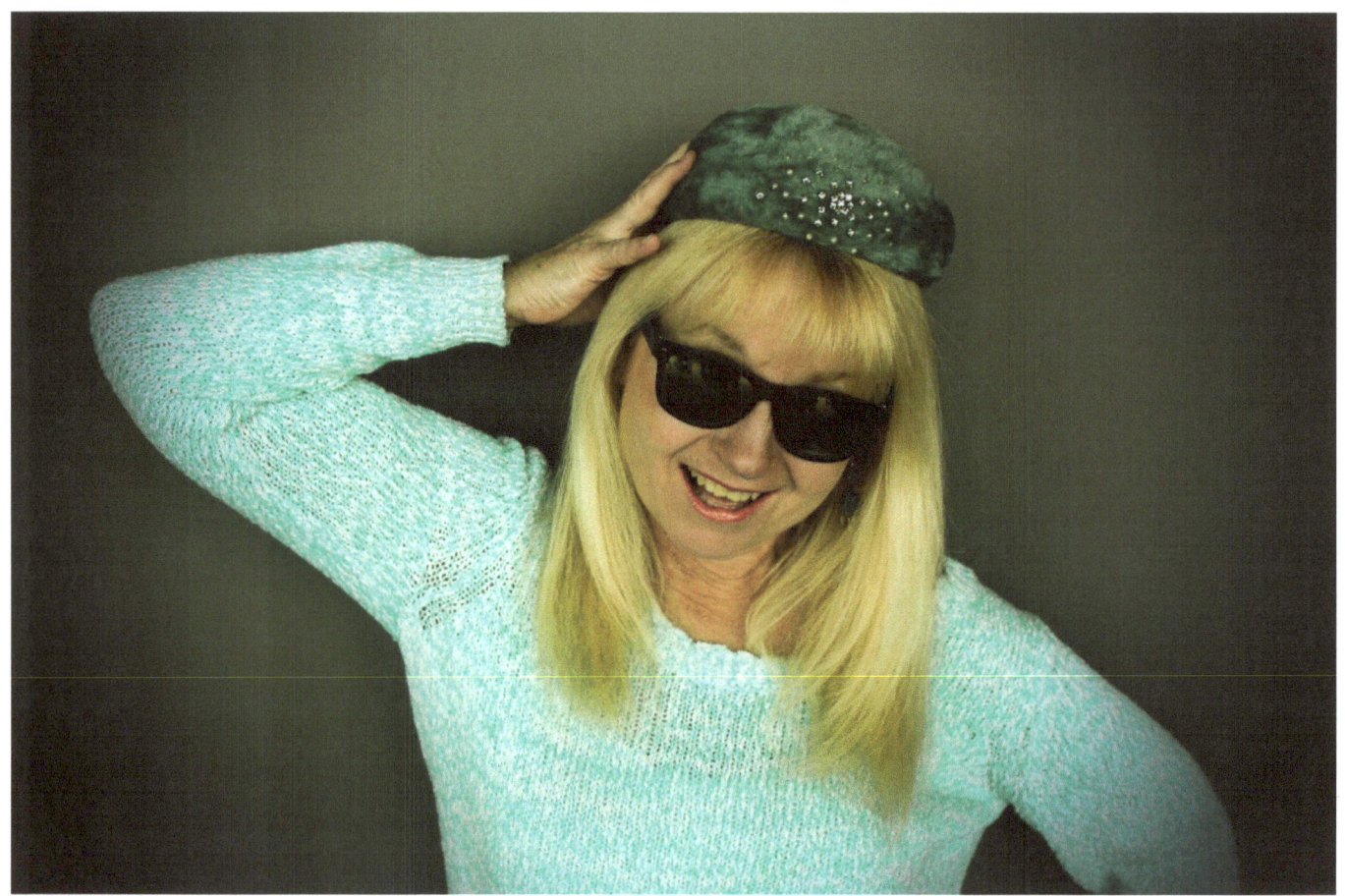

OBJECT:

Hat

WHY IS IT IMPORTANT TO HER?

"What I have here is a hat that used to be my mother's. She passed away in 2000. It's a cute turquoise, furry hat with some pearls on it. She would tell my sister and I this story about how it was in a bin in downtown Rock Island in a nice store and she and another woman spied it at the same time. She grabbed onto it. This other woman grabbed onto it and there was a slight tussle. A physical tussle where they each pulled on the hat and my little 4'10" mother won the hat!

So she would wear it with pride and was pretty happy that she, with her tiny self, was actually able to intimidate someone to actually get this cool hat. So I wound up with it and it reminds me a lot of her. She did some theater and some acting when she was young and I feel I inherited that from her, and that's what I do now and i think she's like it."

Brandy

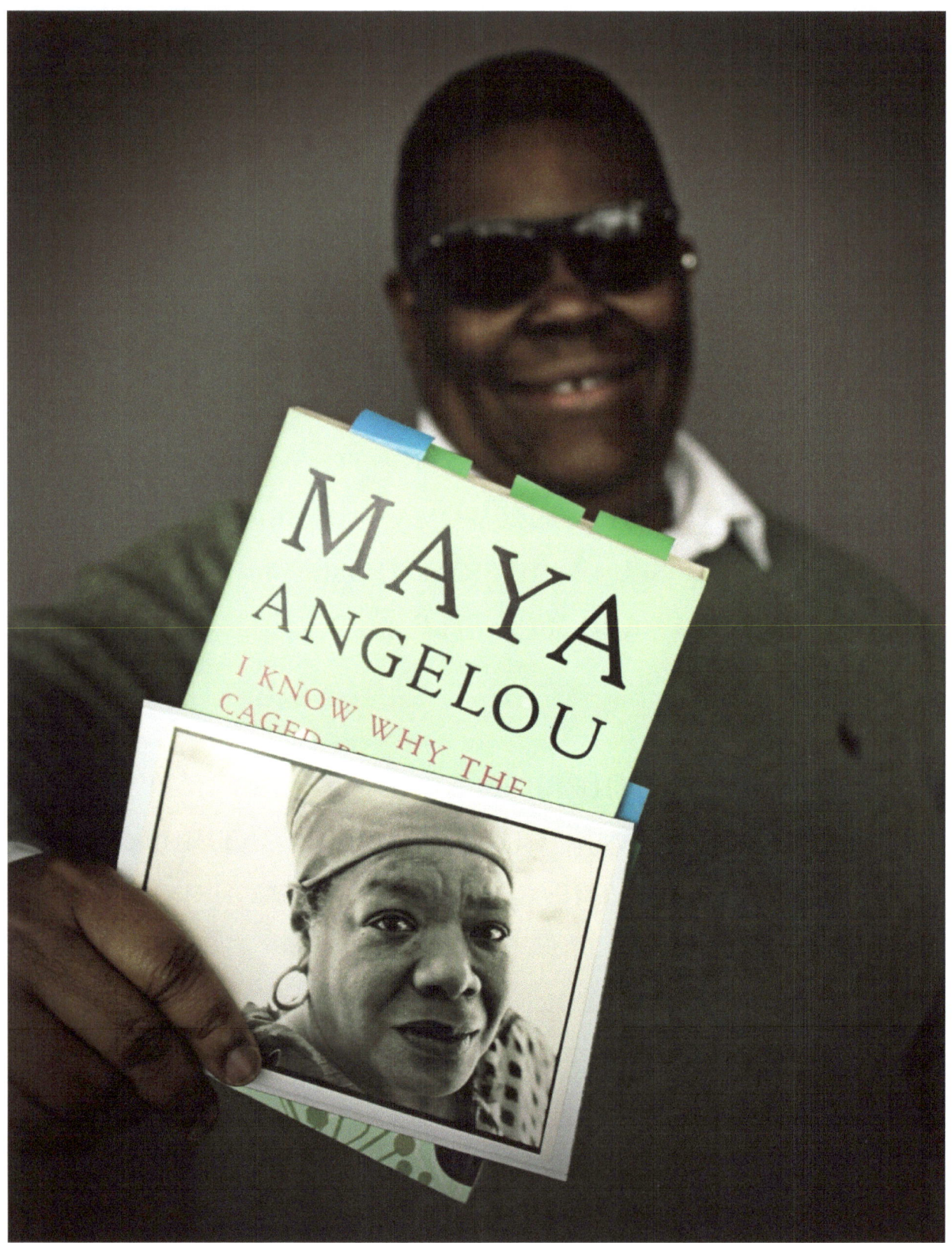

OBJECT:

MAYA ANGELOU PHOTO AND BOOK

WHY IS IT IMPORTANT TO HER?

"I MYSELF AM A WRITER AND I'M ALSO FROM ARKANSAS AS AS MS. ANGELOU WAS. SO WHEN I WAS YOUNG, AND I WAS TRYING TO FIGURE OUT BEING A WRITER, LOVING POETRY, AND ALL THOSE THINGS, I DIDN'T HAVE ANY EXAMPLES OF PEOPLE WHO LOOKED LIKE ME WHO DID THAT. I DIDN'T KNOW ANY POETS THAT LOOKED LIKE ME. WE DIDN'T GET TAUGHT ANY AUTHORS IN SCHOOL THAT LOOKED LIKE ME. THAT WERE BLACK. THAT WERE WOMEN. SO WHEN I DISCOVERED MAYA ANGELOU, THAT OPENED MY EYES TO A COMPLETE DIFFERENT WORLD. I OPENED MY EYES TO THE FACT THAT I COULD DO THIS, BECAUSE SOMEONE LIKE ME IS BRILLIANT AT IT. SO THROUGHOUT THE YEARS OF READING HER AND BEING INSPIRED BY HER, WORDS AND WHAT SHE TAUGHT, AND HOW SHE LIVED HER LIFE, HAS REALLY ADDED A LOT TO WHO I AM TODAY.

THE FIRST BOOK I EVER READ OF MAYA ANGELOU'S WAS 'I KNOW WHY THE CAGED BIRD SINGS.' WHICH IS THE FIRST INSTALLMENT IN HER AUTOBIOGRAPHY SERIES. SHE WROTE HER LIFE STORY IN A SERIES OF NOVELS. IN THAT BOOK, READING HER STRUGGLES, HER SUCCESSES, HER TRIUMPHS, WHAT SHE CAME FROM...WHICH WAS VERY SIMILAR TO WHAT I CAME FROM, THAT JUST REALLY MADE ME A DIFFERENT PERSON FOR THE BETTER. IT REALLY HELPED ME FIGURE OUT WHO I WANTED TO BE AND WHAT TYPE OF LIFE I WANTED TO LIVE. AND NOT TO EVER LET MY STRUGGLES DETERMINE MY FUTURE OR DETERMINE WHAT TYPE OF SUCCESS I COULD HAVE. BECAUSE SHE IS A GREAT EXAMPLE OF THE TYPE OF WOMAN WHO OVERCAME EVERYTHING AND BECAME A WORLD-RENOWNED SUCCESS. I JUST THINK AS A PERSON, SHE WAS ALSO AN INDIVIDUAL THAT LIVED WITH INTEGRITY, WITH PURPOSE, AND NEVER LET ANYONE DERAIL HER PURPOSE. SO, MAYA ANGELOU IS MY BIGGEST INSPIRATION. IN HER BOOK, 'I KNOW WHY THE CAGED BIRD SINGS,' IS PROBABLY THAT ONE BOOK THAT I HOLD ABOVE ALL THE HUNDREDS OF OTHER BOOKS I'VE EVER READ. THIS BOOK LITERALLY DID CHANGE MY LIFE."

ALEXEY

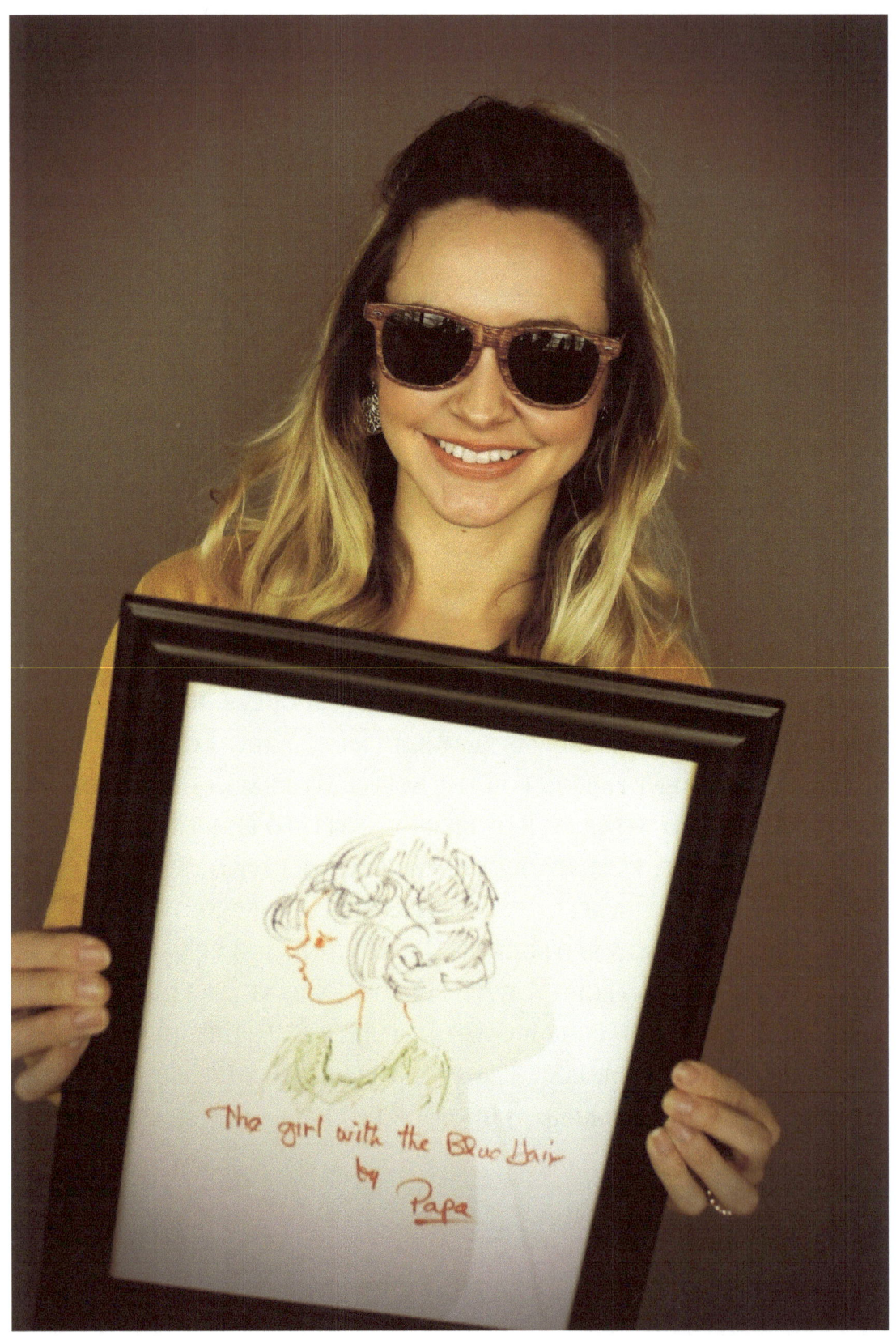

OBJECT:

Drawing from her grandfather

WHY IS IT IMPORTANT TO HER?

"I brought a picture that my grandfather, Jack Anderson, drew for me when I was probably about nine years old. We were drawing at the kitchen table and he just picked up some markers and started drawing it and he gave it to me. I thought it was so cool that I had an original Jack Anderson (drawing), aka Papa as we called him.

I hung it in my room and I've always had it. I've always displayed it in every place I've lived since then. Aside from being a teacher, a counselor, and a coach, my grandpa was a really talented artist and he achieved a lot in his life, but some of the stuff I remember about him is that he was so fun and just really funny. He had a really funny sense of humor. Me and my family can spend hours telling 'Papa stories.' About all the funny stuff that he said and did. So whenever I look at this, I think about him and I really miss him a lot."

DAVE

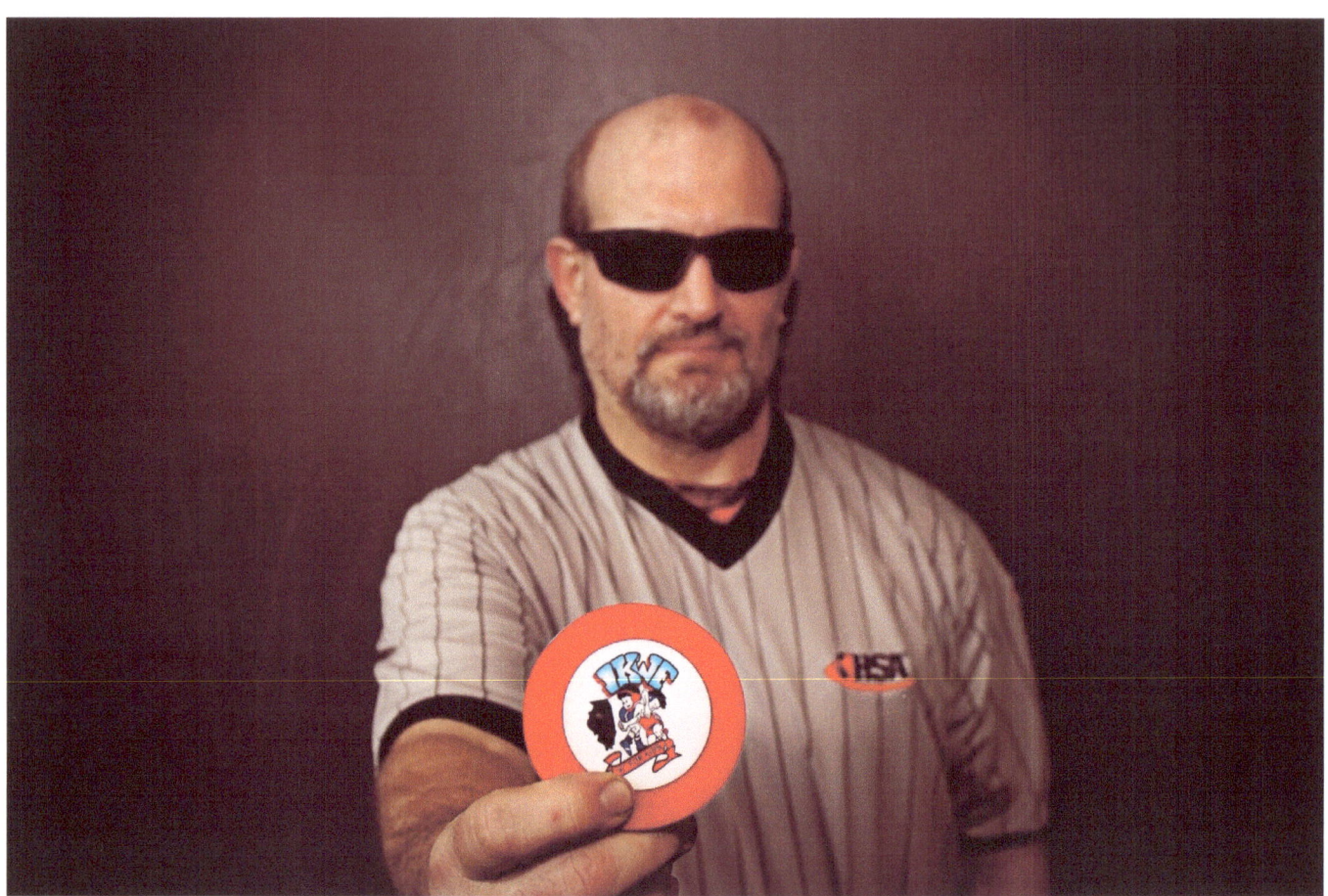

OBJECT:

REFEREE FLIP DISK

WHY IS IT IMPORTANT TO HIM?

"IT WAS GIVEN TO ME BY THE FAMILY OF MY MENTOR. I CALL HIM MY WRESTLING DAD AND I COACHED WITH HIM. I LIVED WITH HIM. HIS SONS ARE LIKE BROTHERS TO ME. HE PASSED AWAY AND THEY GAVE ME THIS DISK TO USE AND THE IRONIC THING IS JUST THIS LAST MARCH, I WAS REFEREEING THIS GRANDSON WITH HIS SON IN THE CORNER COACHING AND I HAD THIS IN MY POCKET. AND WHERE I WAS, WAS THE LAST PLACE THAT I GOT TO TALK TO KEN WHEN HE WAS ALIVE. THE IRONIC THING WAS THAT I WASN'T EVEN SUPPOSED TO BE REFEREE. ONE OF THE REFEREES GOT SICK AND I WAS CALLED TO DO IT AND ACTUALLY GOT TO REFEREE KOLE AND WITH KEVIN IN THE CORNER. KOLE WENT ON TO PLACE SECOND IN THE STATE CHAMPIONSHIP THIS YEAR.

SO, HAVING THIS IN MY POCKET, KEN WAS KIND OF WITH ME AND WITH THE WHOLE FAMILY. I DON'T USE IT VERY OFTEN BECAUSE WHEN I FLIP IT, IT ROLLS. SO I USE A DIFFERENT ONE, BUT I ALWAYS KEEP THIS WHEN I'M DOING MATCHES WHERE I'M A LITTLE NERVOUS. I HAVEN'T HAD A LOT OF HIGH SCHOOL EXPERIENCE, SO WHEN I DO THE HIGH SCHOOL MATCHES, I KEEP IT BECAUSE KEN WAS A REFEREE FOR 25 YEARS SO THAT'S WHY IT'S SPECIAL."

GRETCHEN

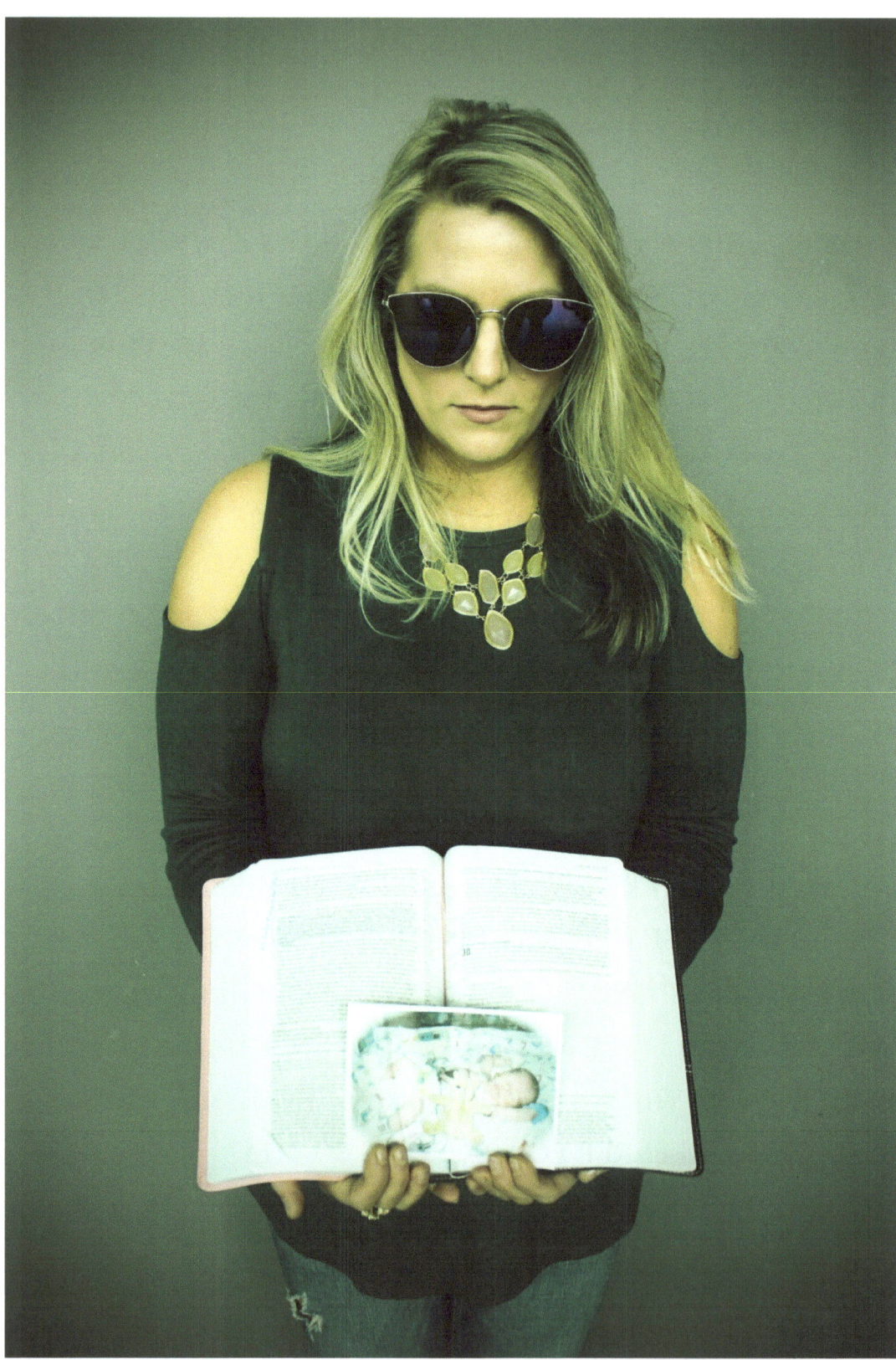

OBJECT:

PHOTO OF SON AND BIBLE VERSE

WHY IS IT IMPORTANT TO HER?

"THE OBJECT I CHOSE WAS THE BIBLE VERSE OUT OF MY VERY FIRST BIBLE FROM MY HUSBAND, WHICH IS JEREMIAH 29:11. THE BIBLE VERSE IS, 'I KNOW THE PLANS I HAVE FOR YOU,' SAYS THE LORD. 'THE PLANS FOR GOOD AND NOT FOR DISASTER. TO GIVE YOU FUTURE AND A HOPE. AND IN THOSE DAYS WHEN YOU PRAY, I WILL LISTEN. AND IF YOU LOOK FOR ME WHOLEHEARTEDLY, YOU WILL FIND ME. I WILL BE FOUND BY YOU AND I WILL END YOUR CAPTIVITY AND RESTORE YOUR FORTUNES.'

SO, THE REASON WHY THIS IS IMPORTANT TO ME IS BECAUSE WHEN I HAD MY FIRST CHILD, HE WAS DIAGNOSED WITH A STROKE IN THE WOMB. I WAS GIVEN SOME VERY GRAVE NEWS THAT HE WOULD PROBABLY HAVE CEREBRAL PALSY AND NOT BE ABLE TO WALK, TALK, OR FEED HIMSELF. A FRIEND VISITED ME IN THE HOSPITAL AND GAVE ME THIS VERSE ALMOST TEN YEARS AGO. IT WAS ON A PLAQUE AND THIS VERSE JUST REPRESENTS THE LORD'S SUSTAINABILITY FOR MY LIFE AND OVER MY LIFE. THAT HE CARES FOR ME AND THAT HE WILL BRING ME OUT OF ANYTHING THAT IS NOT MEANT FOR HIS GOOD. SO IT SHOWS ME THE STRUGGLE AND IT REPRESENTS THE BLESSING AT THE END."

TRAVIS

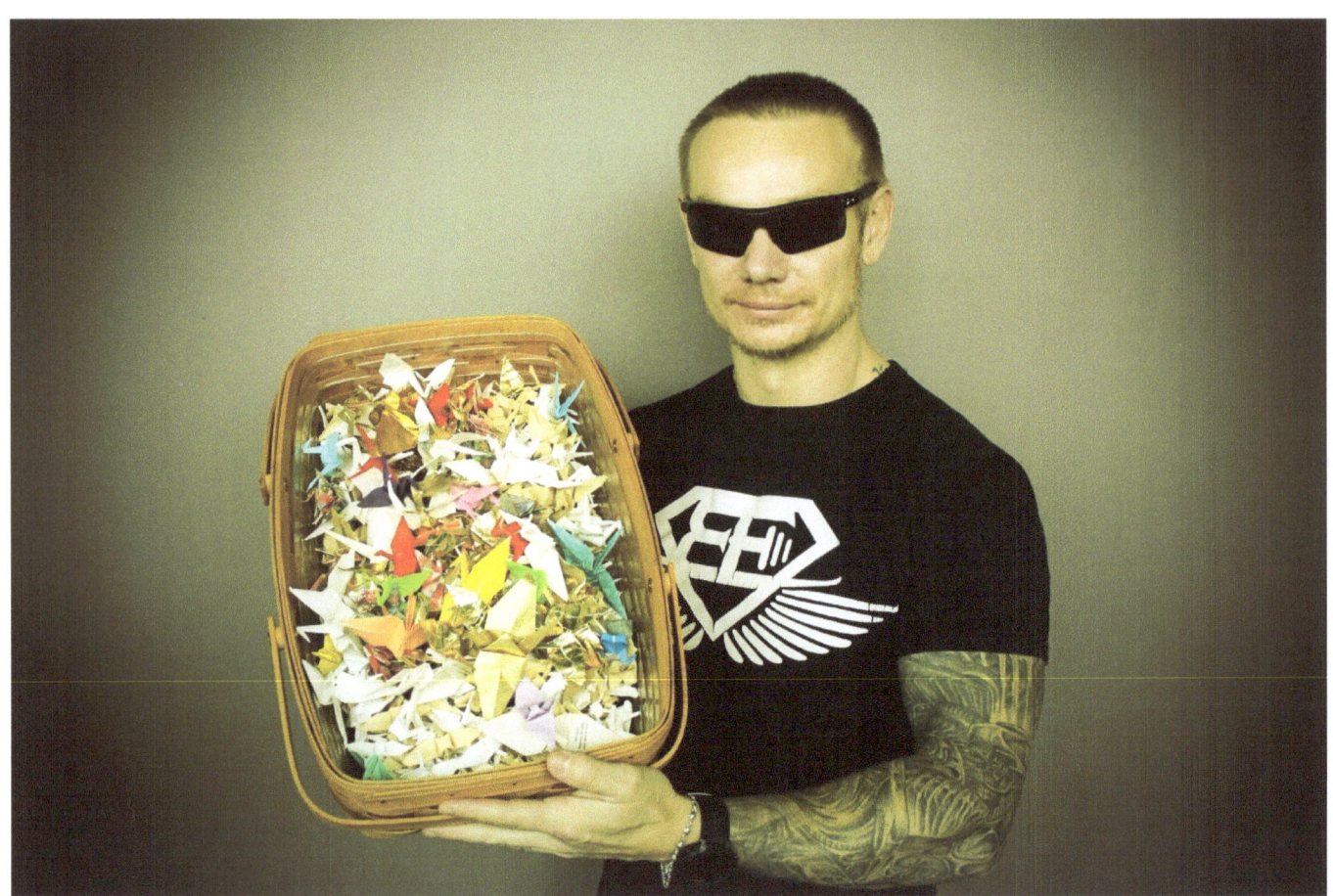

Object:

1000 Origami Cranes

Why is it important to him?

"My wife made these for me right before we got married. I thought a lot about what I was going to bring. What was important to me. I thought things I did. Things I accomplished. What was cool about me. And I realized that she is the most important thing to me. So it's a sign of pure love. A wish for lifelong happiness. Before we were married, we lived in a small apartment and we were just starting out. Didn't have much money. So she wanted to do something for me. So this is the Japanese symbol for 'A thousand cranes is a symbol for a wish lifelong happiness and love.'

So she sat there for hours on end folding each one of these thinking about nothing but me and my happiness. I am blessed with her true love. I don't deserve her. I don't. She is the most selfless, amazing person I could ever ask for and this reminds me of that every time I look at her."

AUBREY

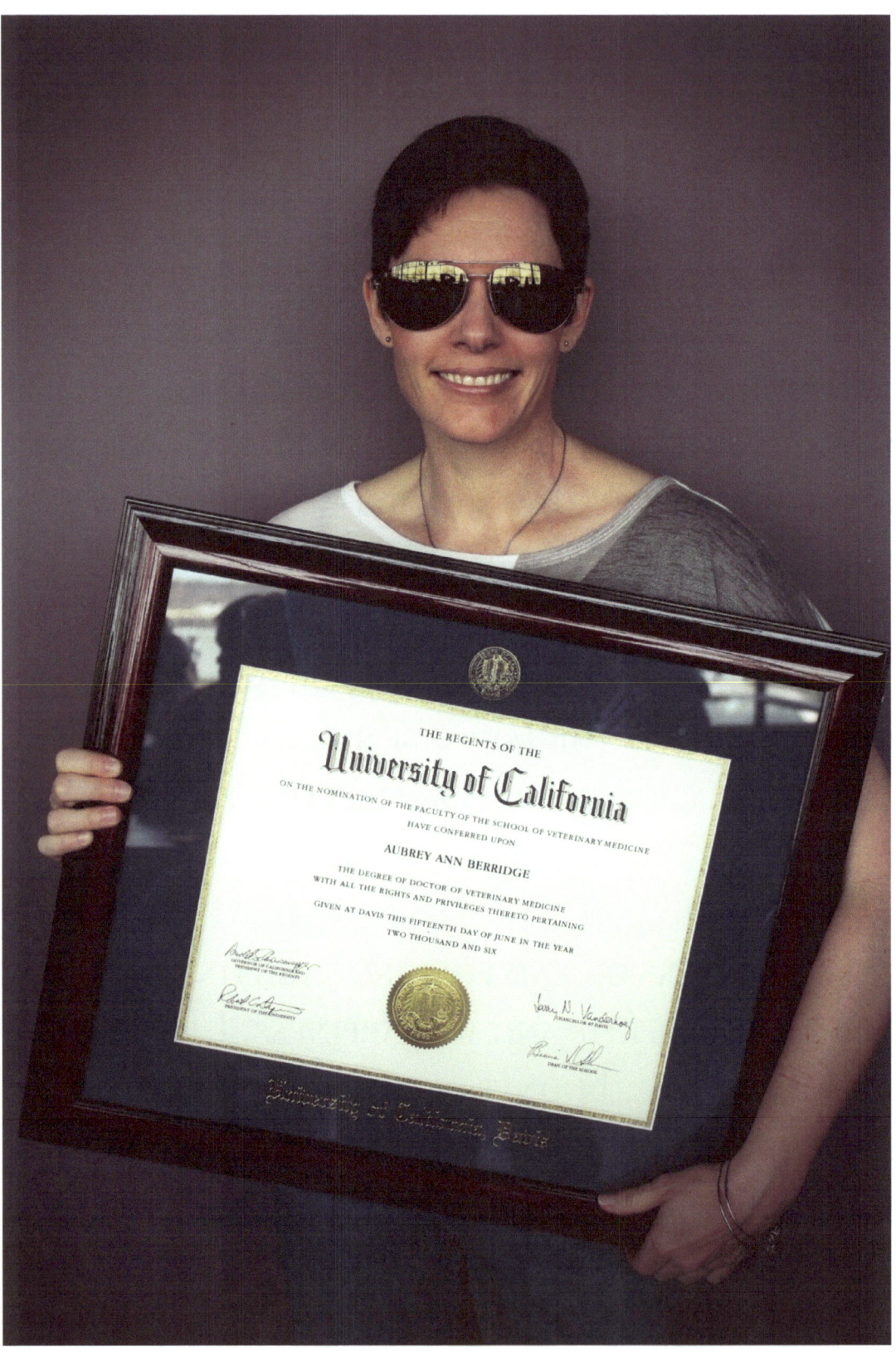

OBJECT:

VET'S SCHOOL DIPLOMA

WHY IS IT IMPORTANT TO HER?

"IT REPRESENTS GOING AFTER YOUR DREAMS AND HOW PEOPLE CAN BELIEVE IN YOU IN THE FACE OF ADVERSITY. I ENDED UP DROPPING OUT OF SCHOOL WHEN I WAS ABOUT 20 YEARS OLD BECAUSE WE HAD SOMETHING HAPPEN IN THE FAMILY WHERE MY BROTHERS AND I WERE ACTUALLY HELD AT GUN POINT AND SOMEBODY WAS SHOT. IT WAS REALLY TRAUMATIC AND ACTUALLY TWO OF THE OTHER PEOPLE INVOLVED AREN'T EVEN ALIVE ANYMORE BECAUSE IT. SO BECAUSE OF THAT, I COULDN'T REALLY HANDLE IT AND I DROPPED OUT OF SCHOOL AFTERWARDS AND IT RUINED MY ACADEMIC RECORD (OR I THOUGHT).

SO I STARTED ANOTHER CAREER AND I DIDN'T THINK THAT GOING TO THAT SCHOOL AFTER THAT WAS AN OPTION ANYMORE. A FEW YEARS LATER I WAS TALKING TO A FRIEND OF MINE AND SHE SAID, 'WELL, I THINK YOU COULD DO IT, BUT YOU REALLY NEED TO BE HONEST WITH THE APPLICATION FOR IT WITH YOUR PERSONAL STATEMENT AND TELL THEM WHAT HAPPENED.'

SO I WENT BACK AND COMPLETED THE COURSES AND GOT STRAIGHT AS AFTER THAT AND WHEN I WROTE MY PERSONAL STATEMENT, I THEM WHAT HAPPENED AND WHY I HAD DROPPED OUT OF SCHOOL AND EVERYTHING. I ENDED UP GETTING ACCEPTED. SO HERE I AM TODAY!"

ANITA

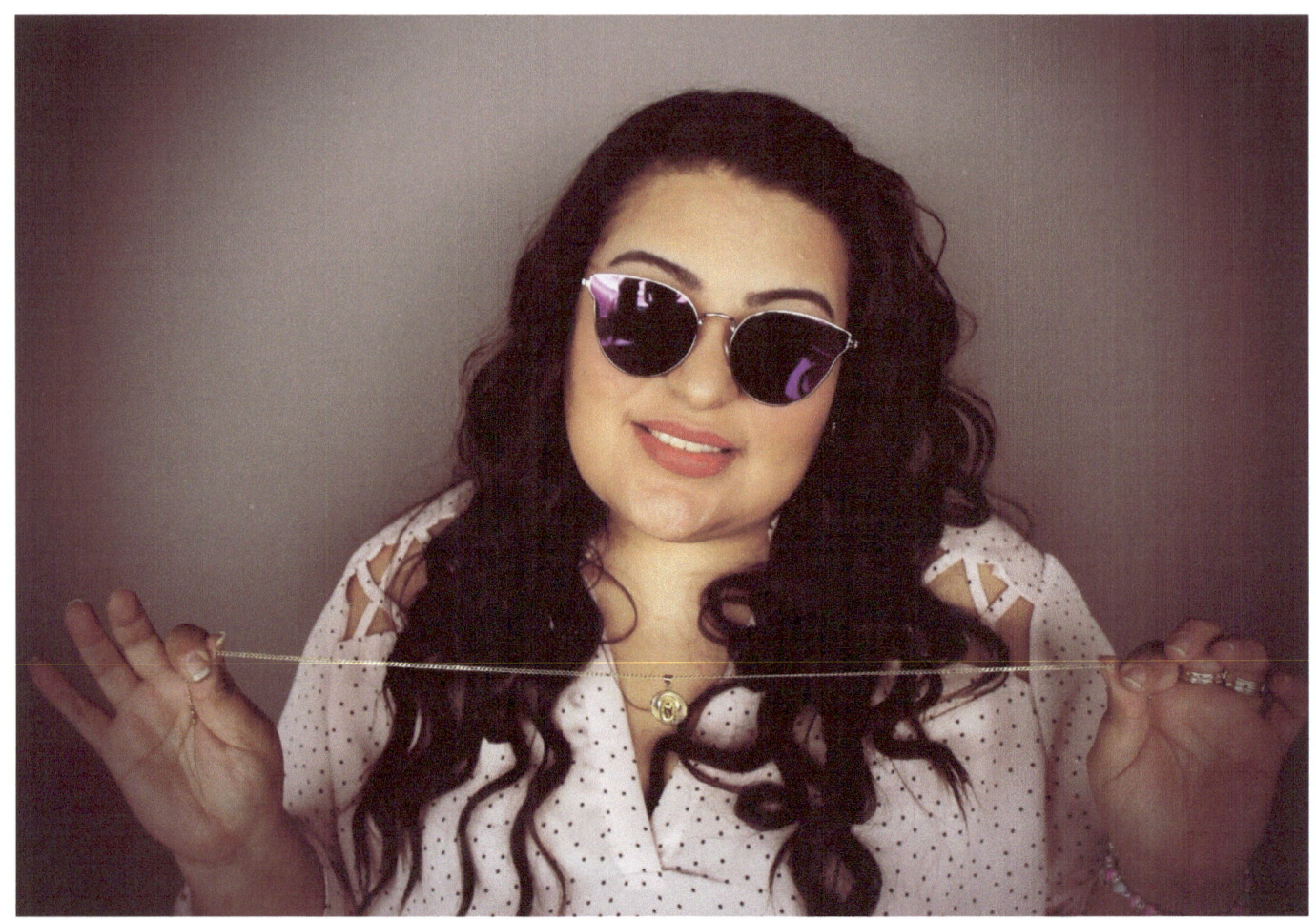

OBJECT:

NECKLACE

WHY IS IT IMPORTANT TO HER?

"IT WAS 1ST GIVEN TO ME WHEN I WAS 10 AND THEN AGAIN AT AGE 15. BY THEN I WAS ABLE TO REALIZE THE SIGNIFICANT MEANING IT HAD. LA VIRGEN DE GUADALUPE IMAGE ON THE MEDALLION HAS BEEN MY PATRON SAINT FOR AS LONG AS I CAN REMEMBER. SHE HAS GOTTEN ME THROUGH MOMENTS THAT I THOUGHT I WOULD NEVER BE ABLE TO GO THROUGH. SHE WAS MY ROCK WHEN MY MOTHER 1ST TOLD ME ABOUT HER CANCER.

I PRAYED TO HER TO GIVE ME STRENGTH. I TURNED TO HER TO GIVE ME THE POWER TO BE STRONG FOR MY MOTHER AND SISTER. SHE SAW ME THROUGH MANY MOMENTS WHEN I DIDN'T KNOW WHERE TO TURN. SHE SAW ME THROUGH A TIME IN MY LIFE WHERE I WAS ALONE AND HELPLESS PRAYING FOR A SAFE RETURN OF SOMEONE I LOVED. SHE HAS ALWAYS BEEN MY ROCK. THE MEDALLION IS A REMINDER OF THE FAITH I HAVE, SHOULD HAVE, AND WILL CARRY EVERYDAY."

DAVID

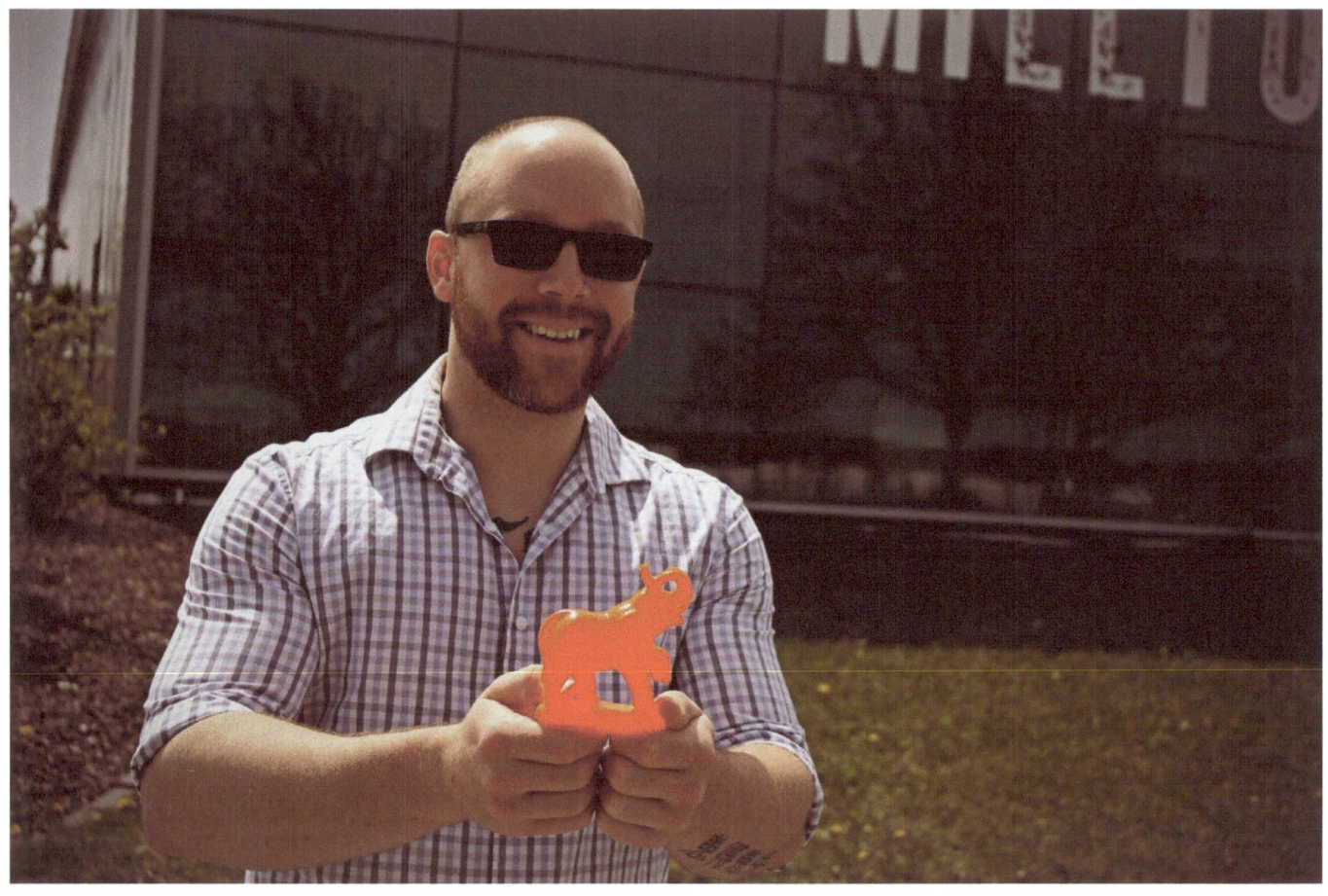

OBJECT:

ORANGE ELEPHANT

WHY IS IT IMPORTANT TO HIM?

"ELEPHANTS ARE EASILY MY FAVORITE ANIMAL, SECOND ONLY TO OWLS. I WAS HAVING A ROUGH COUPLE OF WEEKS AS SOME OF US DO AT TIMES. WHEN A FRIEND OF MINE SAID DURING ONE OF OUR RANDOM CONVERSATIONS THAT SHE HAD NOT BEEN TO THE FIELD MUSEUM(IN CHICAGO) SINCE SHE WAS A KID. I SAID WE SHOULD GO SOMETIME AND WE PLANNED A TRIP WITH HER, MYSELF AND HER SISTER WHO IS ALSO A FRIEND OF MINE. WE HAD A GOOD DAY OF ROAD TRIP MUSIC, FRENCH FOOD, TRAIN RIDES, AND NAVIGATING THE SUBWAY, BEFORE GETTING TO ROAM THE ENTIRETY OF THE MUSEUM. RIGHT BEFORE WE LEFT, MY FRIEND LEA DECIDED TO TOSS $2 INTO A MACHINE THAT MADE A MOLD OF AN ELEPHANT (MY FAVORITE ANIMAL) AS A TOKEN OF OUR DAY THERE.

SMALL GESTURES LIKE THAT MEAN THE WORLD TO ME AND IT REMINDED ME OF HOW FRIENDS CAN KNOW YOU BETTER THAN RELATIVES. THIS ELEPHANT NOW SITS ON MY COFFEE TABLE AS A REMINDER OF THAT DAY. SO AFTER WAKING UP EARLY TO WORK TWO JOBS, RUNNING ERRANDS, DANCE PRACTICE, PHOTOSHOOTS, AND GENERAL ADULTING, I'VE GOT A REMINDER THERE. I KNOW WHEN I SIT DOWN ON MY COUCH AND LOOK AT THAT ELEPHANT, THAT IF MY DAY HAS BEEN STRESSFUL, OR I'M FEELING DOWN, THAT I CAN ALWAYS COUNT ON MY FRIENDS TO PICK ME BACK UP, BECAUSE WE HAVE EACH OTHER'S BACKS."

KIMBERLY

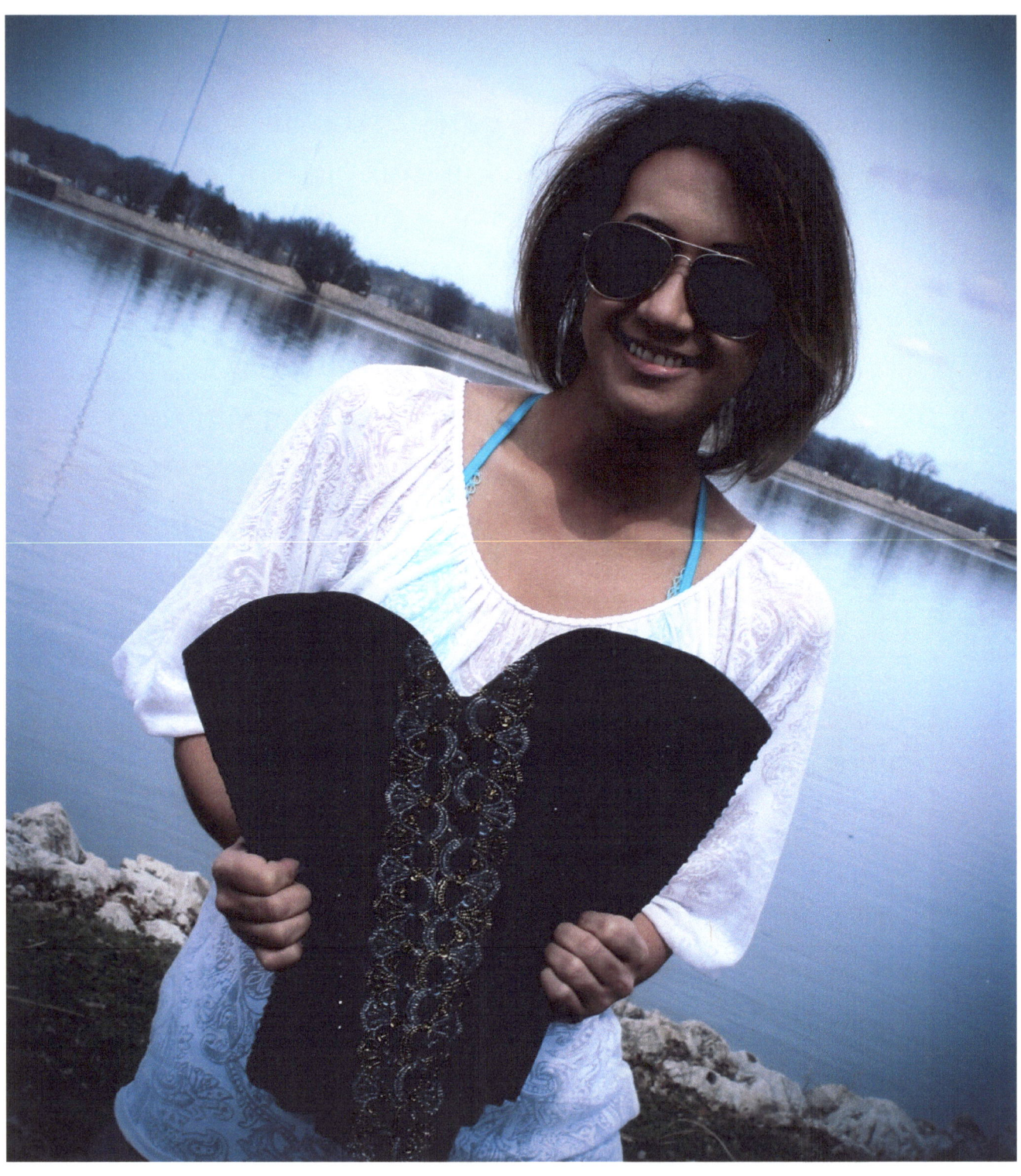

OBJECT:

Corset

WHY IS IT IMPORTANT TO HER?

"I HAVE ALWAYS BEEN FASCINATED WITH DANCE BECAUSE OF THE WAY YOU CAN EXPRESS YOURSELF IN ALL THESE DIFFERENT STYLES. ESPECIALLY INDIVIDUALLY AS A PERSON. I'VE NEVER ACTUALLY BEEN PERSONALLY OR PROFESSIONALLY TRAINED, BUT I HAVE BEEN DANCING IN ONE FORM OR ANOTHER EVEN ON THE PROFESSIONAL LEVEL MY ENTIRE LIFE.

I RECENTLY IN THE LAST COUPLE OF YEARS FOUND MYSELF ASSOCIATED WITH A BURLESQUE GROUP IN THE QUAD CITIES THAT I STARTED TO LEARN A LOT ABOUT MYSELF AND BEING ABLE TO CHALLENGE MYSELF. THEY EVENTUALLY PUT TOGETHER A SCHOOL AND I WAS ONE OF THEIR FIRST STUDENTS. IT WAS THEIR FIRST YEAR AND THE FINAL FOR THAT SCHOOL WAS TO PUT ON A SHOWCASE ENTIRELY PRESENTED BY THE STUDENTS. IN THAT SHOWCASE, I THOUGHT IT WAS GOING TO BE EASY SINCE I'VE BEEN DANCING MY WHOLE LIFE, BUT I LEARNED VERY QUICKLY THAT IT WAS ACTUALLY GOING TO BE ONE OF THE HARDEST THINGS I'VE EVER DONE IN MY LIFE.

I WAS USED TO BEING A VERY SMALL PART OF A VERY BIG PICTURE AND THE WAY THEY DO THINGS IS SO DIFFERENTLY. YOU ARE ABOUT FOUR FEET AWAY FROM PEOPLE AND YOU ARE THE ONLY PERSON ON STAGE. YOU PUT THE OUTFIT TOGETHER, AND YOU PUT THE ROUTINE TOGETHER, AND YOU PUT THE MUSIC TOGETHER. BEFORE YOU KNOW IT, YOU'RE ACTUALLY LOOKING IN SOMEONE'S EYES WHILE YOU'RE TAKING OFF YOUR CLOTHES!

SO, I BROUGHT THE CORSET THAT I WORE IN MY FIRST PERFORMANCE THAT I DID IN BURLESQUE AS A DANCER IN A COMPLETELY DIFFERENT WORLD. I LEARNED ABOUT MYSELF AND I LEARNED THAT I CAN DO THINGS SO MY HARDER THAN I THOUGHT I COULD DO."

BRANDON

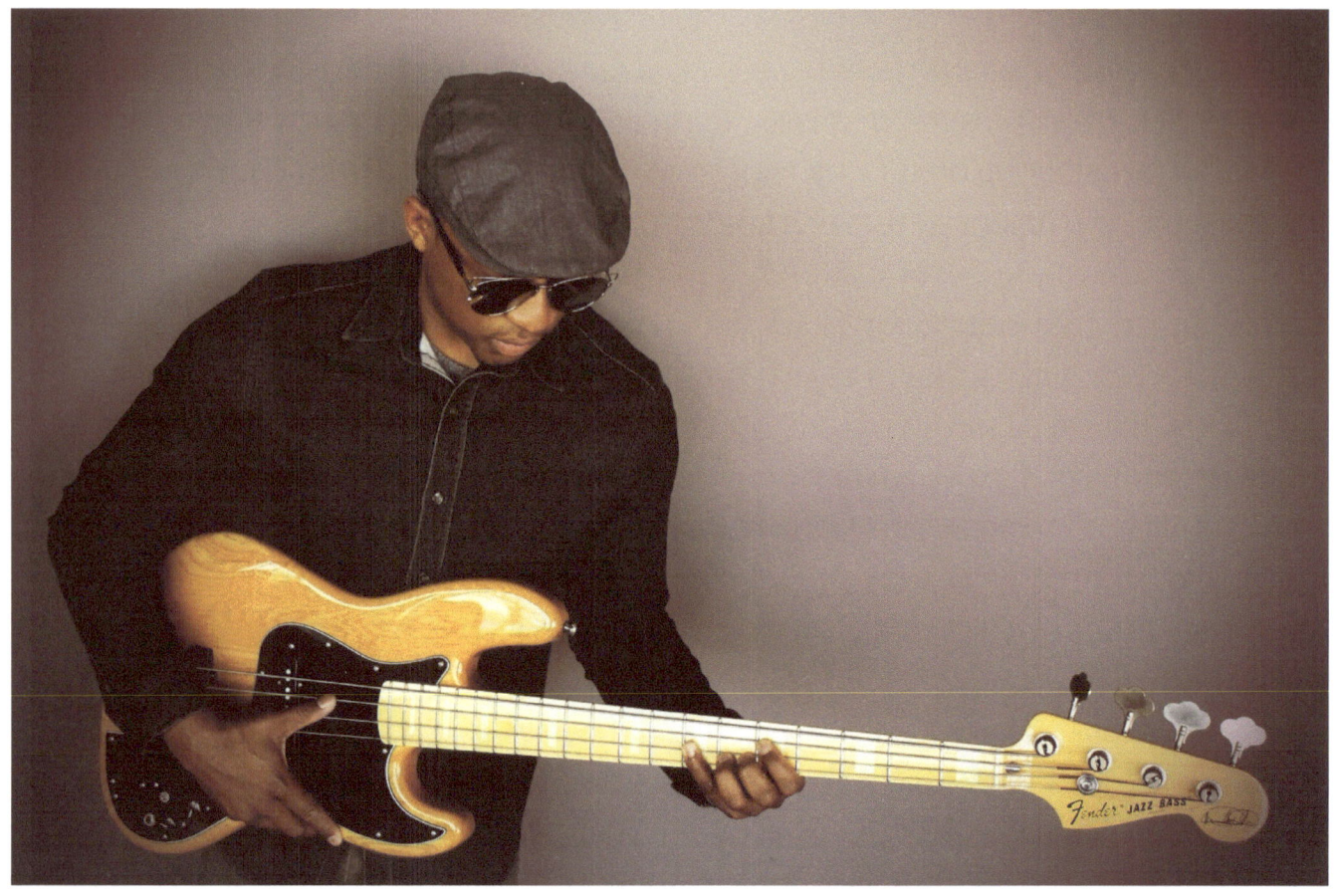

OBJECT:

Bass Guitar

WHY IS IT IMPORTANT TO HIM?

"Bass has been a part of my life since I was about 5 and a half, 6 years old. I actually started out on piano, but I had seen this guy in church playing the bass and I asked my stepdad at the time, 'What is that instrument that he's playing?'

He's like, 'Oh, that's the bass!'

I'm like, 'I really like the sound of that instrument.' It sound really cool. He looks really cool playing it. So I really decided to get into bass playing. He bought me my first bass. I was about the 5 and half, 6 year old age and I've been playing ever since. I really, really, truly love it. It's actually a part of me.

One of my greatest inspirations is Victor Wooten, who I've now met twice. Met him recently again, but a few years back, he was at the Redstone Room and he had a workshop. In that workshop, he said, music is not music until you actually play the music. The instrument is just sitting there until you actually make it become music. He said you are music. It's inside of you. Whatever's inside of you, you bring that out and interpret that in whatever instrument you're playing. That's a part of me and the bass is a part of me."

Cassie

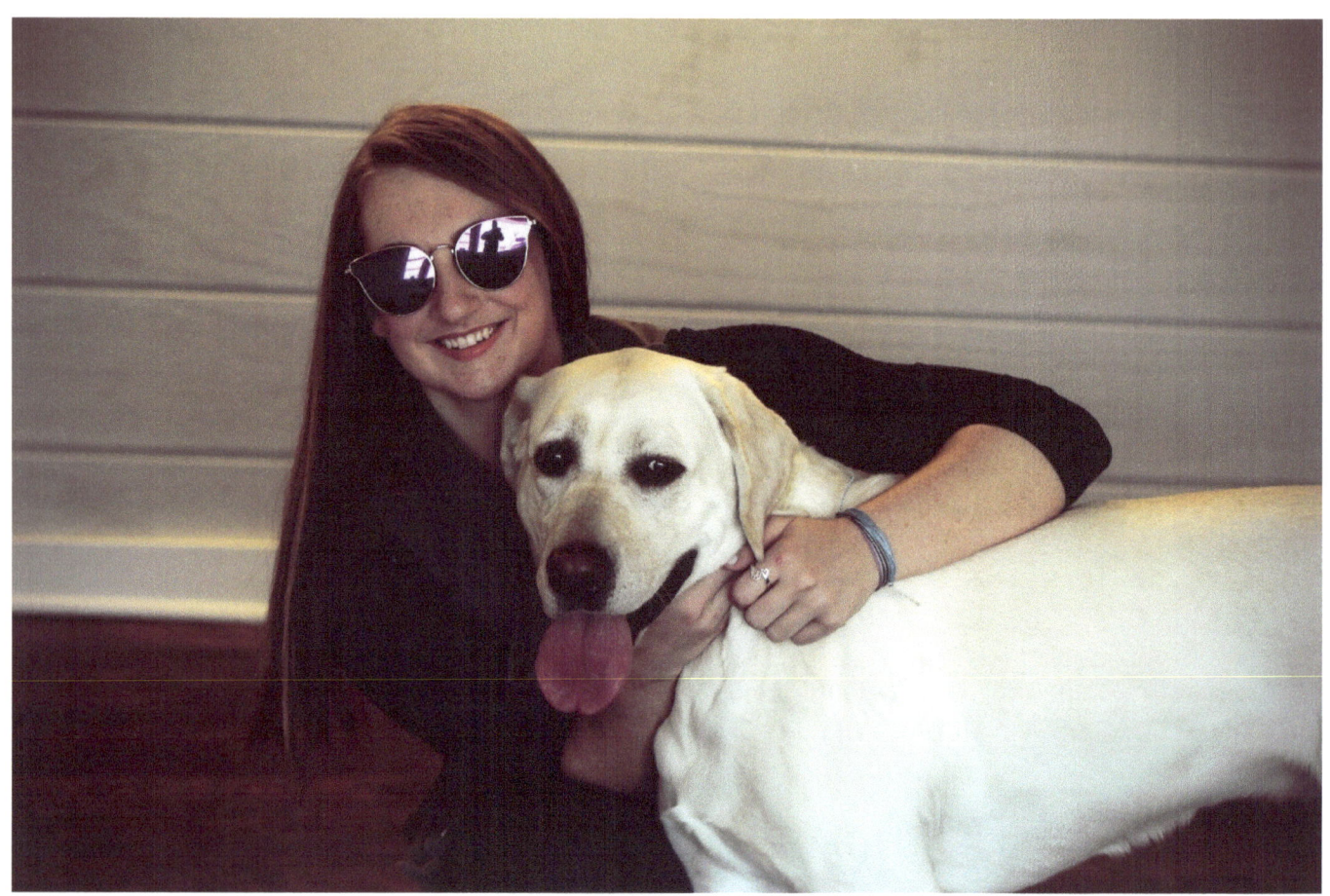

OBJECT:

Her dog, Mia

WHY IS SHE IMPORTANT TO HER?

"To me, Mia is a true angel in the form of fur. Having a mental illness and being in your early 20's is stressful, but being able to come home to something that doesn't even speak the same language as you, yet loves you like you're the absolute best human on this planet is insanely stress relieving. Every heartbreak I have been through, every tear shed from the loss of someone close, every failure, and every panic attack that forces me to curl up onto the couch and avoid the world has been comforted by this sweet girl. And on the other hand, Mia is always down to celebrate the good times with me, even if she doesn't know why she is jumping or getting extra treats! She can sense my feelings, and she somehow always knows how to approach the situation.

She has taught me more about responsibility, love, and loyalty than anything else could. I walked into the shelter a year and a half ago thinking that I knew that I did not want the responsibility of a dog at the time. Three days and three visits later, there was no way that I could leave without her. She is one of the best decisions I have ever made."

DEREK

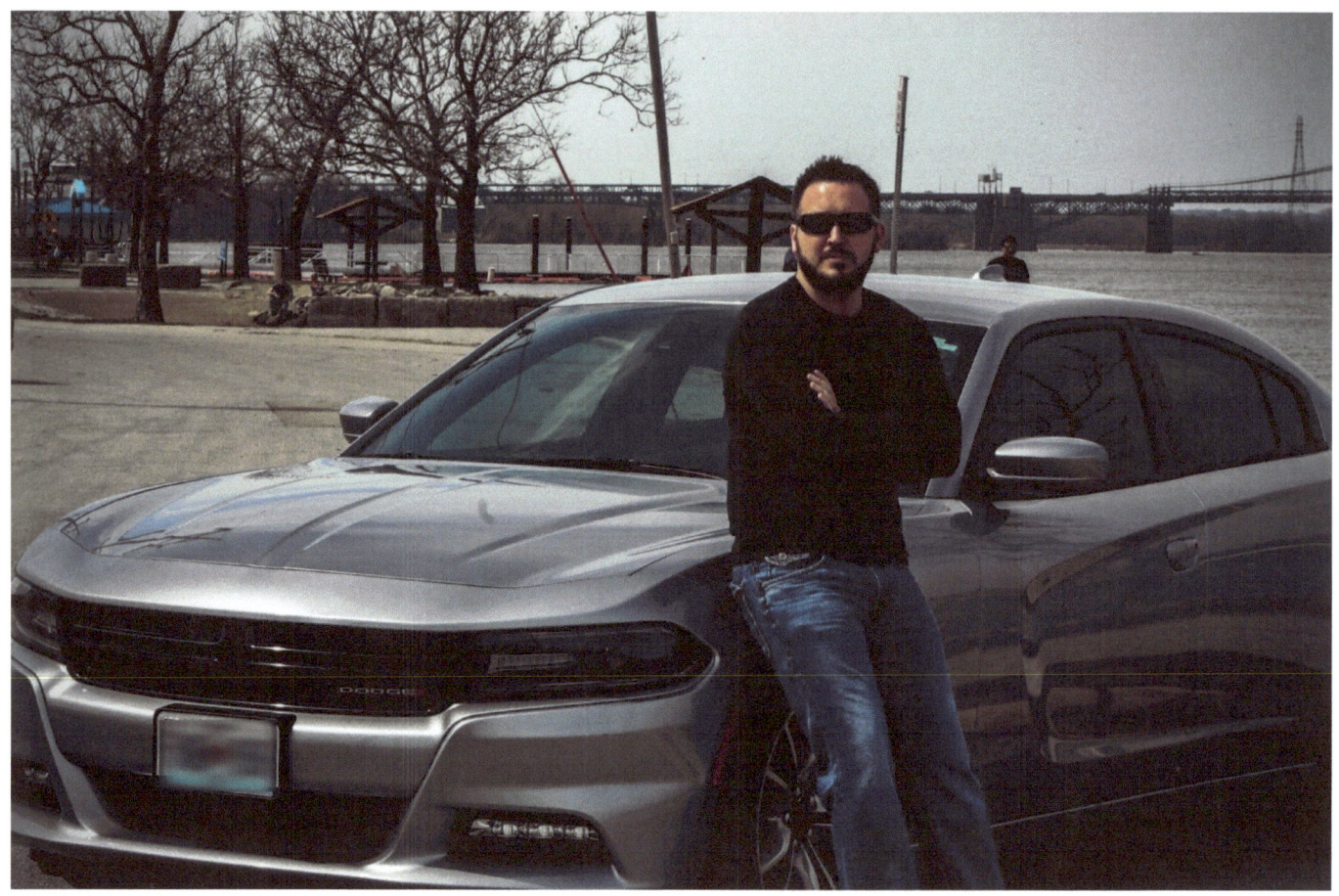

OBJECT:

His Car

WHY IS IT IMPORTANT TO HIM?

"I HAVE AN APPRECIATION FOR AUTOMOBILES BUT I'M NOT REALLY A CAR GUY. I WON'T TALK TO YOU FOR HOURS ABOUT CARS BECAUSE EVEN THOUGH THEY ARE AMAZING PIECES OF MACHINERY AND ARTISTIC MASTERPIECES; AT THE END OF THE DAY IT'S A TOOL. GO TO BUY A CAR BASED SOLELY ON YOUR NEEDS AND YOU'LL LEARN A LOT ABOUT YOURSELF AND WHERE YOU ARE AT WITH LIFE.

FOR ME IT'S ALWAYS BEEN MY BIGGEST TOOL FOR LIFE'S ADVENTURES. WITH THE AMOUNT OF TIME I SPEND IN MY VEHICLE FOR WORK AND PLEASURE I WANTED SOMETHING THAT WAS SPACIOUS AND COMFORTABLE FOR LONG ROAD TRIPS. IT FOR SURE NEEDED A COMFORTABLE DRIVER SEAT TO SLEEP IN. I ALSO DESIRED A DECENT STEREO; WHAT'S LIFE WITHOUT GOOD MUSIC?

BEFORE THE INVENTION OF THE AUTOMOBILE, PEOPLE TRAVELLED BY FOOT OR WITH THE USE OF ANIMALS. IT WAS COMMON THAT PEOPLE MAY NEVER TRAVEL FARTHER THAN THE TOWN THEY GREW UP IN THEIR ENTIRE LIVES. COMPARATIVELY, WE CAN CROSS STATES IN HOURS, NOT DAYS. I'VE BEEN FORTUNATE ENOUGH TO LIVE ACROSS SEVERAL DIFFERENT STATES AND THAT STARTED BY PACKING UP MY CAR AND DRIVING HALFWAY ACROSS THE COUNTRY. I KNOW MY NATURE; I WOULD NOT HAVE ACCOMPLISHED THAT WITH A HORSE.

IN MY LIFE, I HAVE LIVED IN MY CAR. NOT IN A DESTITUTE MANNER, RATHER IT WAS PART OF THE ADVENTURE I WAS ON. SOME OF THE BEST CONVERSATIONS I HAVE EVER HAD HAVE TAKEN PLACE BEHIND A WINDSHIELD. THE PRIVACY OF A COUPLE PEOPLE TALKING IN A CAR IS PRICELESS.

MY CAR HAS BEEN WITH ME ON SEVERAL ADVENTURES AND THERE'S MORE PLANNED.

OH! AND PLANES.. DON'T EVEN GET ME STARTED ON PLANES..."

ALEX

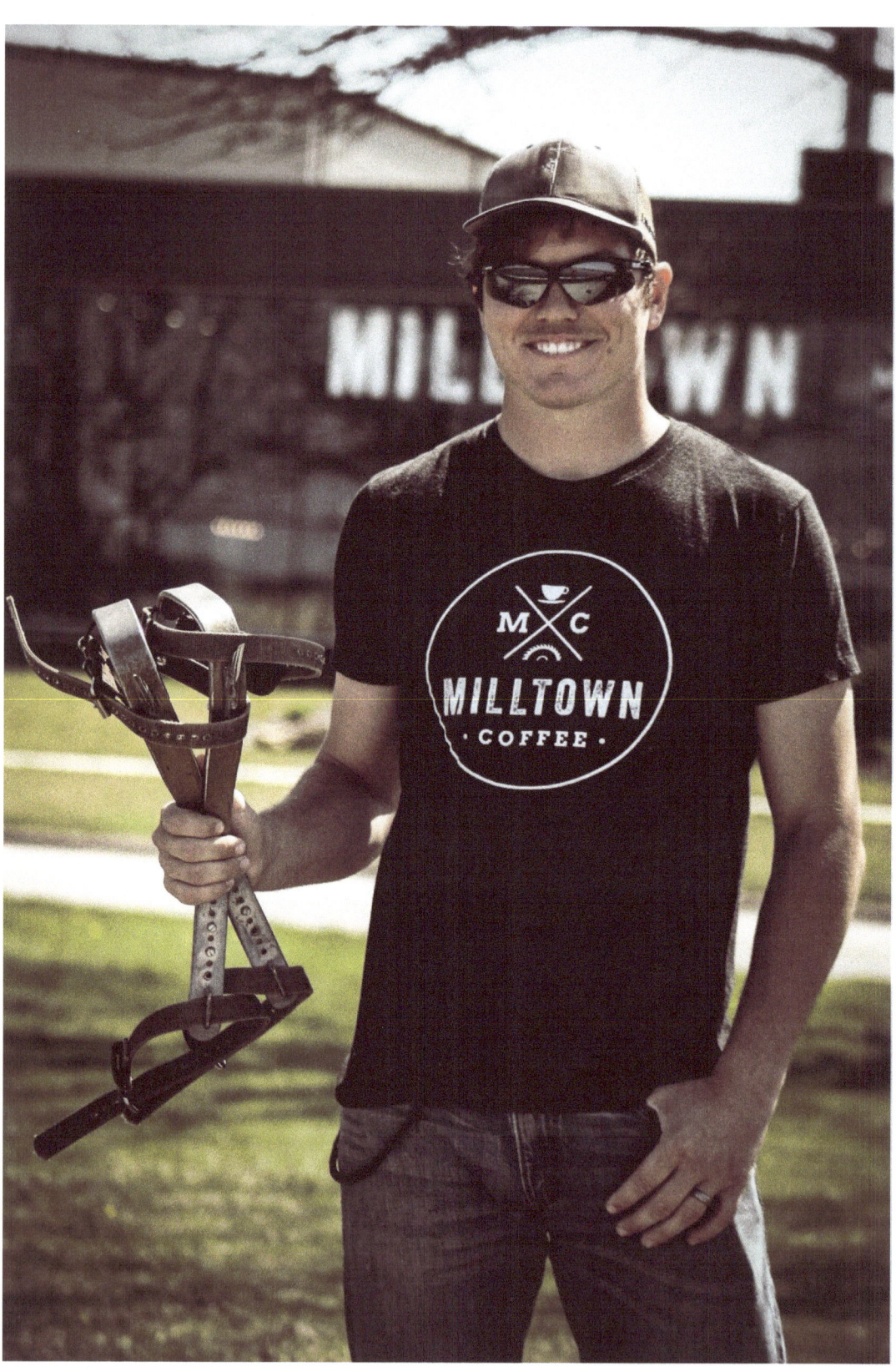

OBJECT:

CLIMBING HOOKS

WHY IS IT IMPORTANT TO HIM?

"TO ME THEY SYMBOLIZE HARD WORK AND STRIVING FOR YOUR GOALS. WHEN MY WIFE AND I FIRST GOT TOGETHER WE WERE POOR, LIKE NOT ABLE TO AFFORD ENOUGH FOOD POOR. NO CABLE NO INTERNET NO NOTHING. WE READ BOOKS I HAD FROM WHEN I WAS YOUNGER AS ENTERTAINMENT, BUT WE WERE MADLY IN LOVE AND DETERMINED TO MAKE IT WORK.

WHEN OUR FIRST BABY WAS ON THE WAY I KNEW I NEEDED A JOB, AND WITH LITTLE TO NO REAL JOB EXPERIENCE THE ONLY THINK I COULD FIND WAS A JOB MAKING PIE DOUGH AT 12 AM- WHENEVER THEY DIDN'T NEED ME. IT WAS HORRIBLE HOURS AND LITTLE PAY, BUT IT WAS WORK AND I WAS GRATEFUL. I KEPT WORKING AND PUSHING TO FIND SOMETHING BETTER ANYTHING. THAT CAME IN THE FORM OF A LEG UP.

MY SOON TO BE FATHER IN LAW NOTICED MY HARD WORK AND PUT ME IN TOUCH WITH A TREE TRIMMING JOB. HE ALSO GAVE ME MY FIRST (AND STILL USING) PAIR OF HOOKS. THAT LANDED ME INTO THE IBEW, INTERNATIONAL BROTHERHOOD OF ELECTRICAL WORKERS, FROM THERE I LEARNED OF AN APPRENTICESHIP AND IMMEDIATELY STARTED WORKING TOWARDS THAT. I WAS VERY BLESSED, ESPECIALLY WHEN IT SEEMED EVERY TIME WE HAD A KID, I ACCOMPLISHED A MILESTONE AND MADE MORE MONEY.

6 YEARS LATER, I NOW HAVE 4 CHILDREN. MY WIFE AND I ARE STILL MADLY IN LOVE, WE GET THE OPPORTUNITY TO TRAVEL ALL OVER THE COUNTRY AND I'M STILL STRAPPING THE SAME SET OF HOOKS TO MY FEET AND CLIMBING EVER HIGHER."

MAX

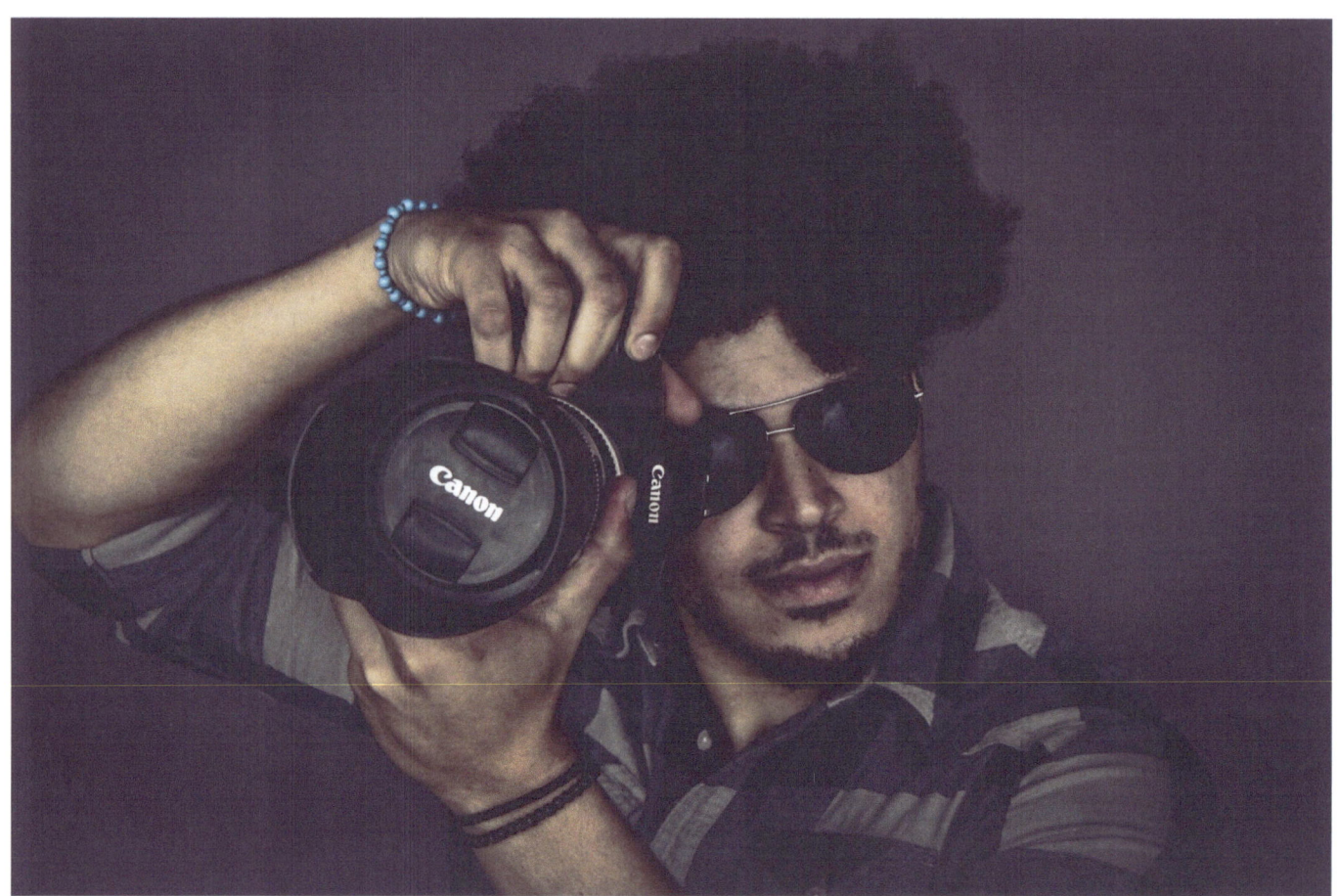

OBJECT:

Canon 5d Mark III

WHY IS IT IMPORTANT TO HIM?

"What I enjoy in life is capturing moments. Taking a piece of life. Especially nature. I love taking pieces of nature and then showing people that things exist outside their normal reality or normal everyday life. Because a lot of people don't see a lot of certain things.

I was fortunate enough to be able to travel a lot around the world and I come back always to the Quad Cities and try to explain it to somebody and it's very hard to. They can't really conceptually picture what I'm saying in their head or at least they probably try to.

So that's what I love. Capturing moments. First it was photography. Taking pictures of things and whatnot, and then it morphed into videography. Taking videos of everything. I started doing a little bit of blogging. I have terabytes and terabytes and terabytes of of absolutely useless footage that I just capture every day because I keep this thing with me.

I one day want to put all this kind of footage together and show people life from my point of view. But it also expands into I just want to show people that there are interesting things out in the world."

Katie

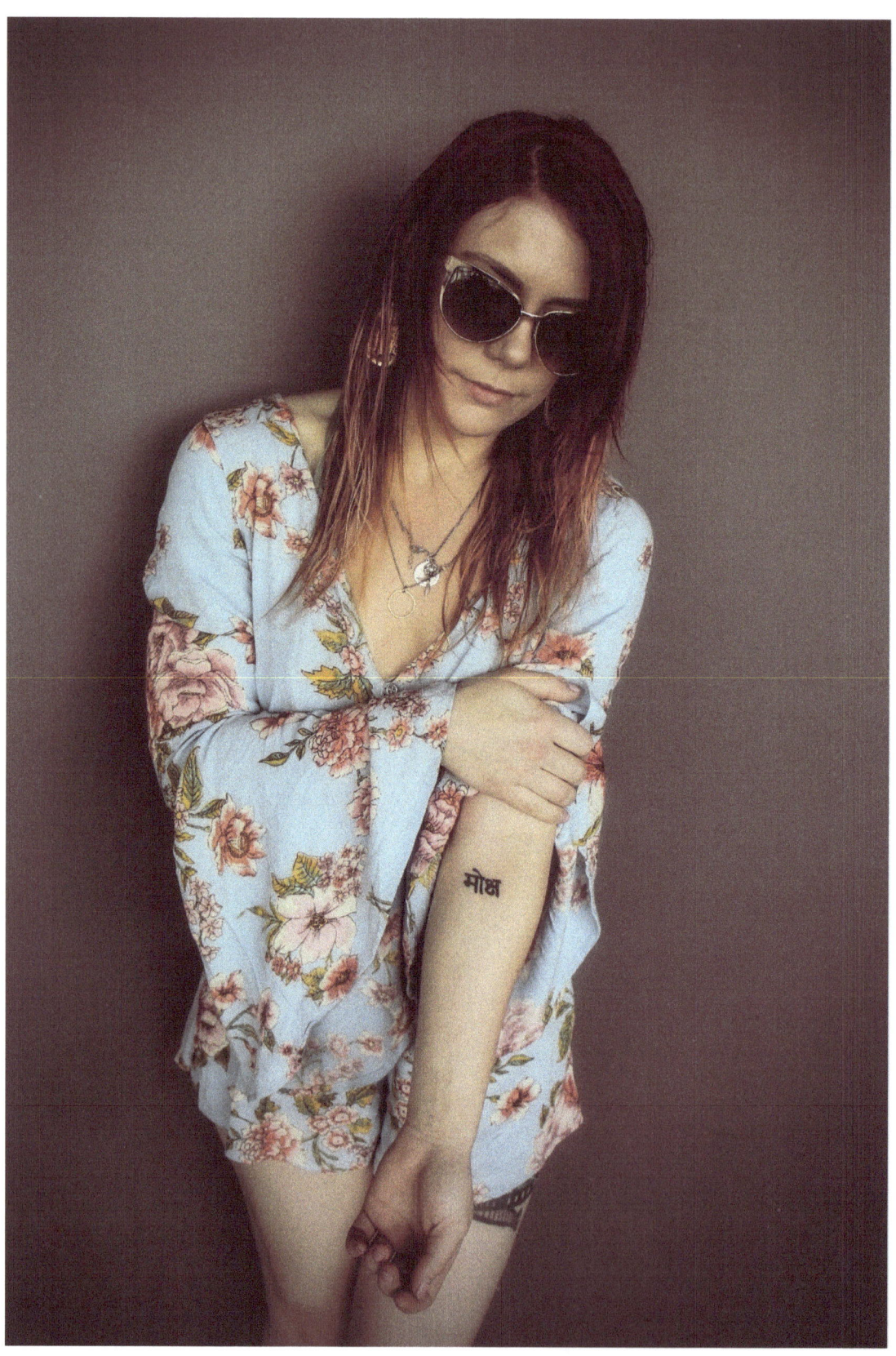

OBJECT:

Arm Tattoo

WHY IS IT IMPORTANT TO HER?

"It's Sanskrit for Moksha, which means 'I am emotionally free.' I got it actually after my mom passed away a couple years ago. It was hard. She was technically my stepmom, but she did more for me than anyone ever has. She was always there. She was always really supportive. My dad has a bad habit of disappearing and she was always there to make sure that he would call us. He would talk to us. He would make sure he would come visit us and just make sure he was a part of our lives.

It's really a lot more difficult not having her around during the really, really good times. So that's why I got it, because she was always really happy for us and was always telling us when we do something good, she would always be the first one to sit there and be like, 'Congratulations.' Or if anything was really hard, she would always be like, 'Let it go. Don't let it hold you down. Make sure it's a moment that you learn and you move past. Be emotionally free about it. Don't let your emotions control you.'

That's why I got it. Because she always a lot like that. She was always very happy and emotionally free. So I got that after her passing so that way I would always remember and always look down and control my own life."

DALTON

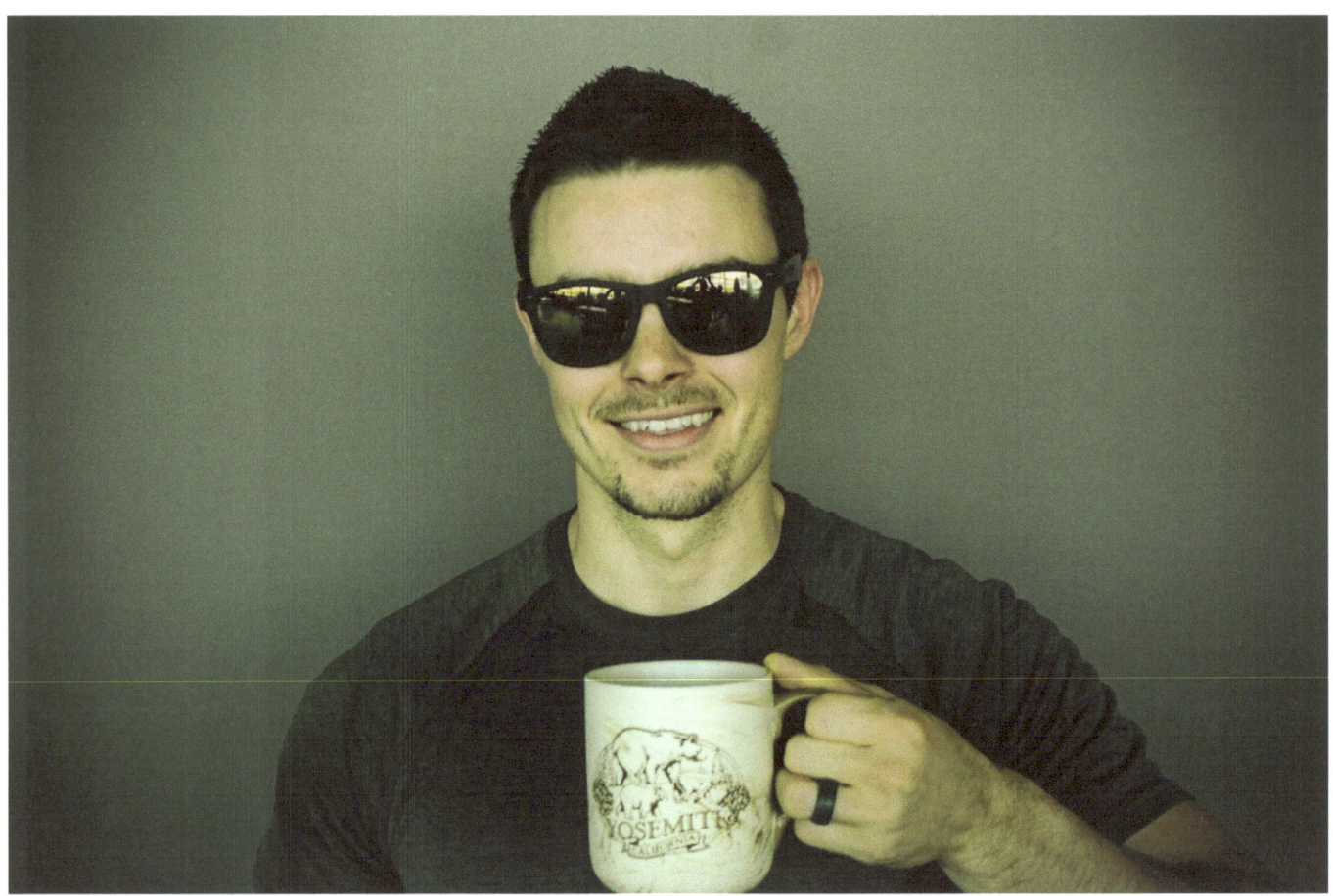

Object:

Collectible Coffee Mug

Why is it important to him?

"Maddy (his wife) and I, when we first started dating, we started collecting coffee mugs wherever we went places. We've actually gotten six or seven other ones. So we just get a mug whenever we on a small vacation or something somewhere. Actually, one of my buddies made me a coffee stand, where you can display all your mugs. So we're just gonna keep adding to it as we go and as we get older and before too long, we'll have a big whole wall and have all of our coffee mugs in there.

It's something I think will be cool for us to remember and then our kids and grand-kids. I think it's something cool to look at. And we both love coffee! So why not coffee mugs? This was my favorite one so I just picked this one.

We've also have a Lake of the Ozarks one. We have a Wisconsin Dells one. We have a Mesa, Arizona one. The Yosemite one. And I just picked this one because it was my favorite one and it was really cool.

We went out there to meet her (his wife's) brother and went to Half Dome, a mountain we hiked. I was an 18-mile round trip hike to the very top of the mountain and back down and it was just really cool. I really enjoy stuff like that so I decided we'd bring this one!"

TANNER

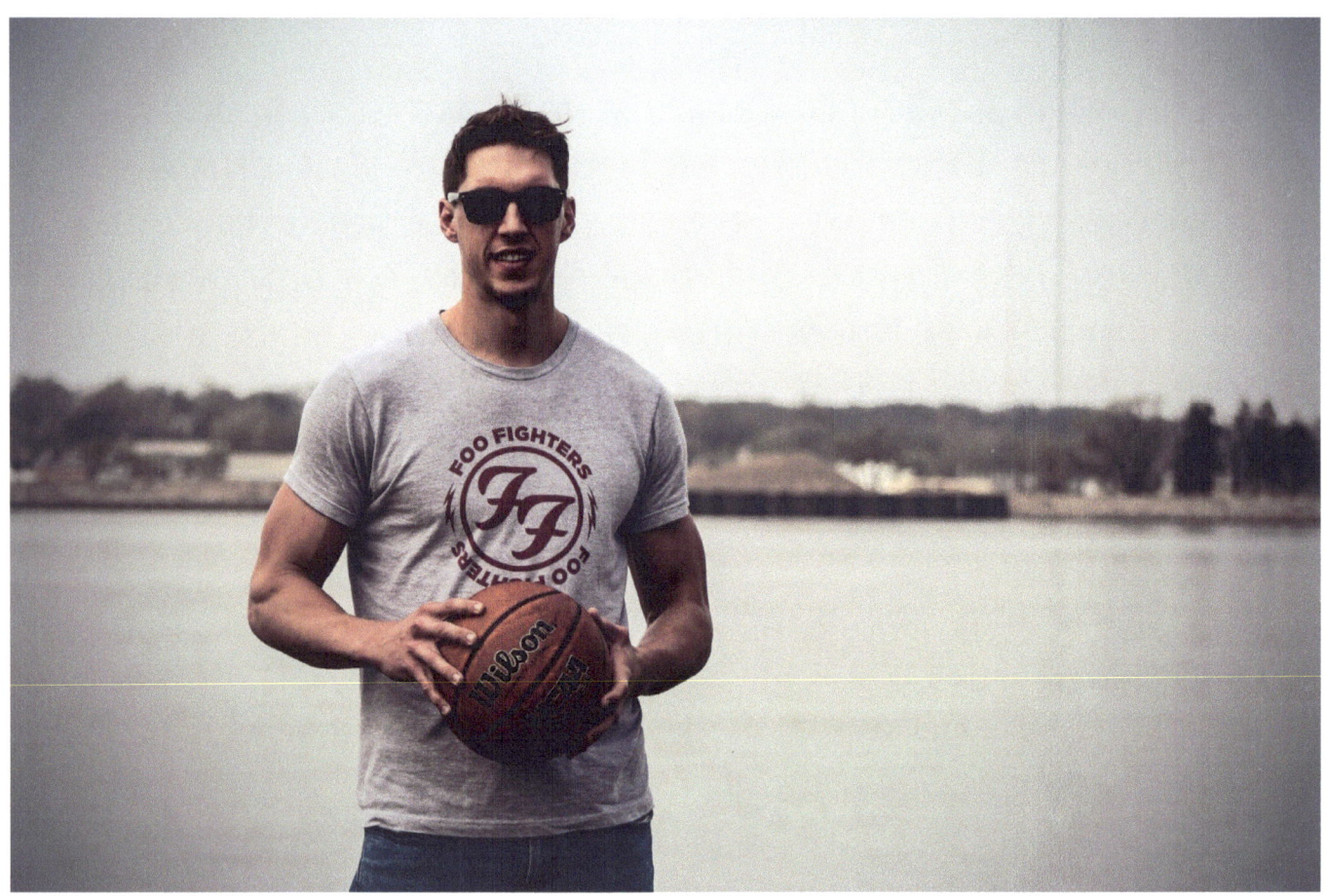

OBJECT:

BASKETBALL

WHY IS IT IMPORTANT TO HIM?

"A GOOD MAJORITY OF MY LIFE I SPENT TRYING TO ACHIEVE A GOAL. THAT WAS EARNING A FULL RIDE SCHOLARSHIP TO COLLEGE TO PLAY BASKET BALL. I PUT IN COUNTLESS HOURS TOWARDS THAT, EVEN IN MIDDLE SCHOOL AND HIGH SCHOOL. I LOST SOME FRIENDSHIPS BECAUSE OF IT. I WAS TREATED BAD BY OTHER PEOPLE SOMETIMES BECAUSE OF THE AMOUNT OF WORK I PUT IN. BECAUSE I WASN'T ABLE TO GO OUT AND PARTY OR GO OUT WITH FRIENDS.

TRYING TO EARN THAT SCHOLARSHIP REALLY MADE ME VALUE DEDICATION, HARD WORK AND MOTIVATION, BECAUSE IT TOOK A LOT OF THAT. SINCE I'M GRADUATED NOW, IT'S REALLY HELPED ME GET THROUGH COLLEGE AND TO WORK HARD IN THE CLASSROOM. SO IT DIDN'T JUST TEACH ME ATHLETIC SKILLS.

A LOT OF PEOPLE MAY BE LIKE, 'OH. YOU'RE JUST AND ATHLETE. YOU'RE JUST IN COLLEGE TO PLAY SPORTS.'

WELL, I WASN'T. I WANTED TO PLAY BASKETBALL, BUT I WANTED TO BE GOOD IN THE CLASSROOM TOO. SO PRETTY MUCH THOSE SKILLS JUST TRANSFERRED OVER."

LIZA

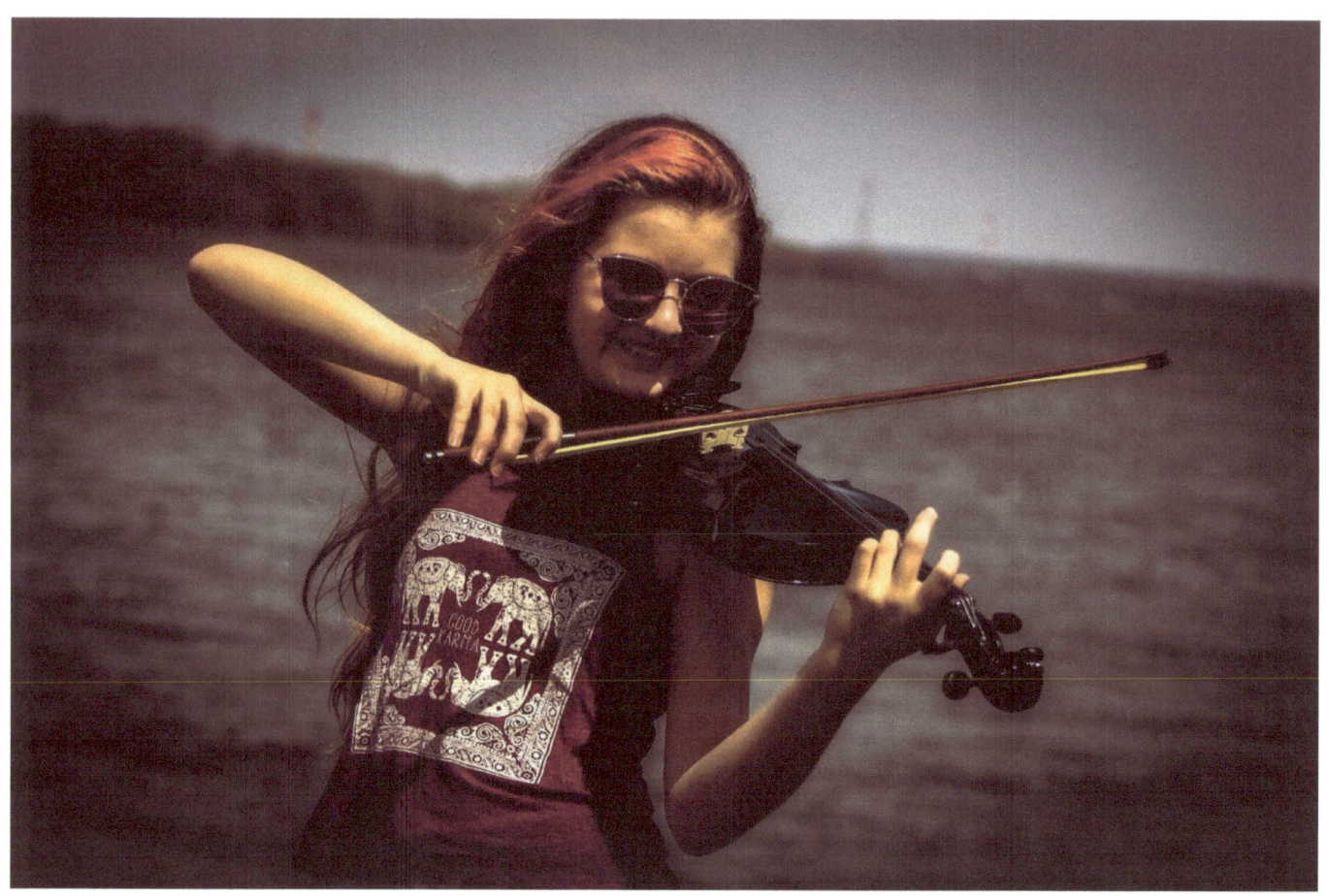

OBJECT:

VIOLIN

WHY IS IT IMPORTANT TO HER?

"MUSIC HAS ALWAYS BEEN A HUGE PART OF MY LIFE AND I GET TO PLAY THE VIOLIN IN PARTICULAR WITH THE FLUTE. SOME OF MY ROLE MODELS USE LOTS OF DIFFERENT INSTRUMENTS, ESPECIALLY THE VIOLIN. IT'S A JUST A WAY FOR ME TO BE ABLE TO INTERPRET WHAT I FEEL INTO MUSIC AND PERFORMING."

JAMES

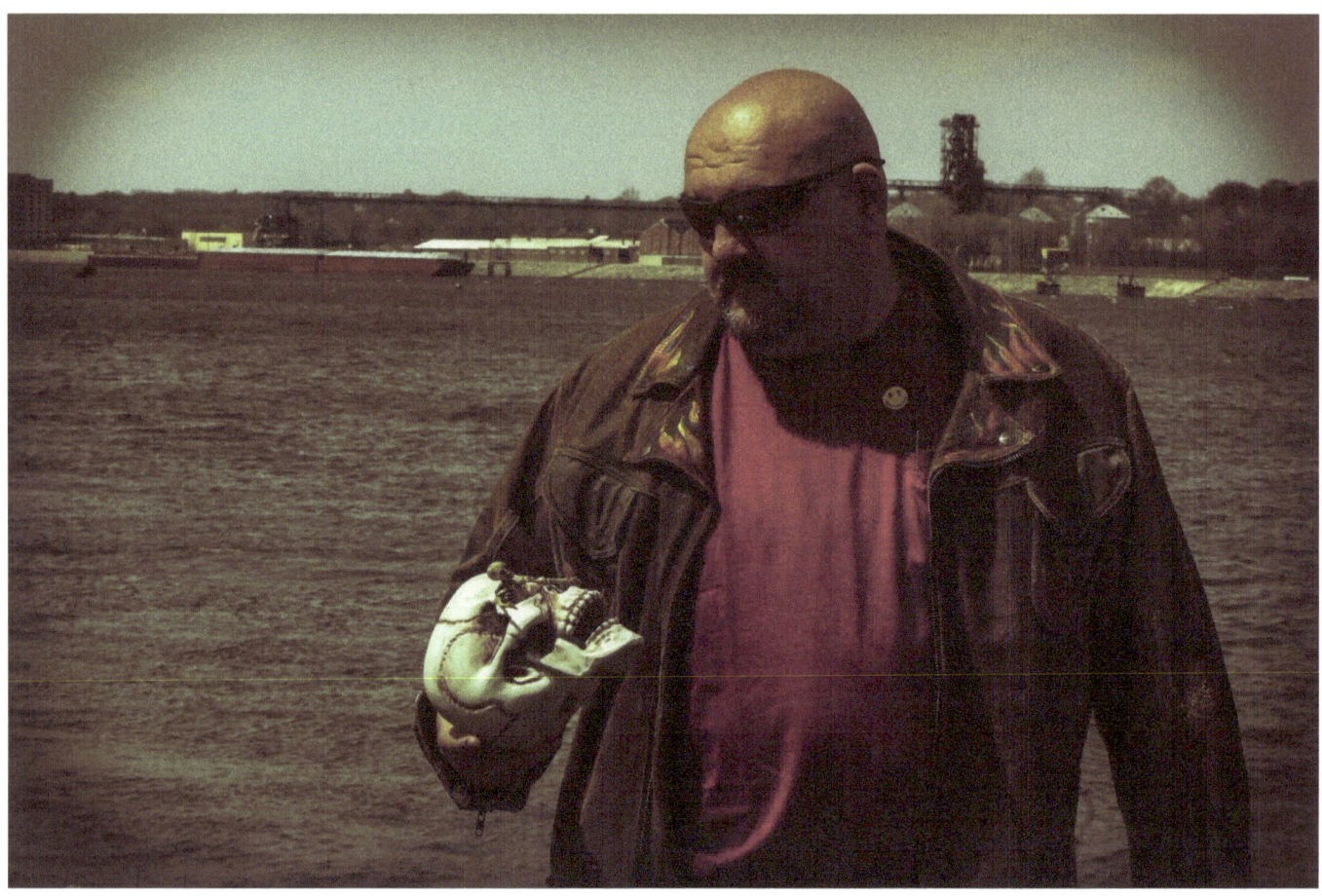

OBJECT:

Prop Skull

WHY IS IT IMPORTANT TO HIM?

"'Memento Mori,' is a Latin phrase that's basically translated as remember that you will die and it reminds me to keep in mind that we're never promised tomorrow. The whole idea is that "I dance burlesque. I do improv. I enjoy performing almost in ways that will be a performance that will never be duplicated. So I enjoy taking a little slice in time and making it special and then when the moment passes, it's over for always and the skull reminds me like Yorick in Shakespeare, once he was full of life and happy, but now he's gone."

JULIET

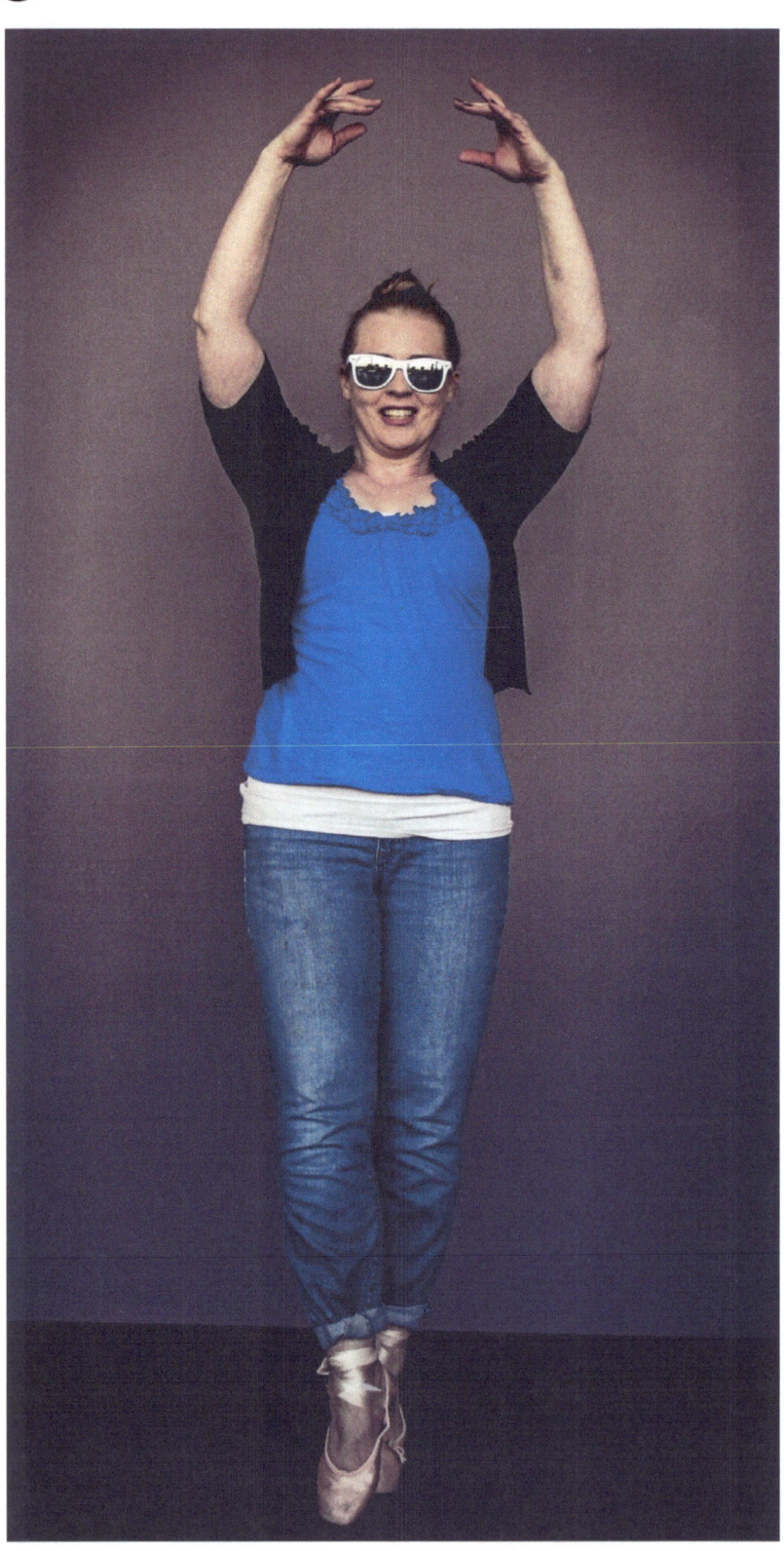

OBJECT:

Point Shoes

WHY IS IT IMPORTANT TO HER?

"For many years, even though I wanted to be a dancer, a lot of people told me I was going to be too old to dance on point because most people start as children. And it was my number one bucket list item that I dreamed always of growing up and becoming a dancer and I didn't have an opportunity to dance as a child. So I started dancing as an adult and over the years I kept thinking, 'I really want to do this.'

Eventually I talked to my dance teacher and she said if I was willing to put in work, that she'd be willing to teach me...as long as I gave it my best and I did everything I could and It was really hard. I had to put myself in an uncomfortable situation, taking beginning point classes with 11 and 12 year olds, but it was the thing I wanted to do most. So I put myself out there and I learned that if you put yourself out there, you can accomplish anything you want.

I learned that if you work your hardest at it, you can accomplish anything you want, and you have to overcome those obstacles. Sometimes, I literally lost three toe nails the first year I was doing it! It was really painful, but I didn't give up. And I now know how to dance in point shoes. Which for somebody at my age, is pretty phenomenal, because most girls quit by the time they're 40 and I started at 40!

I've been doing this for about five years now and I still dance with a company and it's just one of the greatest things I've ever done. Last year at our recital, one of our graduating seniors, even said in her speech that one of the most important lessons she learned from dance was learning never to give up and to always go after your dreams. No matter how silly or how strange they may have seemed to other people. And she said that she learned that from me, because she saw how hard I worked and she saw that I never gave up!"

MICHAEL

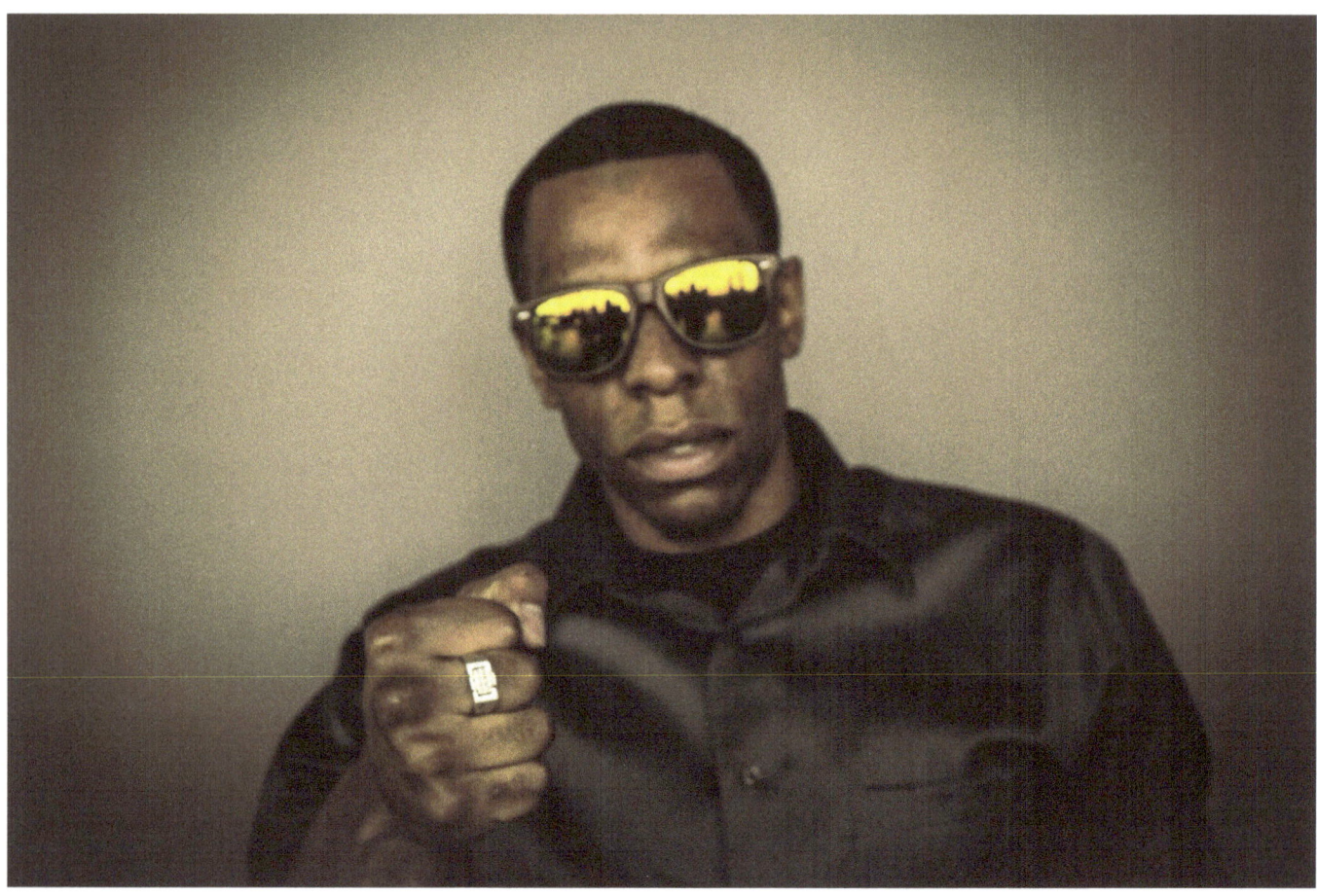

OBJECT:

RING GIVEN TO HIM BY HIS FATHER

WHY IS IT IMPORTANT TO HIM?

"MY FATHER GOT ME A RING. CHRISTMAS, ABOUT FOUR YEARS AGO. IT'S ONE OF THE MORE SENTIMENTAL THINGS THAT I HAVE IN MY LIFE AND WHEN HE PRESENTED IT TO US (HIS BROTHER GOT ONE AS WELL), HE SHOWED HIS APPRECIATION AND TO TELL US THAT WE WERE VERY VALUABLE IN HIS LIFE. EVER SINCE THEN, I HAVE VALUED MYSELF A LOT MORE AND APPRECIATED HIM AS WELL A LOT MORE."

HEATHER

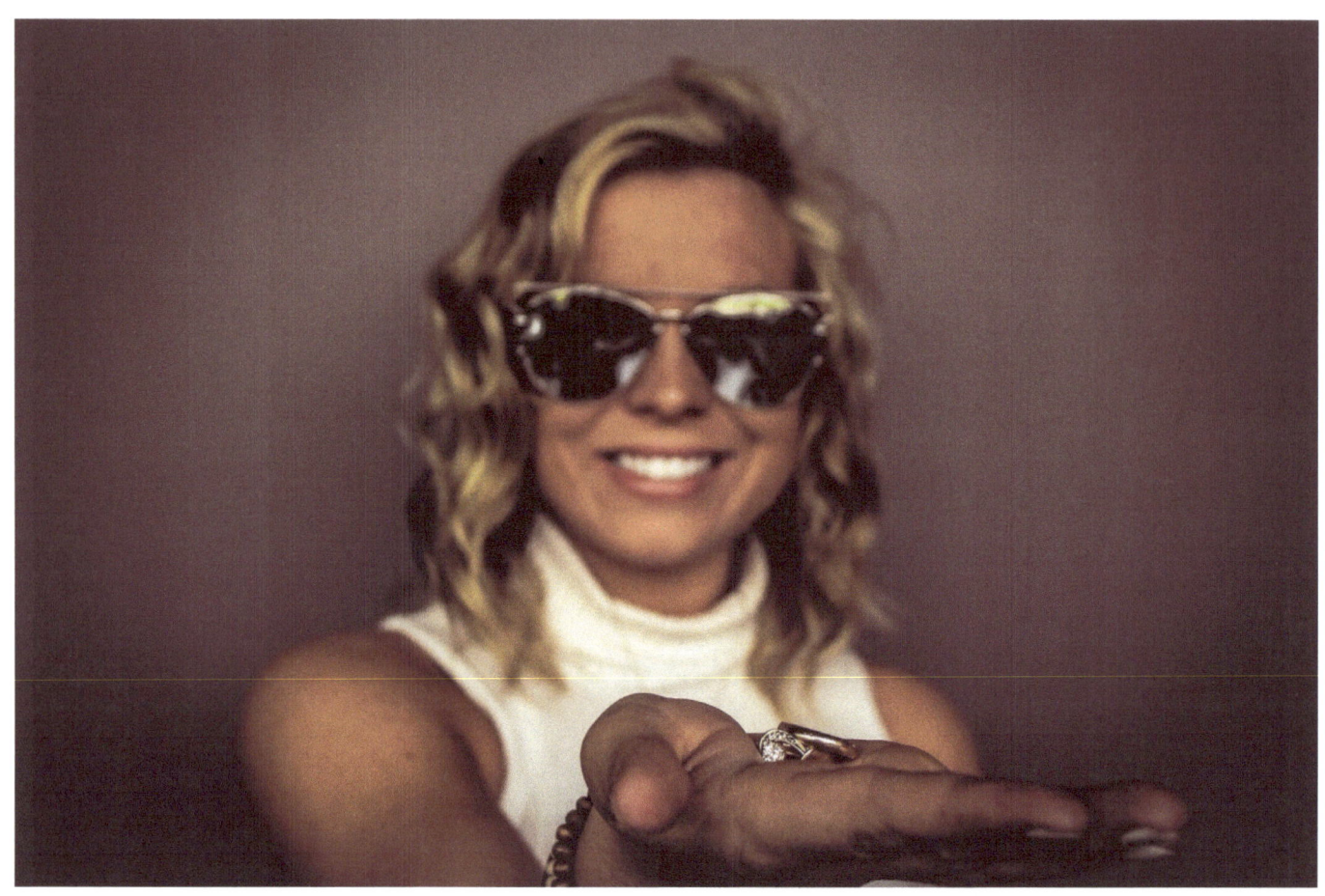

Object:

Two rings

Why is it important to her?

"One of them is a manly wedding band. The other one is a feminine wedding band. They were both my parents' actually. I lost my mom to cancer when I was only 15 years old. She was diagnosed three weeks before she passed away before we ultimately decided to have her taken off the ventilator.

Just two years later, when I was 17, I lost my dad to cancer as well. They both struggled. They both fought bravely, but it was their time to go home to heaven. But there's another part of the story with my dad's ring. My boyfriend, Kasey Hodge, took me to Lake Michigan in summer 2016 and I actually lost my dad's wedding band in the lake, so I was heartbroken. So for my birthday he bought me a new one! Bought me a new wedding band! Although he knows he can't replace it, but he engraved my parents anniversary on the inside. September 6th, 1986.

It's probably the most meaningful gift I've ever received because although it's not the original band that my dad wore, for his wedding, it's still very impactful and it's just a great gift. I wear them every single day. I fidget with them when I'm nervous. But every time I look down, it reminds me of my parents, and I love having them."

EMILY

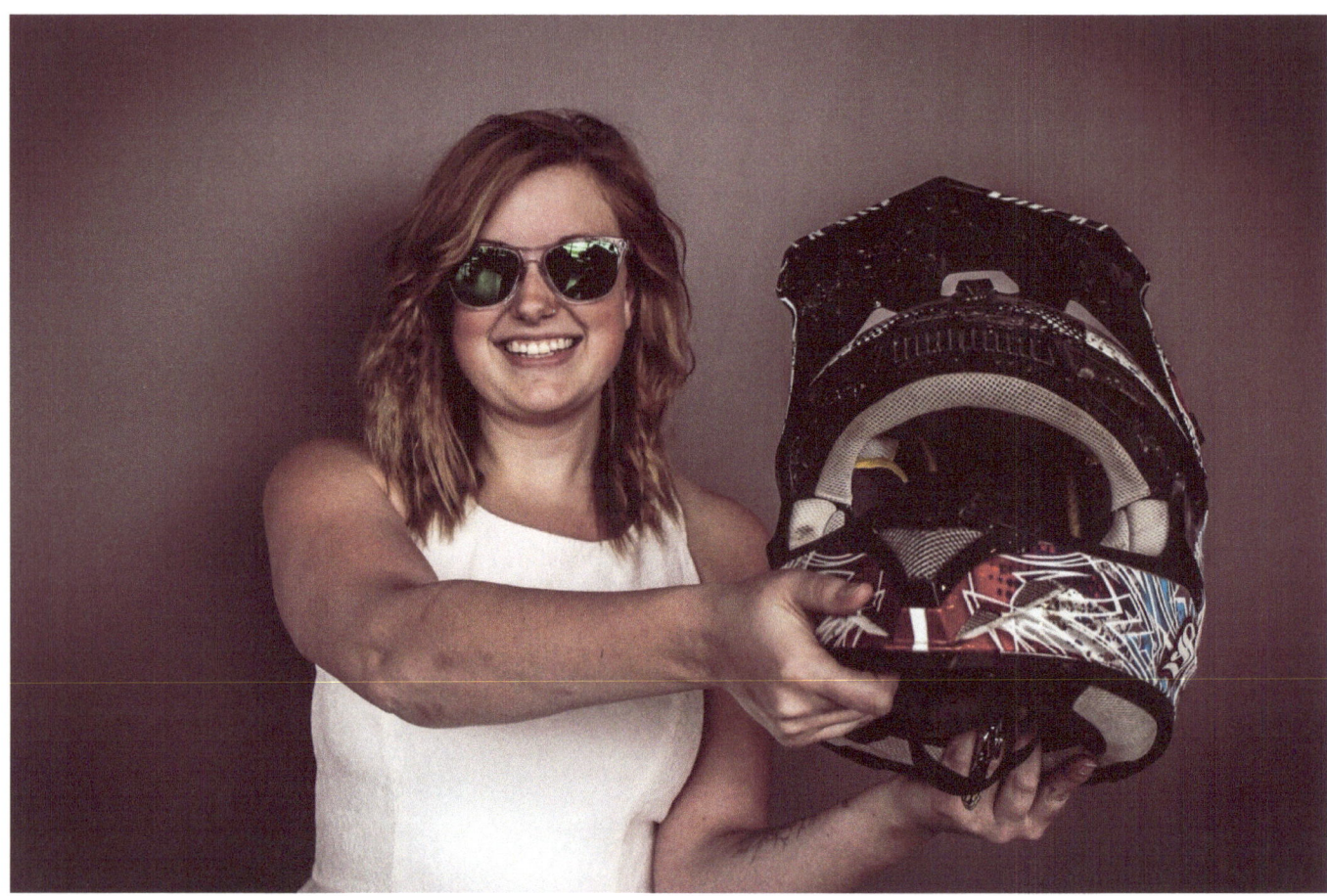

OBJECT:

Dirt bike Helmet

WHY IS IT IMPORTANT TO HER?

"My older brother gave it to me, so it's very sentimental. I have been riding dirt bikes since I was in high school and it's the one thing my entire family does together. So it's very important to me. I just started racing at the end of last year and this is my first season racing Hare Scrambles with WFO Promotions and I love it. It is my life and if I'm not racing, I feel lost.

It's a great stress reliever. I just get on my bike and I don't have to think about anything but where I'm going and trying not to fall. It's important to me because it's something that not only does my family and I do together, but it's something that my husband and I can always do together. We have fun with it and we look out for each other. I race and then he races. I get hurt and I wait because I'm waiting for him to race before I want to go to the hospital to get checked out. It's a lot of fun and It brings us a lot of enjoyment."

CRAIG

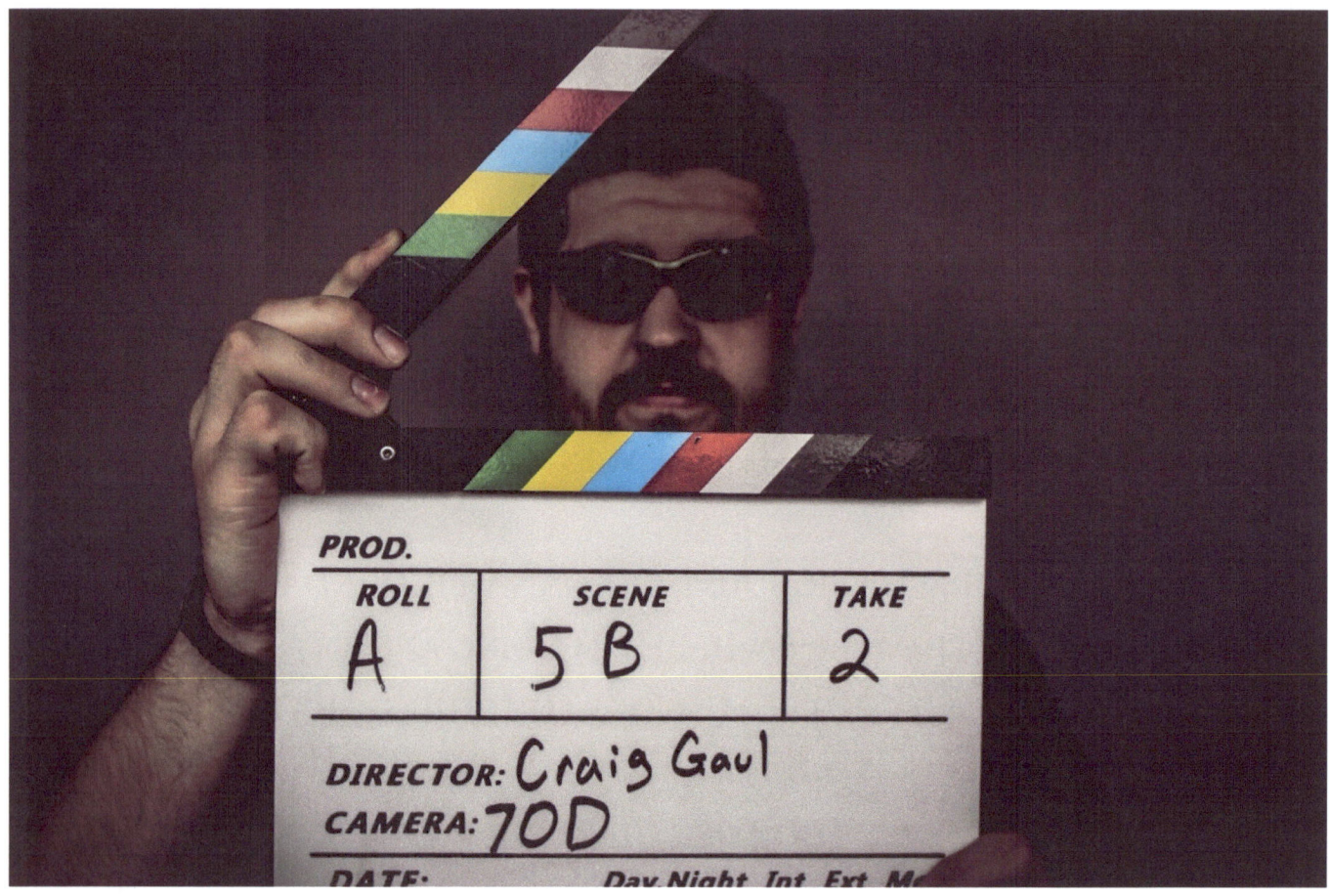

OBJECT:

MOVIE SLATE

WHY IS IT IMPORTANT TO HIM?

"IT'S SOMETHING THAT REMINDS ME OF WHERE I WANT TO BE, WHERE I AM, AS WELL AS WHERE I WANT TO GO. WANTING TO MAKE IT BIG IN THE FILM INDUSTRY IS A DREAM OF MINE AND I'M DOING EVERYTHING I CAN TO GET THERE. JUST THINKING ABOUT BEING ON A MAJOR PRODUCTION, HOLLYWOOD, THE MULTI-MILLION DOLLAR FILMS IS GOING TO BE AMAZING JUST TO EXPERIENCE. TO BE A PART OF THAT AND TO REALLY MAKE A MOVE.

THE ULTIMATE GOAL FOR ME IS TO BECOME AN OSCAR WINNING DIRECTOR, WHICH IS A STRETCH, BUT I'M WORKING TOWARDS IT AND IT'S REALLY WHERE I WANT TO BE. THIS OBJECT IS REALLY IMPORTANT TO ME JUST BECAUSE IT'S CONTINUING TO MOTIVATE ME EVERYDAY. TO LEARN SOMETHING NEW. TO BE MORE CREATIVE. TO TRY DIFFERENT THINGS OUT. SINCE CHOOSING TO DO FILM, I'VE ALSO GROWN A LOT MYSELF AND LEARNING MORE ABOUT MYSELF. SO IT'S DEFINITELY A GOOD REMINDER OF WHERE I WANT TO GO AS WELL AS WHERE I'VE BEEN."

ELIZABETH

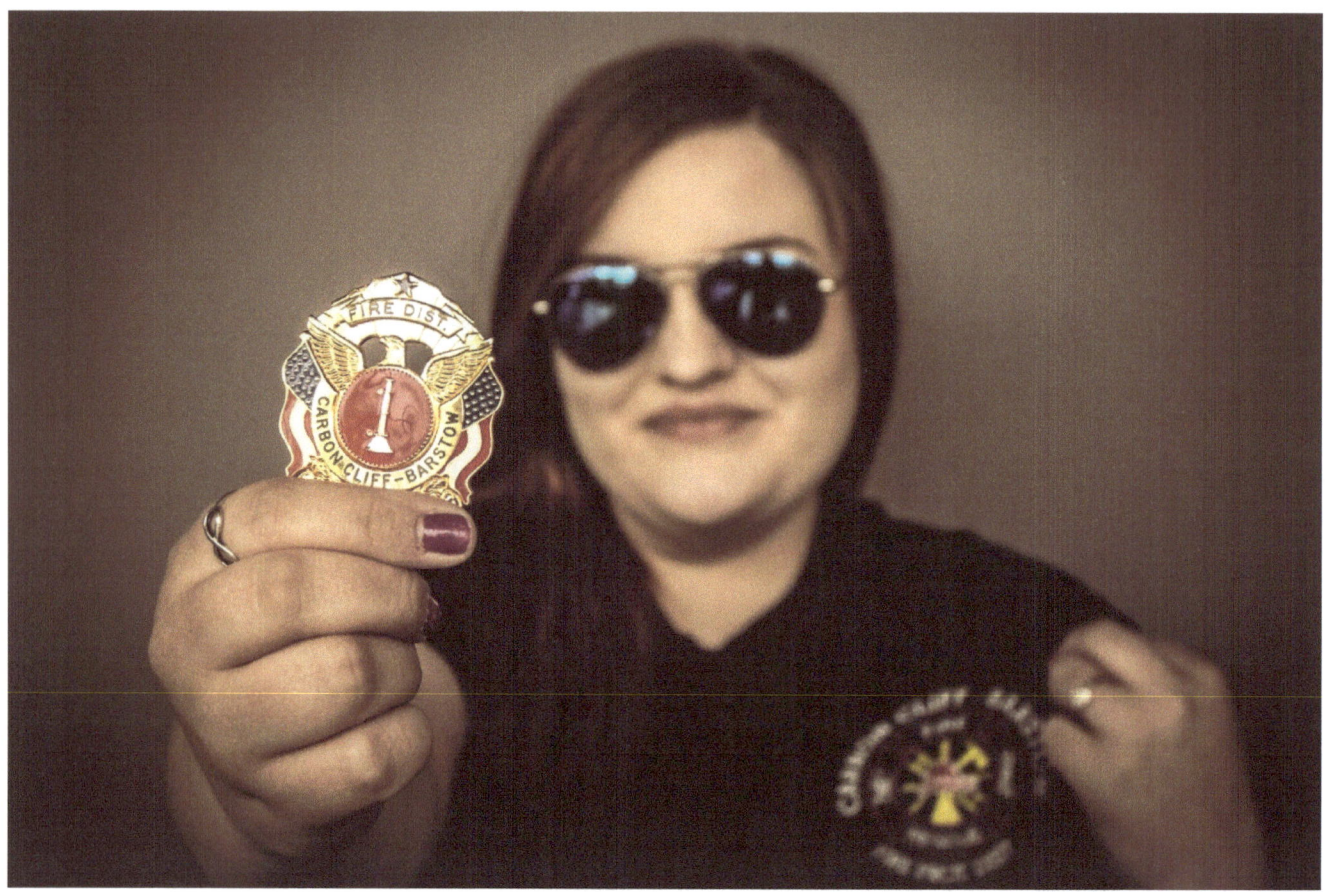

OBJECT:

FIRE DEPARTMENT BADGE AND SHIRT

WHY IS IT IMPORTANT TO HER?

"This shirt and the badge represent the family at the fire house, they represent the good times and the bad times, the wins and the losses. For me it represents the patients I've saved and the many that I've lost. This shirt holds the pain of a family losing their house two days before Christmas, but also the joy we were able to bring when the fire department replaced the presents the children had lost in that fire.

I've worn this shirt on some of my absolute happiest days and also on some of the darkest days of my career. Being a volunteer means in a split second things can, and they will, change for the worse. I've learned that throughout my 8 years in the Fire service.. One second you can be driving down the road on your way to a bonfire and the next second you're telling someone's husband you'll do everything in your power to save his wife's life. You don't win every fight, but you give it your all every single time.

I wear this shirt proudly because it represents the good fight. It represents the struggles, the losses, the saves and the lessons learned. It reminds me everyday where I've come from and where I have yet to go."

TIFANI

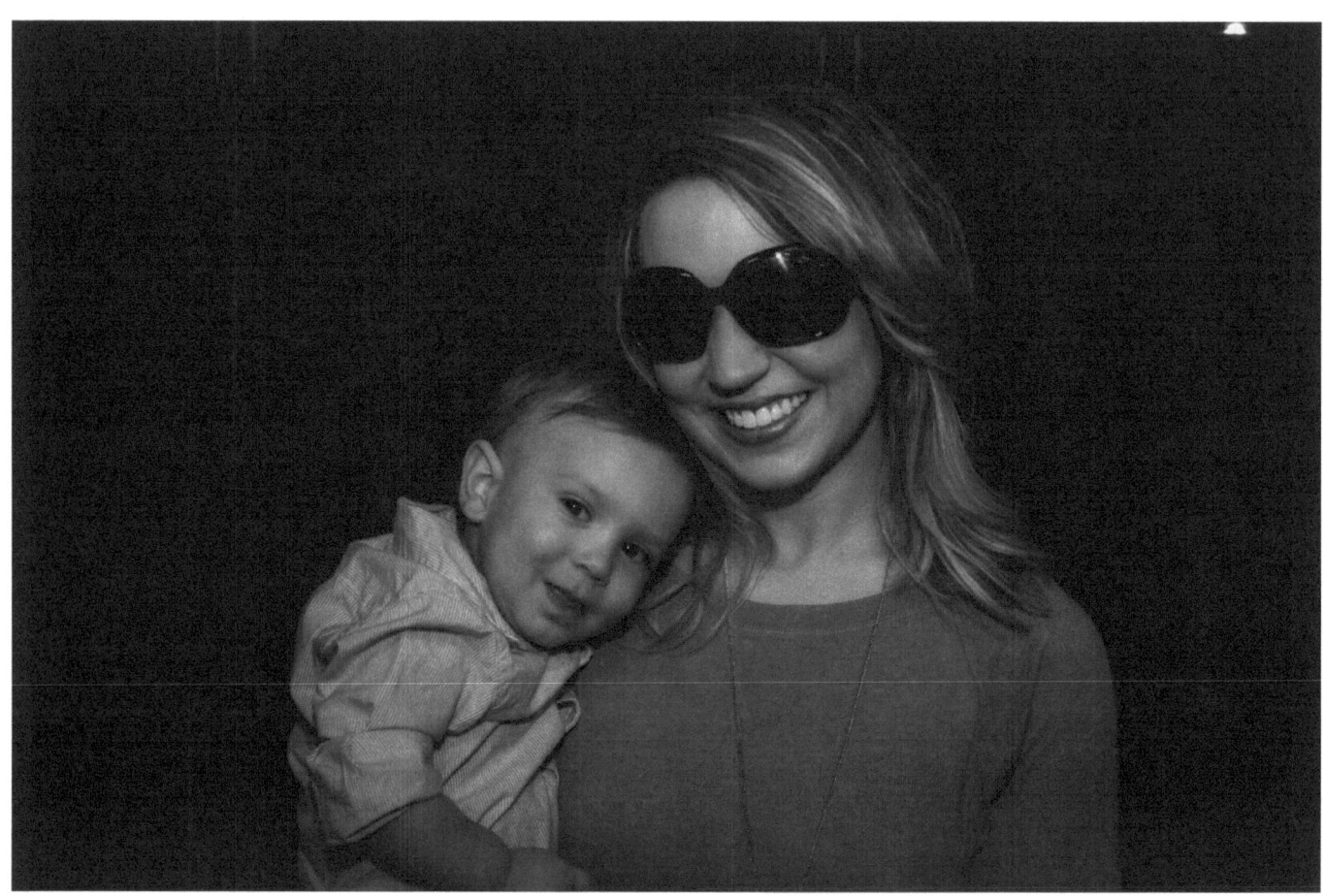

Why she chose to pick her son for this project:

"When you initially asked me to be a part of your 100 Shades project, I started thinking of sentimental items I have held on to through the years. There are hundreds of things I could've chosen but, at the end of the day, I know that God put me on this Earth for several reasons, but the biggest ones are: 1) to be a Godly wife, encourager, and supporter to my husband, and 2) to be a mommy.

Braylan represents all things good about life. He represents promises from God that have come to fruition. Promises that I had second guessed not too long ago. He's my constant reminder that God always takes care of me, answers me when I cry out to Him, and cares about every single thing- even the things that may seem small. Braylan also represents many sleepless nights where I chose to worship and sing to God instead of live in fear- both before, during and after his birth.

Labor with Braylan was the most incredible experience of my life to date. Despite the pain, I have never known the presence of God could be so thick and tangible. I literally felt like I could reach out and touch Him during the entire process. I will never be able to thank God enough for trusting me to be his mommy."

DERRICK

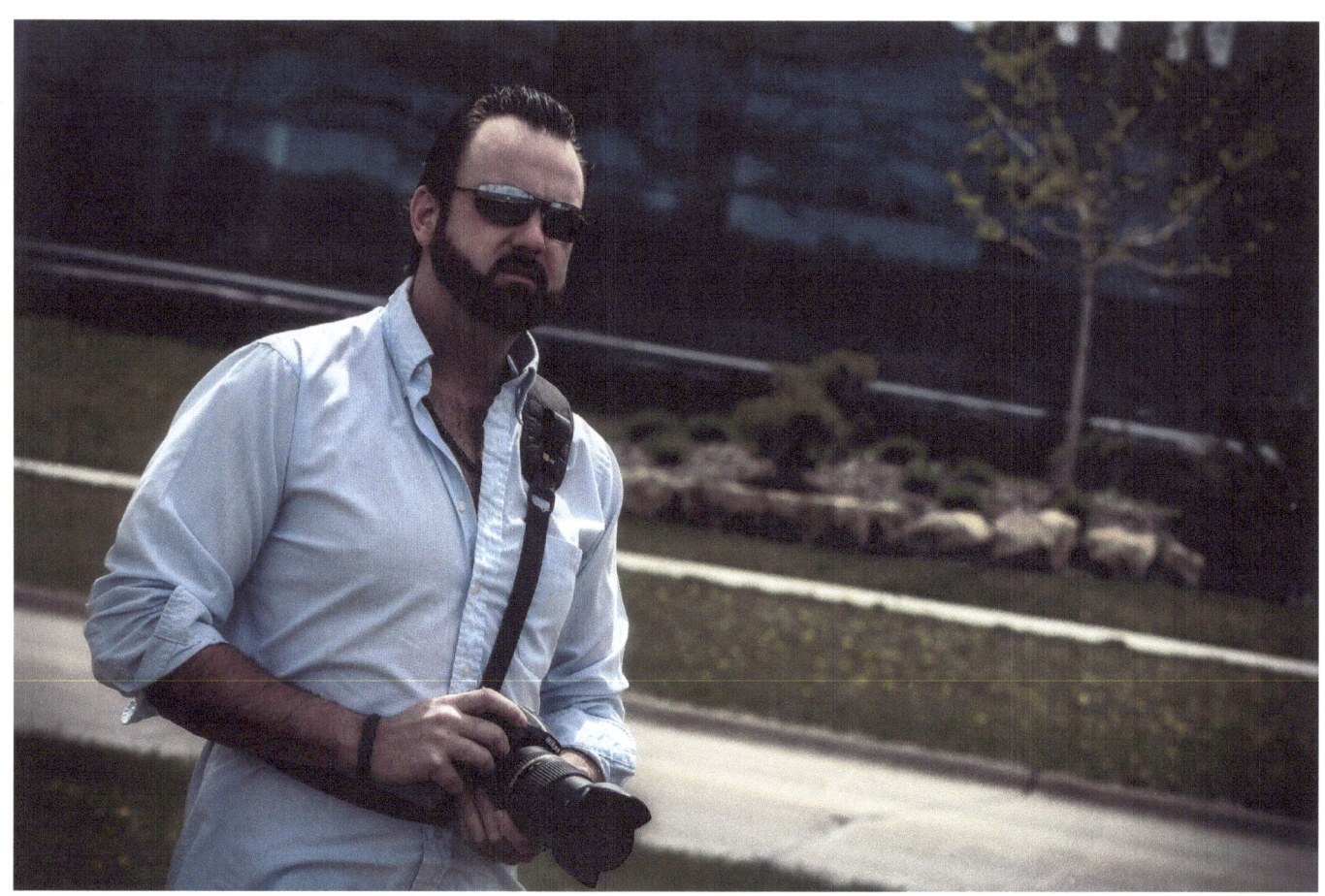

OBJECT:

CAMERA

WHY IS IT IMPORTANT TO HIM?

"MY CAMERA IS IMPORTANT TO ME BECAUSE IT IS AN EXTENSION OF MYSELF AND MY IMAGINATION. IT HELPS ME SHOW OTHERS THEIR TRUE BEAUTY; ESPECIALLY WHEN THEY HAVE A HARD TIME SEEING IT THEMSELVES.

I TRULY ENJOY SEEING THE REACTION WHEN PEOPLE RECEIVE THEIR FINAL IMAGES FROM ME. SEEING THEM HAPPY AND EXCITED MAKES ME HAPPY, IN ADDITION TO REITERATING HOW A WORK OF ART CAN CHANGE SOMEONE'S LIFE."

ALICE

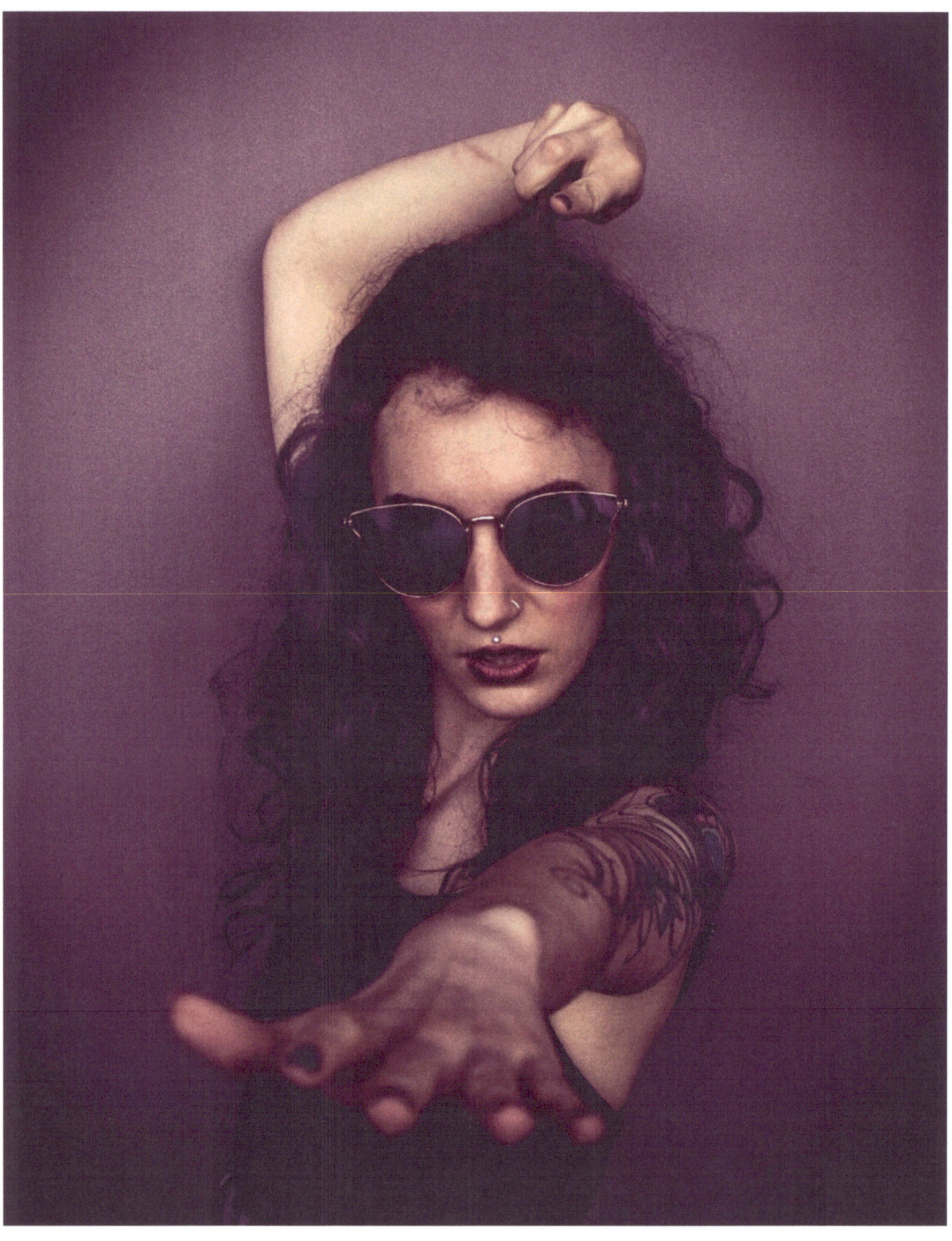

OBJECT:

WAND

WHY IS IT IMPORTANT TO HER?

"ANYONE WHO KNOWS ME KNOWS OF MY OBSESSION WITH HARRY POTTER. IT IS, WITHOUT A DOUBT, THE WORK OF LITERATURE THAT HAS HAD THE MOST IMPACT ON MY LIFE. IT IS SINGLE HANDEDLY RESPONSIBLE FOR SO MANY ASPECTS OF MY PERSONALITY, AND HAS SHAPED WHO I AM MORE THAN ANYTHING ELSE. I GREW UP READING IT, AND WAS THE SAME AGE AS HARRY WAS IN THE SERIES. I CAN'T TELL YOU HOW MUCH I WISHED THAT UNIVERSE WERE REAL. NOT GONNA LIE, I STILL KIND OF DO.

WHEN I TURNED 23, I WENT TO UNIVERSAL THEME PARK IN FLORIDA. ALTHOUGH THE PARK WAS HUGE, AND HAD MANY OTHER FRANCHISES TO VISIT, I SPENT MY ENTIRE TIME IN HARRY POTTER WORLD. I WAS SO OVERWHELMED WITH EXHILARATION, THAT I CRIED MORE THAN YOU SHOULD IN A THEME PARK. WE WENT TO OLIVANDER'S, AND THERE I PICKED MY FAVORITE CHARACTER'S WAND, LUNA LOVEGOOD. I IDENTIFY WITH HER MOST IN THE BOOKS, SHE IS ECCENTRIC, DIFFERENT, AND MISUNDERSTOOD. SHE IS BRAVE, INTELLIGENT, INTUITIVE, QUIRKY, AND ODD. AS A FELLOW RAVENCLAW, AND AN ODDBALL MYSELF, IT WAS EASY FOR ME TO IDENTIFY WITH HER CHARACTER. GROWING UP, I WAS VERY THANKFUL TO HAVE A ROLE MODEL THAT DIDN'T FIT SOCIETY'S MOLD. I ASPIRE TO FOREVER BE AS OPEN MINDED, SUPPORTIVE, AND WILD AS HER."

CARL

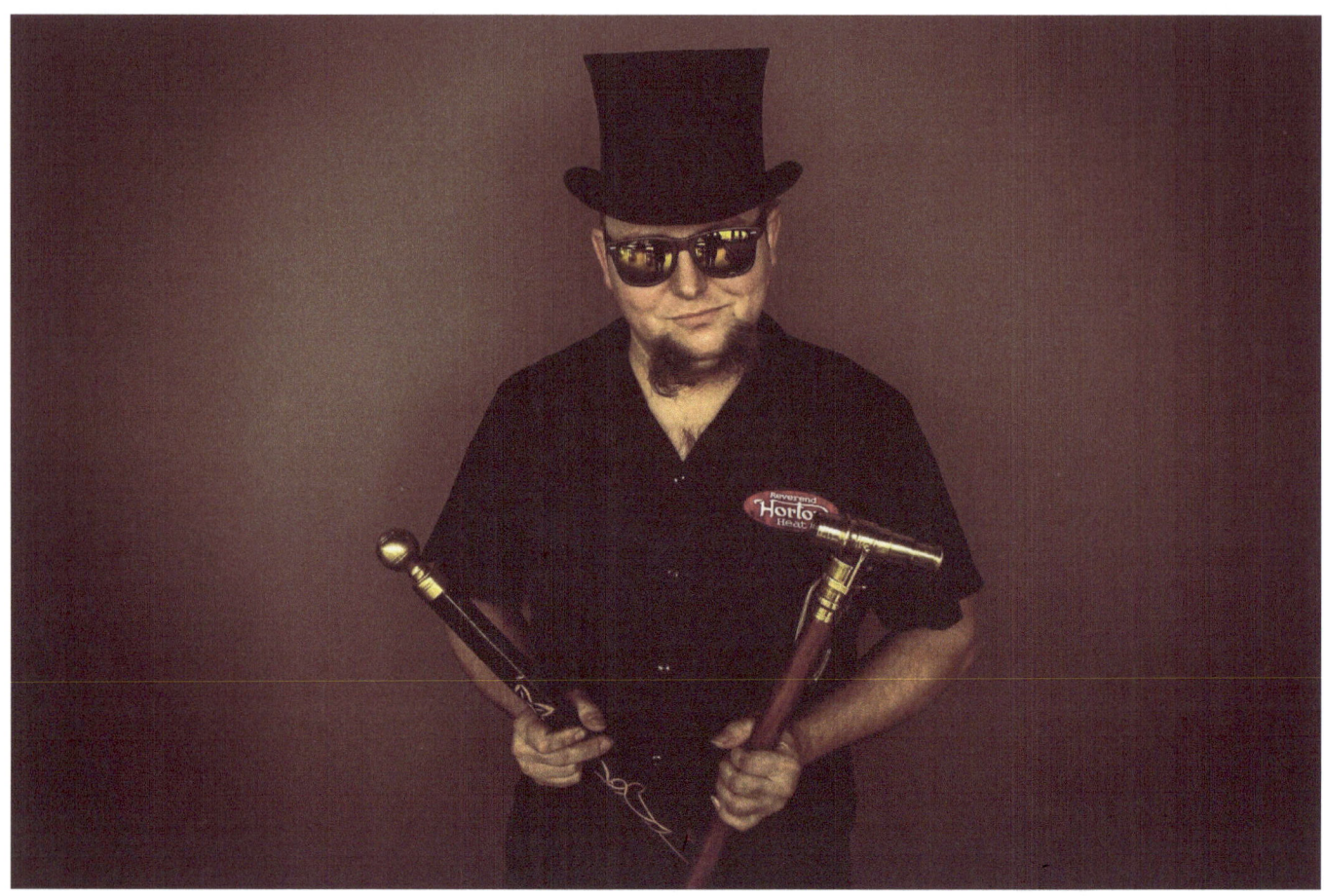

OBJECT:

CANES AND TOP HAT

WHY IS IT IMPORTANT TO HIM?

"They represent the vintage style and the vintage look that I've been acquiring over the years. They create my own style and my own unique look here for the Quad Cities.

One is from the 1800's and it was one of the most expensive retro pieces I've ever gotten, but it's a pop up top hat, which is something I've been wanting to have ever since I was younger. So it was an acquired goal.

The canes are so unique because one represents my time when I was in Okinawa, Japan, which I bought over there. I like holding it with me because of those times. The other one is a unique piece. It's a little spyglass. If you look at it from the beginning, it's just a cane, but until I pull out that spyglass, then everyone's impressed! That's who I am. I'm one of those people where I'm quiet and I don't really get out there like most people think I do. I'm just out there doing my own thing and keeping quiet about it and great things happen around me. this piece represents that. It's a hidden treasure. You think it's one thing, but it turns out to be something so much more! Just like me. Most people get misunderstood because they think one thing of me, I then I usually just impress them."

NIKKI

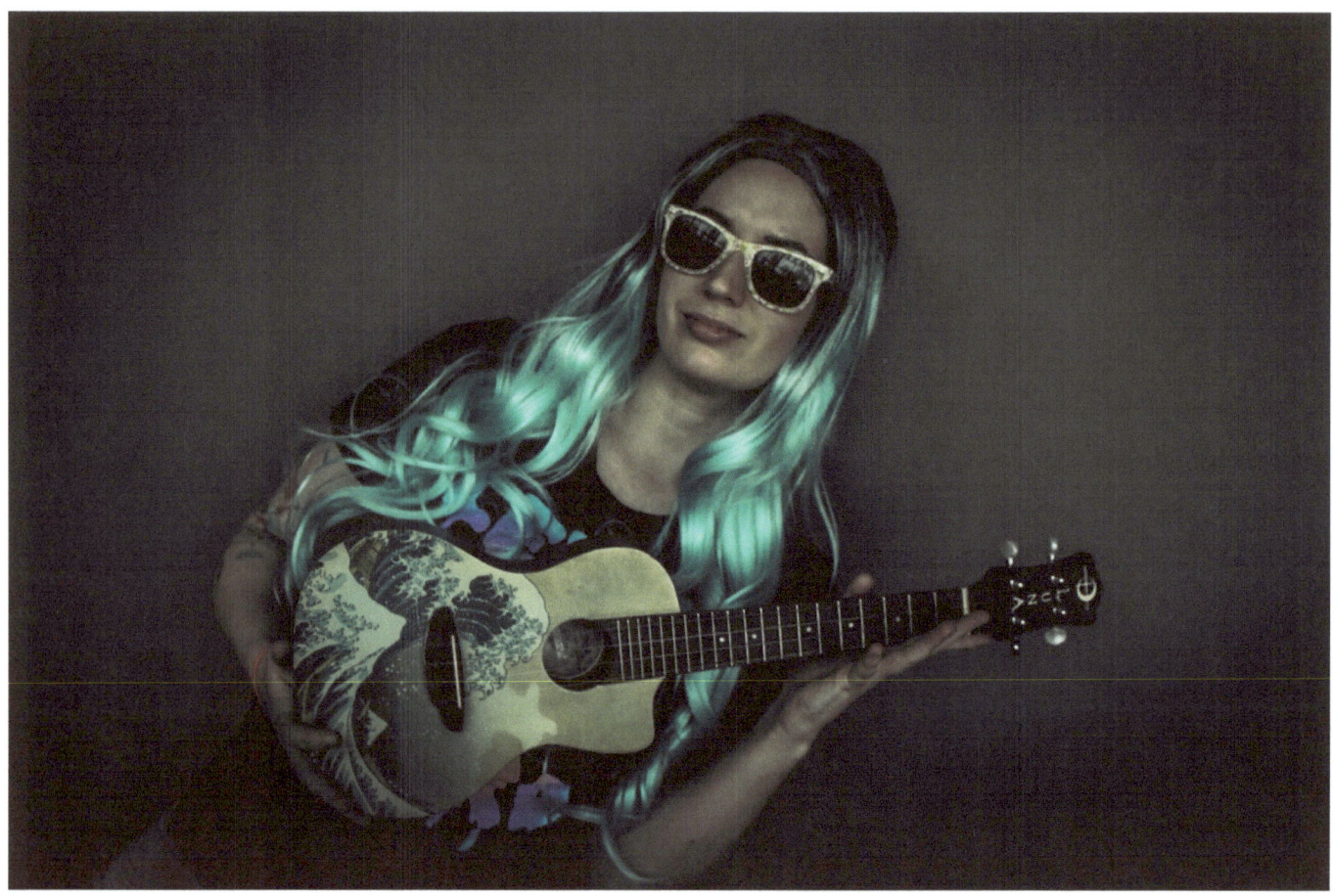

Object:

Ukulele

Why is it important to her?

"To represent how important comedy has been in my life. I started doing stand up in June 2013 and then I started doing comedy music in February 2014. So that following February is when I started doing it. Once I got into it, it was pretty much my love and that's all I wanted to really do.

I have depression and anxiety and something that slowly helps me get through that is being able to help make people laugh. So being able to write jokes and write songs that make people happy, has helped me feel better about things that are going on in my life. Because when don't feel really good about myself, or things that are going on in my head, it's nice to be able to help people feel better in case their going through some things, because I don't know what people are going through.

So that's I picked my ukulele and it was an easy choice. Just to represent how much good comedy has done in my life and that it's something that I hope to keep pursuing and keep getting better at and hopefully maybe someday get bigger with it!"

DAN

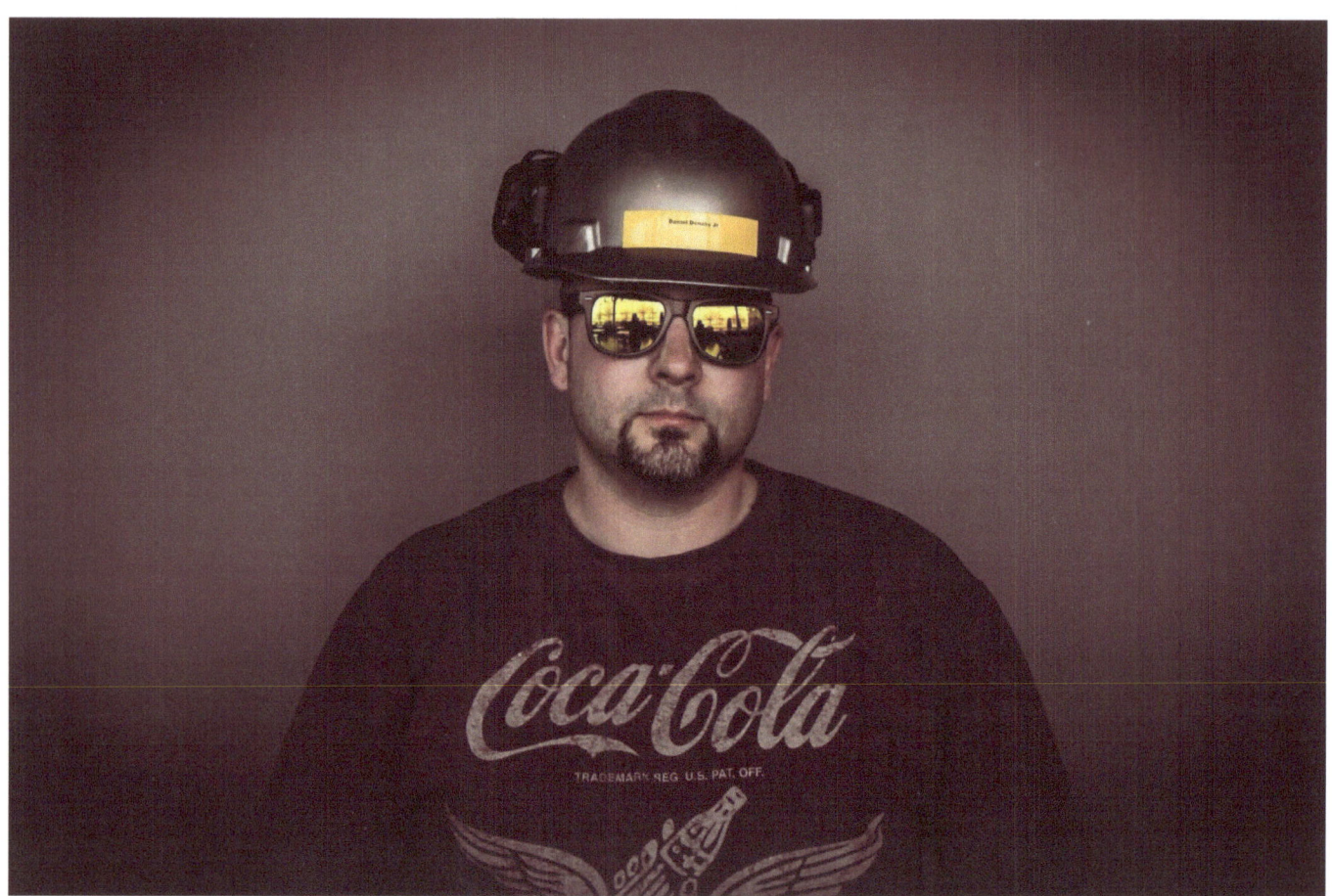

OBJECT:

UNION STEWARD HELMET

WHY IS IT IMPORTANT TO HIM?

"THIS DEFINES ME AS TO WHAT I DO AT WORK AND WHO I AM. I'VE BEEN A UNION STEWARD FOR 15 YEARS AND I'M ACTUALLY A CHIEF STEWARD. WHERE THERE ARE OTHER STEWARDS WHO ARE UNDERNEATH ME AND I HELP GUIDE THEM.

AS A UNION STEWARD, WHAT I DO IS I HELP OTHER PEOPLE STAND UP FOR THE WORKERS. I ALSO MEDIATE BETWEEN WORKERS IN THE COMPANY TO BRING A RESOLUTION SO THAT WAY IF PEOPLE HAVE ISSUES, I CAN HELP SEE THEM THROUGH THEIR ISSUES AND GUIDE THEM. WHETHER IT BE THROUGH WAGES, OUTSIDE ISSUES THAT THEY MAY HAVE, SAFETY CONDITIONS, WORK CONDITIONS, OR GRIEVANCES WITH TEAM MEMBERS. I'VE BEEN DOING THIS FOR SO LONG THAT IT REPRESENTS WHO I AM AT WORK."

AMANDA

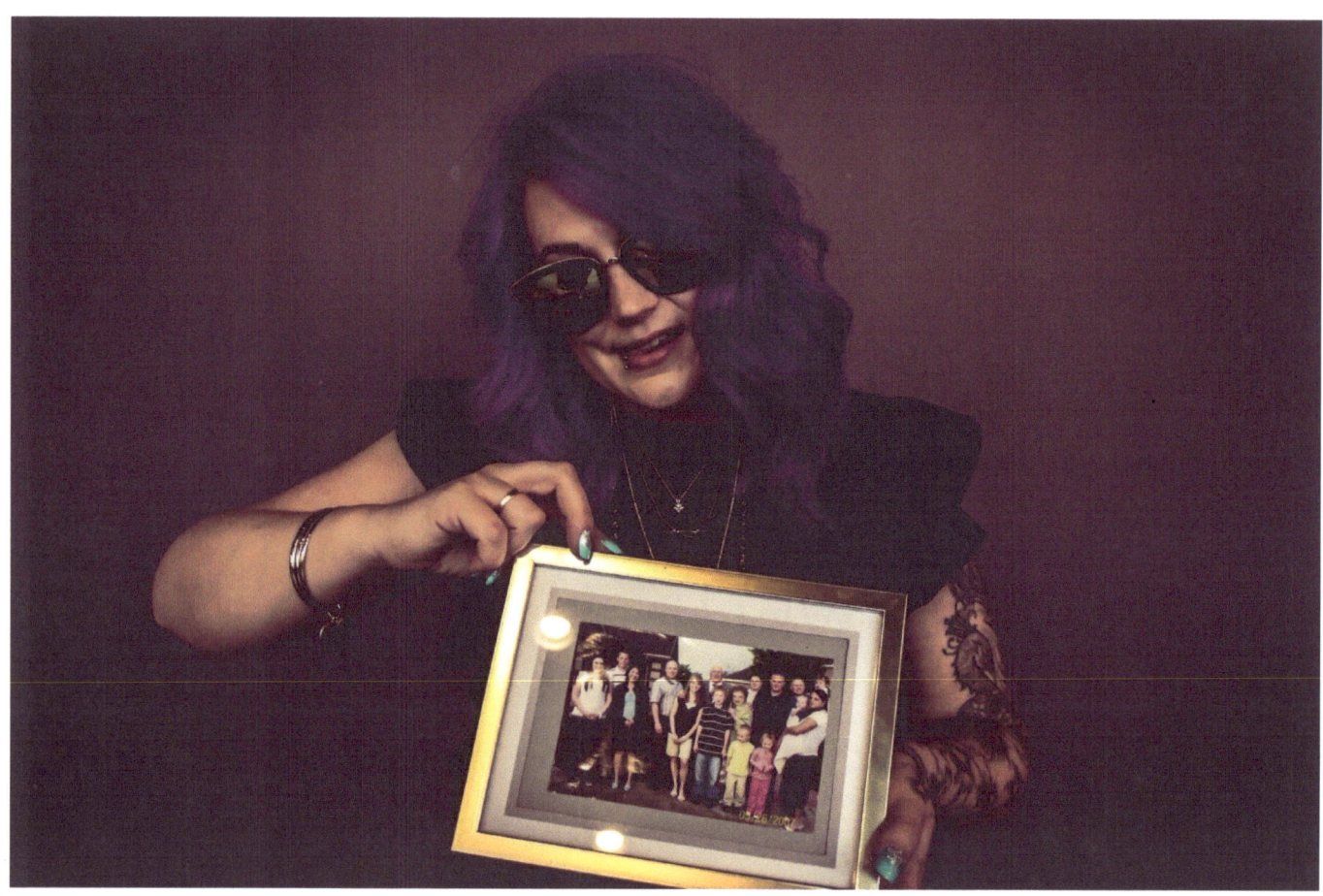

Object:

Her grandmother's Jewelry

Why is it important to her?

"I cherish the jewelry that my grandmother left to me when she passed last year. Its greatest value lies in its emotional and sentimental worth. I never take her wedding band off. She and my grandfather were married in 1952. May 27th would have been their 65th anniversary.

I brought with me a picture of all the grandkids with them at their 55th anniversary vow renewal ceremony. I can only dream of living a life so full of love and knowing the true meaning of, 'Til death do us part.'

Looking at her ring reminds me of one of the things she taught me as a child. She taught me how to sew and that sticking your tongue out a little helps with concentration. Or how to use hairspray to clean ink off her counter when I made a mess drawing in her kitchen.

Looking at her ring also gives me strength. She coped with various adversities to her health throughout her long life. It reminds me to never take a day for granted and to live life to its fullest while I have my health. She's the strongest lady I've known. She is my grandma."

Toño

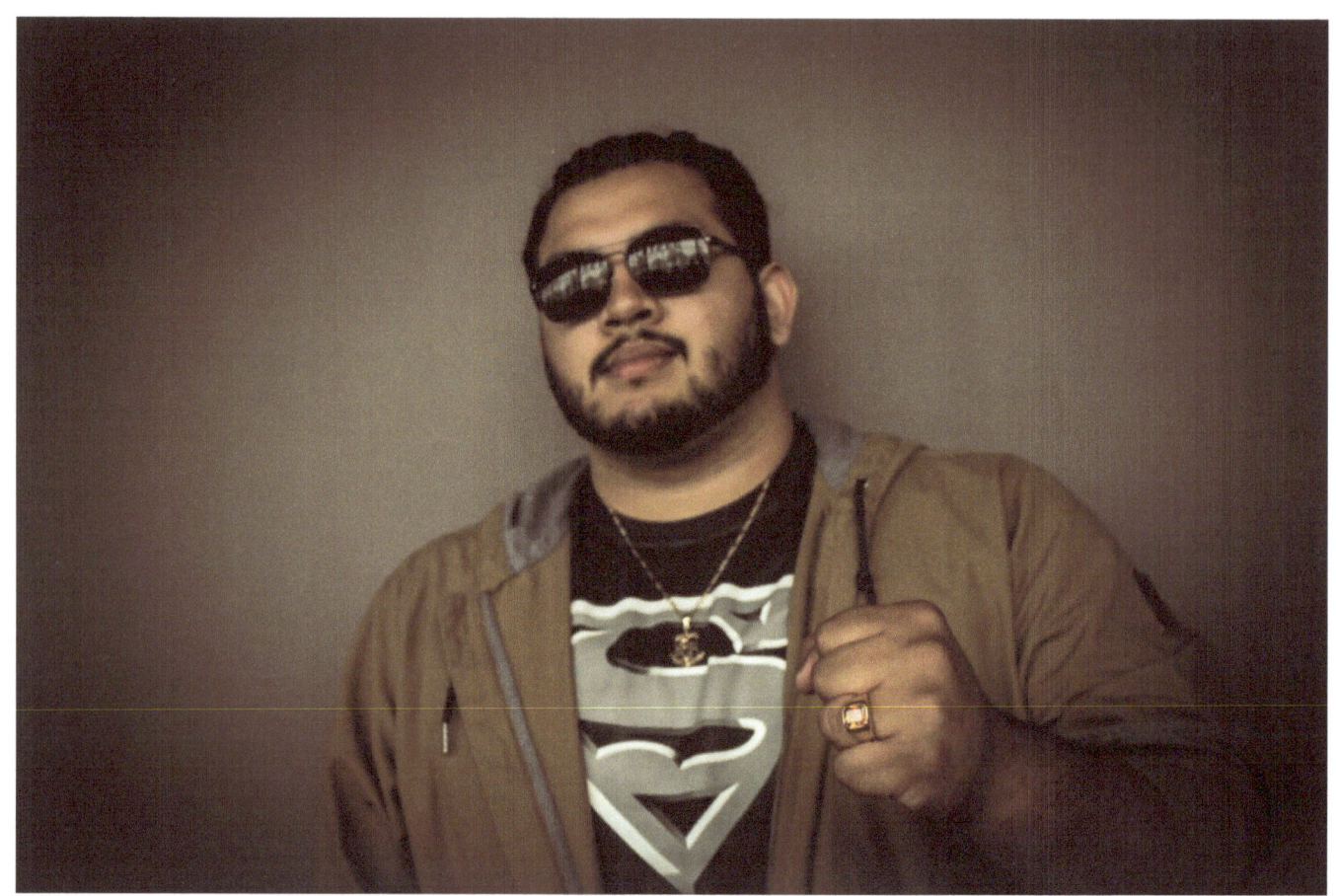

OBJECT:

RING AND MEDALLION

WHY IS IT IMPORTANT TO HIM?

"I BROUGHT A MEDALLION THAT MY FATHER PASSED ON TO ME. JUST TO ALWAYS LET ME KNOW THAT HE'S WITH ME ALL THE TIME. IT REMINDS ME THAT I HAVE A STANDARD TO MEET AND THAT'S MY FATHER'S STANDARD. I HAVE HIM UP ON A HIGH PEDESTAL AND SOMETIMES I CAN'T MEET THAT STANDARD AND THIS NECKLACE REALLY PUTS ME IN CHECK SOMETIMES WHEN I'M NOT DOING MY BEST.

IT REMIND MYSELF THAT I HAVE TO DO THE BEST TO MEET THOSE STANDARDS OR EXCEED THEM. THERE ARE SOMETIMES WHERE I DO EXCEED THEM AND IT REMINDS ME THAT I GOT TO DO MY BEST.

THEN, MY RING. MY GRANDFATHER PASSED AWAY AND GAVE IT ME BEFORE I PASSED AWAY, AND HAS BEEN WITH ME SINCE I WON HOMECOMING KING TO GETTING THE COMMUNITY HERO AWARD. EVEN THOUGH HE PASSES AWAY, HE HAS BEEN WITH ME IN EVERY ACCOMPLISHMENT AND EVERY HARDSHIP."

ANNA

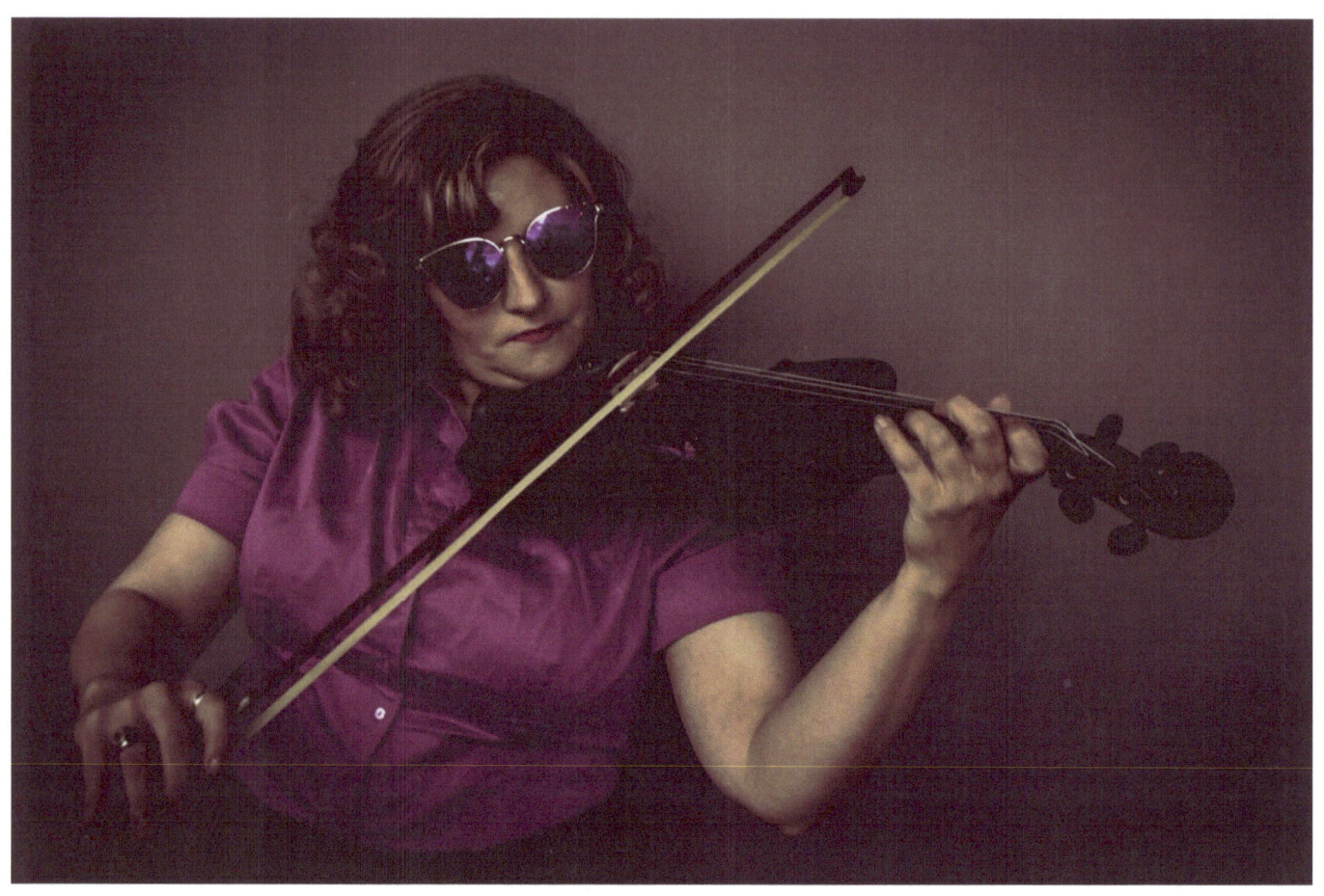

OBJECT:

VIOLIN

WHY IS IT IMPORTANT TO HER?

"THIS IS MY 6TH VIOLIN THAT I HAVE OWNED IN MY LIFETIME. THIS PARTICULAR VIOLIN IS SPECIAL TO ME BECAUSE IT SHOWED ME THAT QUITTING IS NOT AN OPTION AND TO NEVER GIVE UP.

I BEGAN PLAYING THE VIOLIN AT THE AGE OF 6 YEARS OLD. I WAS A FAIRLY TIMID AND SHY LITTLE GIRL. I HAD AN OLD SOUL. I LOVED TO PLAY AND MAKE MUSIC. BY THE TIME I WAS A TEENAGER I HAD PLAYED AT THE FESTIVAL OF TREES, SEVERAL COMPETITIONS AND MANY RECITALS. I ALSO ENJOYED PLAYING FOR THE ELDERS IN THE NURSING HOMES LOCALLY. I WAS AN UNUSUAL GIRL. I WAS TAUGHT FROM AN EARLY AGE THAT IT IS OK TO BE DIFFERENT AND THAT MAKING OTHERS HAPPY WAS VERY IMPORTANT. BY THE TIME I WAS 23 DUE TO WORK, RELATIONSHIP ISSUES AND OTHER OBLIGATIONS I WAS FORCED TO STOP PLAYING. I WAS FORCED TO SELL MY VIOLIN.

FAST FORWARD TO MAY 2015. I NOW WORK AS AN EMERGENCY MEDICAL TECHNICIAN FOR A PRIVATE AMBULANCE SERVICE AND I AM A SINGLE MOTHER. LIFE ISN'T TERRIBLE BUT THERE WAS DEFINITELY SOMETHING MISSING. I HAD A CRAVING. ONE THAT WOULD ONLY BE SATISFIED BY SHEET MUSIC AND A VIOLIN; I KNEW WHAT I HAD TO DO. SO, THE HUNT BEGAN FOR AN AFFORDABLE OPTION. EBAY WAS MY SOLUTION. I TOOK THE PLUNGE AND ORDERED A SHINY BLACK VIOLIN AND FOUND MY SHEET MUSIC THAT HAD BEEN PUT AWAY IN MY BASEMENT. I WAS AT FIRST WORRIED I WOULD NOT REMEMBER. THE MIND AND MUSCLES MAKE AN AMAZING PAIR. MUSCLE MEMORY TO THE RESCUE! I TUNED THIS VIOLIN AND STARTED PLAYING. OF COURSE I DID NOT SOUND THE GREATEST BUT IT WAS A START. I WOULD NOT ALLOW MYSELF TO BE PUT IN A BOX. NEVER AGAIN WOULD I ALLOW SOMEONE TO DESTROY ME TO THE POINT OF GIVING UP SOMETHING THAT I LOVE. I HAVE THE POWER TO BE WHOEVER AND WHATEVER I PLEASE AND THE POWER TO BE AN EXAMPLE TO MY SON TO NEVER GIVE UP. I AM ANNA BIXBY."

ELIJAH

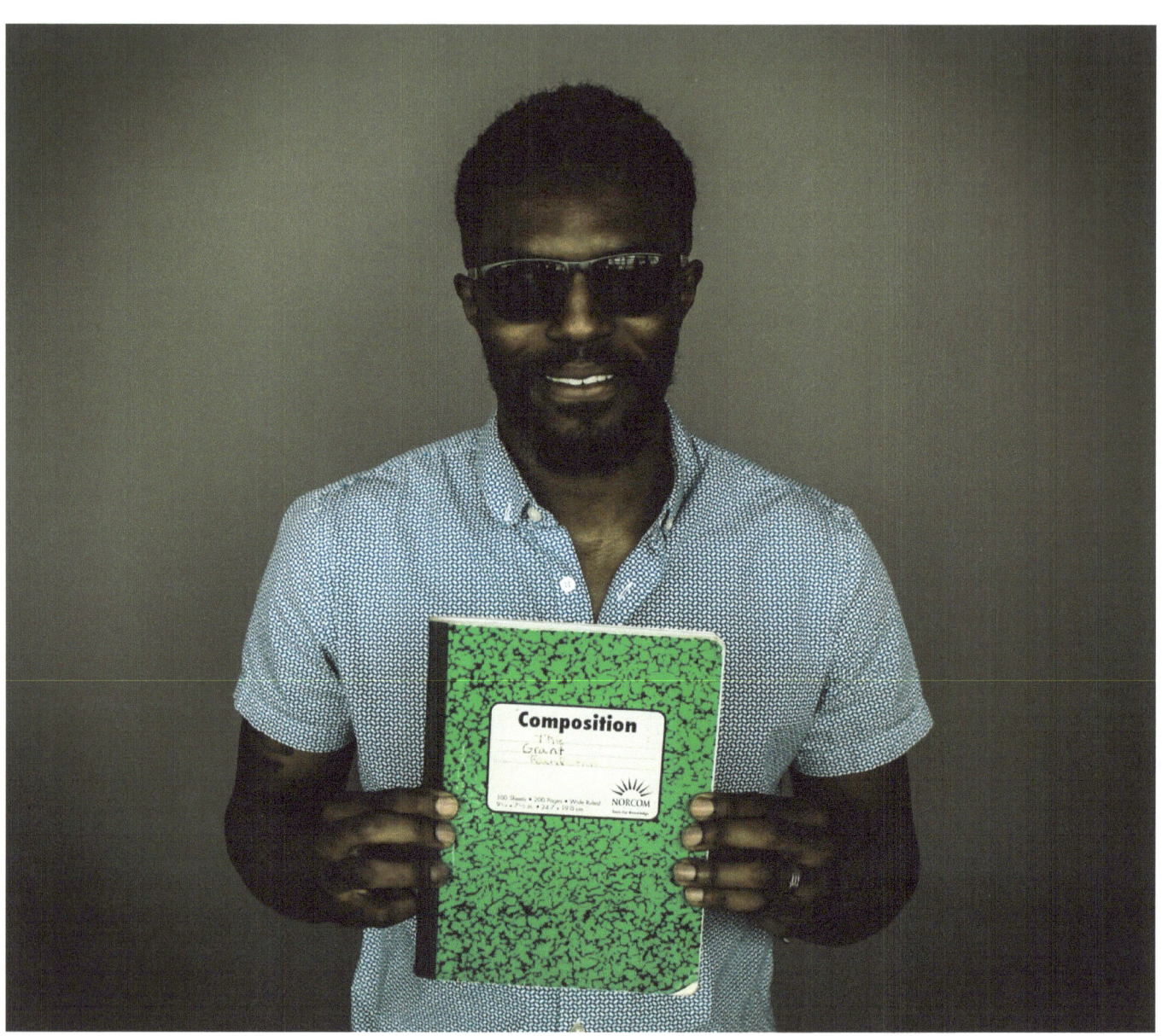

OBJECT:

NOTEBOOK

WHY IS IT IMPORTANT TO HIM?

"I brought my notebook that says 'The Grant Foundation' because this is my ultimate end goal. This is my business focus. I think it can have huge impacts on the world. The Grant Foundation is essentially this business that's going to reinvest in other businesses, and with those profits, invest in other businesses. Ultimately changing the economy, but also it'll be fun!

I bring it with me literally everywhere and every notebook I get, I write this on the front (The Grant Foundation) as a reminder, because this is full of my ideas, thoughts, to dos, pretty much anything that's on my mind. And this is a reminder of where all that energy and power is going to."

PRIMROSE

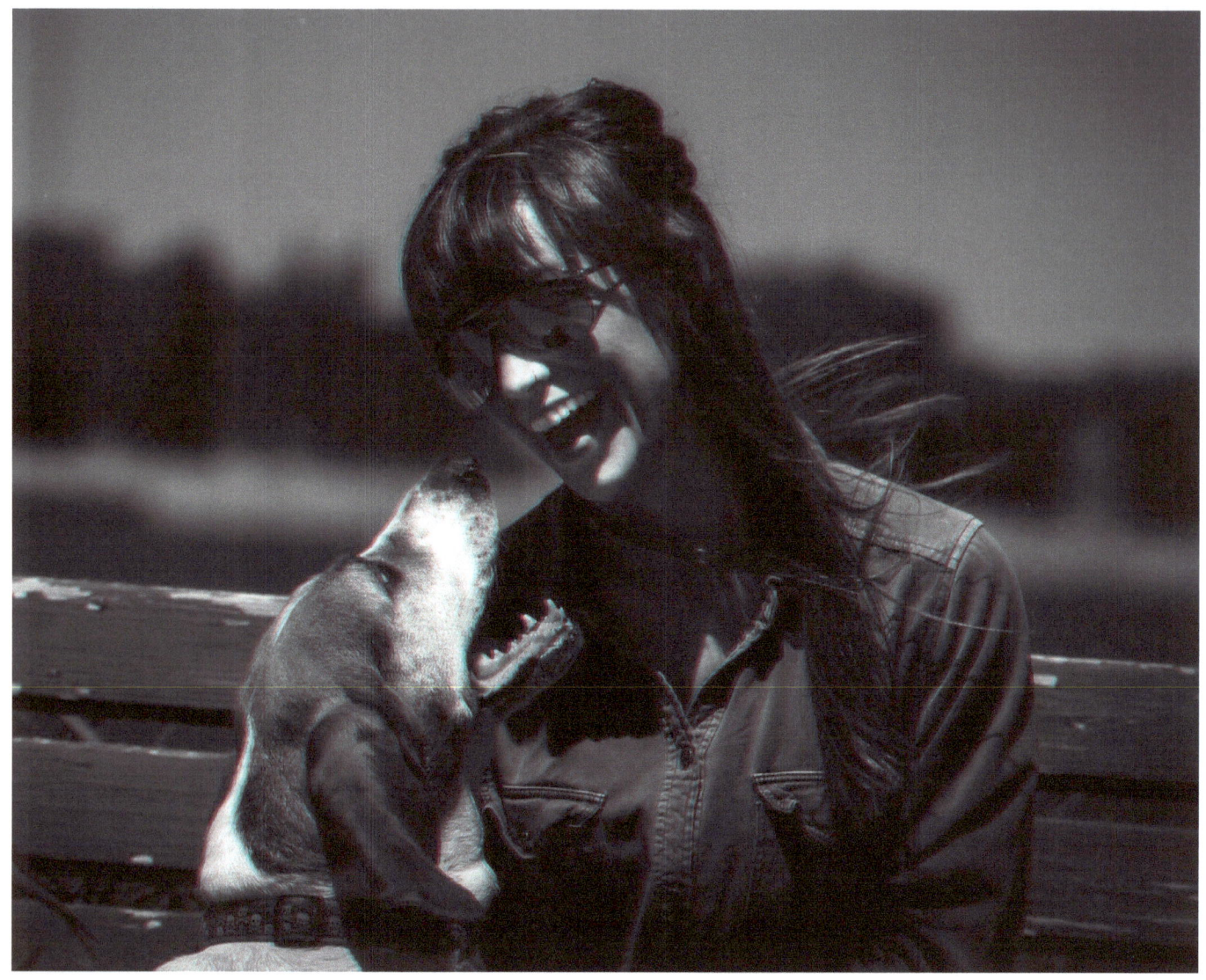

OBJECT:

Her therapy dog, Charlie

Why is he important to her?

"We go all over the Quad Cities helping different people with all sorts of different things. Kids read to him to build up their confidence. They know a dog is not going to judge them for if they miss a word or if they mispronounce a word, or if they don't even know how to say it.

So they build up that confidence and then he just brings joy to other people. When we go visit, if they're having a bad day, make them happy if they're in rehab for something, broken hip or whatever. And just knowing how happy he makes me is why we need to go out and spread that happiness to other people for whatever reason. They don't have a dog, can't have a dog, or they're just missing their dog while they're getting better from surgery or something like that. Just our way to give back to people who need it."

MITCH

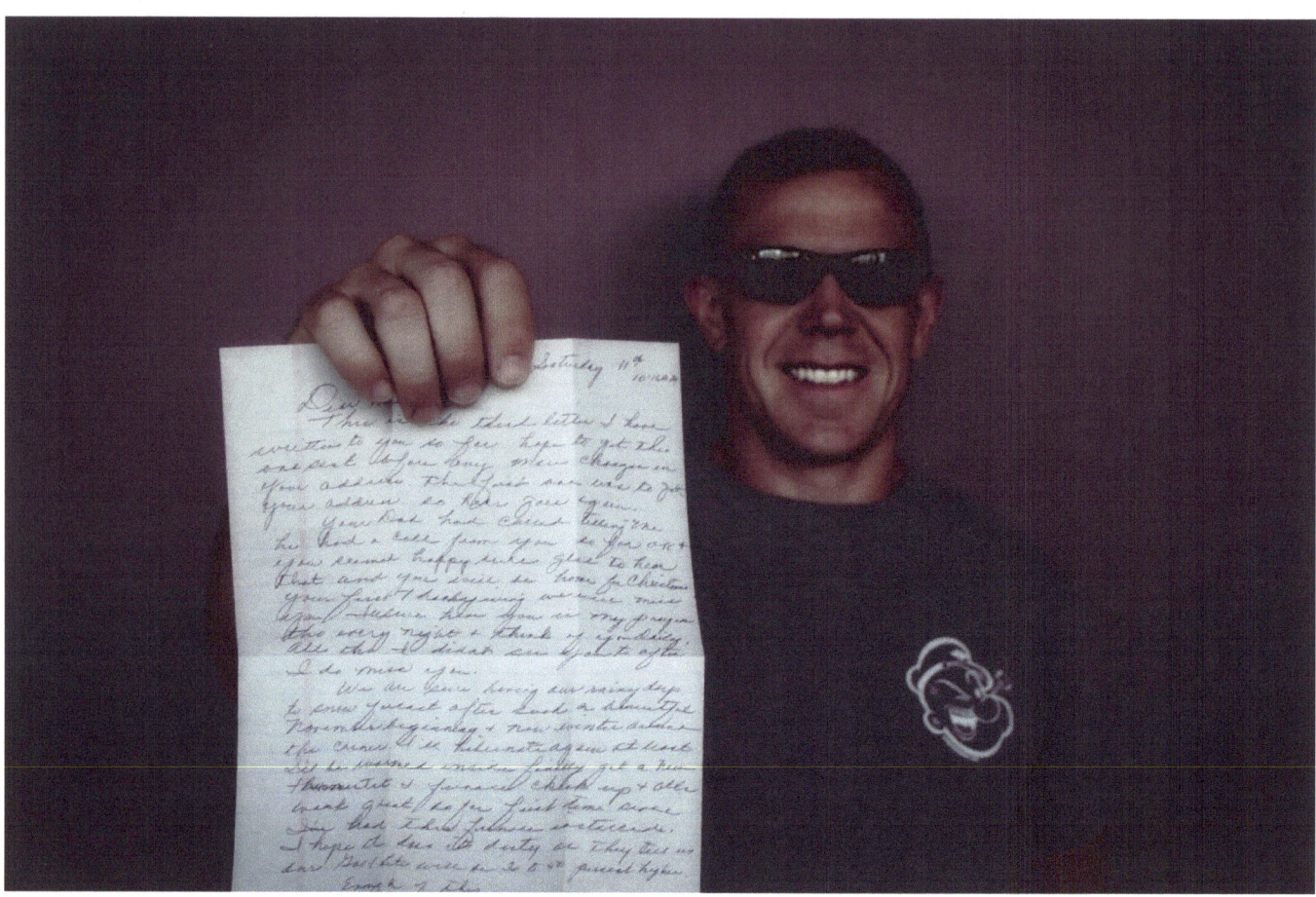

OBJECT:

LETTER FROM GREAT GRANDMOTHER

WHY IS IT IMPORTANT TO HIM?

"THE LETTER WAS WRITTEN BY MY GREAT GRANDMA WHILE I WAS IN BASIC TRAINING FOR THE MILITARY. I LOOKED FORWARD TO HER LETTERS EVERY WEEK MORE THAN ANYTHING ELSE DURING THAT TIME OF MY LIFE. ANYTIME I WOULD GET DISTRACTED OR GET TO THINKING ABOUT HOME TOO MUCH I WOULD READ HER LETTERS TO GET ME REFOCUSED. SHE HAD A HUGE IMPACT ON MY CHILDHOOD AS I SPENT A LOT OF TIME WITH HER DURING THE SUMMER AND WEEK DAYS AFTER SCHOOL WHILE I WAS IN ELEMENTARY SCHOOL. SHE TAUGHT ME A LOT DURING MY TIME WITH HER, FROM HOW TO MAKE A BUDGET AND SAVE MONEY TO UNDERSTANDING THE ASPECT OF HARD WORK AND NOT RELYING ON OTHERS FOR WHAT I WANT OUT OF LIFE. SHE WAS A VERY STRONG, BUT COMPASSIONATE WOMAN WHO LED BY EXAMPLE. I WAS FORTUNATE ENOUGH TO HAVE HER AROUND FOR MOST OF MY LIFE AS SHE LIVED TO BE 100 YEARS OLD.

ONE OF THE BEST MEMORIES I HAVE IS RIDING IN THE CAR WITH HER. SHE HAD A 1972 PONTIAC LEMANS THAT HAD WAY MORE POWER THAN WHAT SHE KNEW WHAT TO DO WITH. QUITE OFTEN SHE WOULD SPIN THE TIRES WHEN TAKING OFF FROM A STOP LIGHT WITHOUT EVEN KNOWING SHE WAS DOING IT. BUT I DEFINITELY KNEW IT WAS HER AND I COULDN'T WAIT FOR HER TO DO IT. I WOULD JUST SIT THERE IN THE PASSENGER SEAT AND GRIN FROM EAR TO EAR AS I THOUGHT I HAD THE COOLEST GREAT GRANDMA IN THE WORLD. I CREDIT THESE TIMES WITH HER AS PLAYING A ROLE INTO MY LOVE OF CARS AND DRIVING FAST. GREAT GRANDMA FAYE WAS A WONDERFUL WOMAN AND I MISS HER DEARLY. "

AMANDA

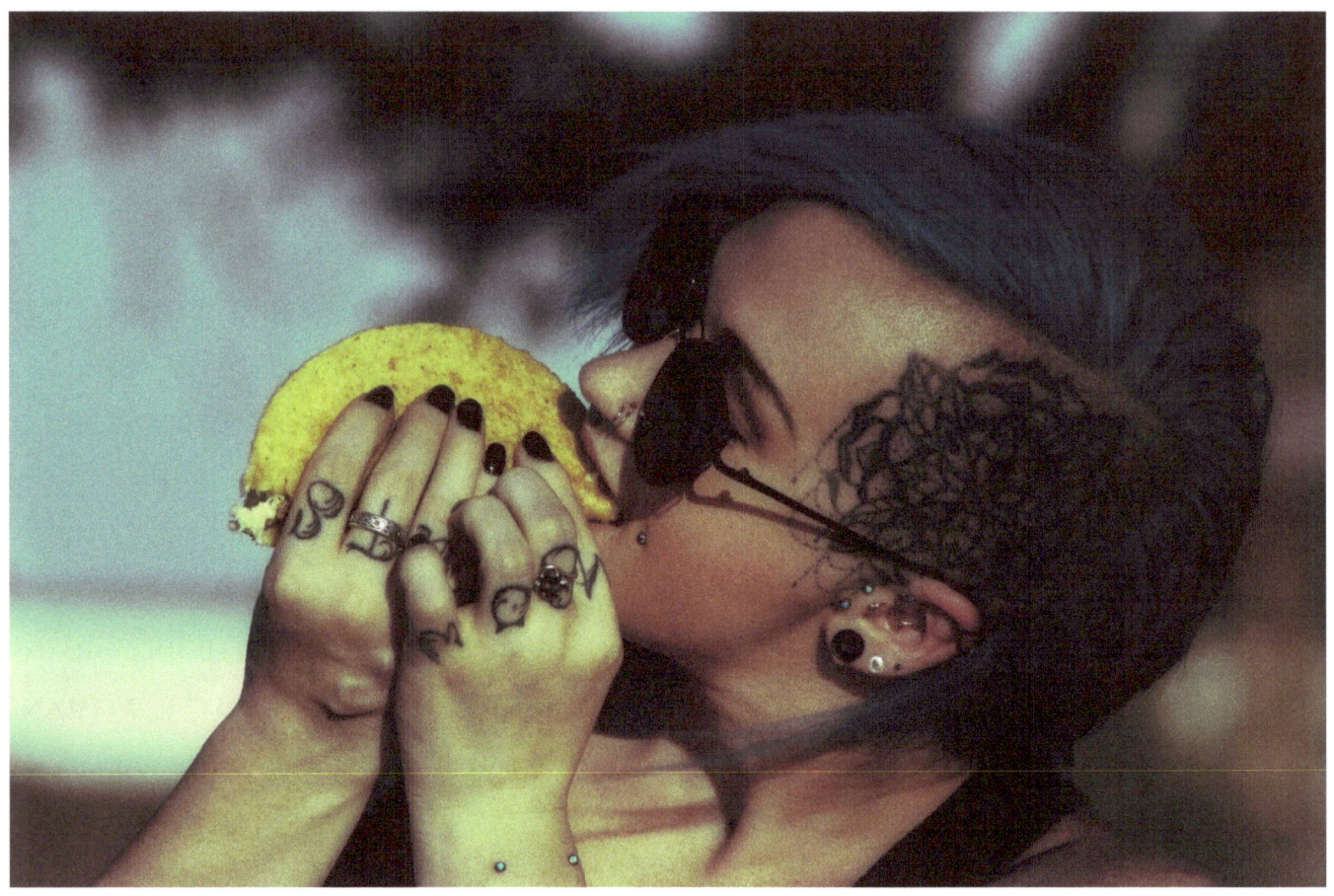

OBJECT:

TACOS

WHY IS IT IMPORTANT TO HER?

"TACOS ARE LIKE ME BECAUSE THEY'RE FUN AND THEY CHANGE. YOU CAN HAVE THEM IN DIFFERENT WAYS. A LOT OF MY FRIENDS SAY THAT SHREK IS LIKE AN ONION AND HE HAS DIFFERENT LAYERS AND TACOS ARE LIKE ME BECAUSE THEY HAVE LAYERS. THEY HAVE FUN, DIFFERENT TOPPINGS AND I'M FUN AND I CHANGE TO DIFFERENT SETTINGS AND ENVIRONMENTS AND TRYING TO BE MYSELF ALL THE TIME, BUT ADAPT TO WHATEVER IS AROUND ME AND MY SURROUNDINGS."

TORIA

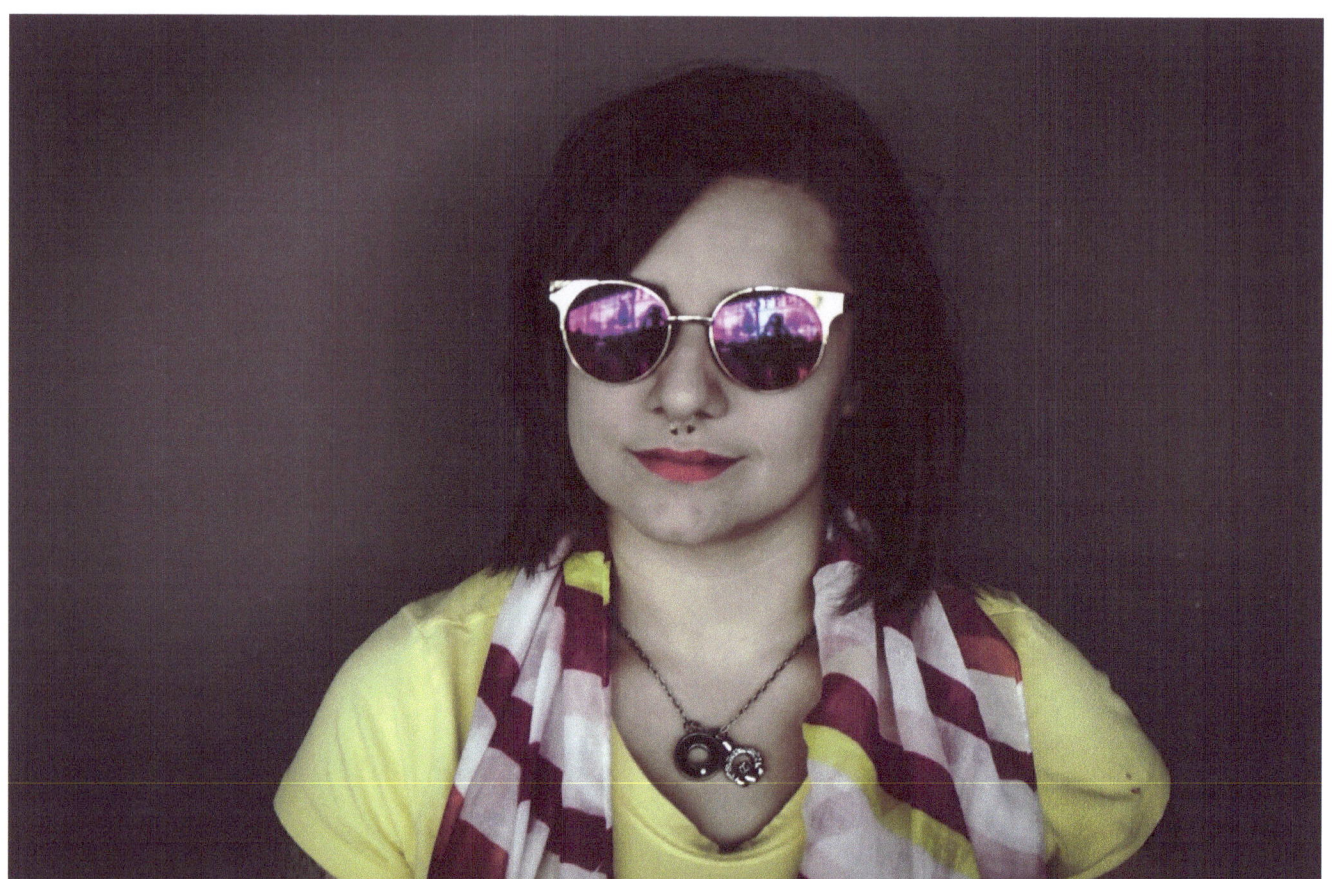

OBJECT:

NECKLACE URNS

WHY IS IT IMPORTANT TO HER?

"MY SISTER DIED FIVE YEARS AGO AND MY MOM DIED SIX MONTHS AGO. IT'S BEEN HARD. GRIEF HAS NOT BEEN EASY OVER THE PAST FIVE YEARS, BUT A COUPLE MONTHS AFTER MY SISTER DIED, MY MOM HAD FOUND THESE ONLINE. THESE LITTLE URNS. SO MY MOM AND MY DAD SURPRISED ME. THEY CAME DOWN FOR HOMECOMING WEEKEND DOWN AT WESTERN (ILLINOIS UNIVERSITY) AND THEY GAVE ME A LITTLE THING WITH TRALEE'S ASHES IN IT.

IT MEANT SO MUCH TO ME AND SO WHEN MY MOM DIED, I ALREADY HAD MY SISTER'S SO I DECIDED I WANTED MY MOM'S WITH ME TOO. I'M NOT A BIG BELIEVER IN GOD OR RELIGION, BUT THEY'RE RIGHT HERE. THEY'RE RIGHT NEXT TO MY HEART. SO THEY'RE WITH ME EVERYWHERE I GO. EVERY CONCERT. EVERY MAJOR LIFE DECISION. EVERYTHING. THEY'VE BEEN RIGHT BY MY SIDE. THEY'RE NOT FAR AND THEY NEVER WILL BE BECAUSE THEY'RE RIGHT HERE. BY MY HEART."

Caleb

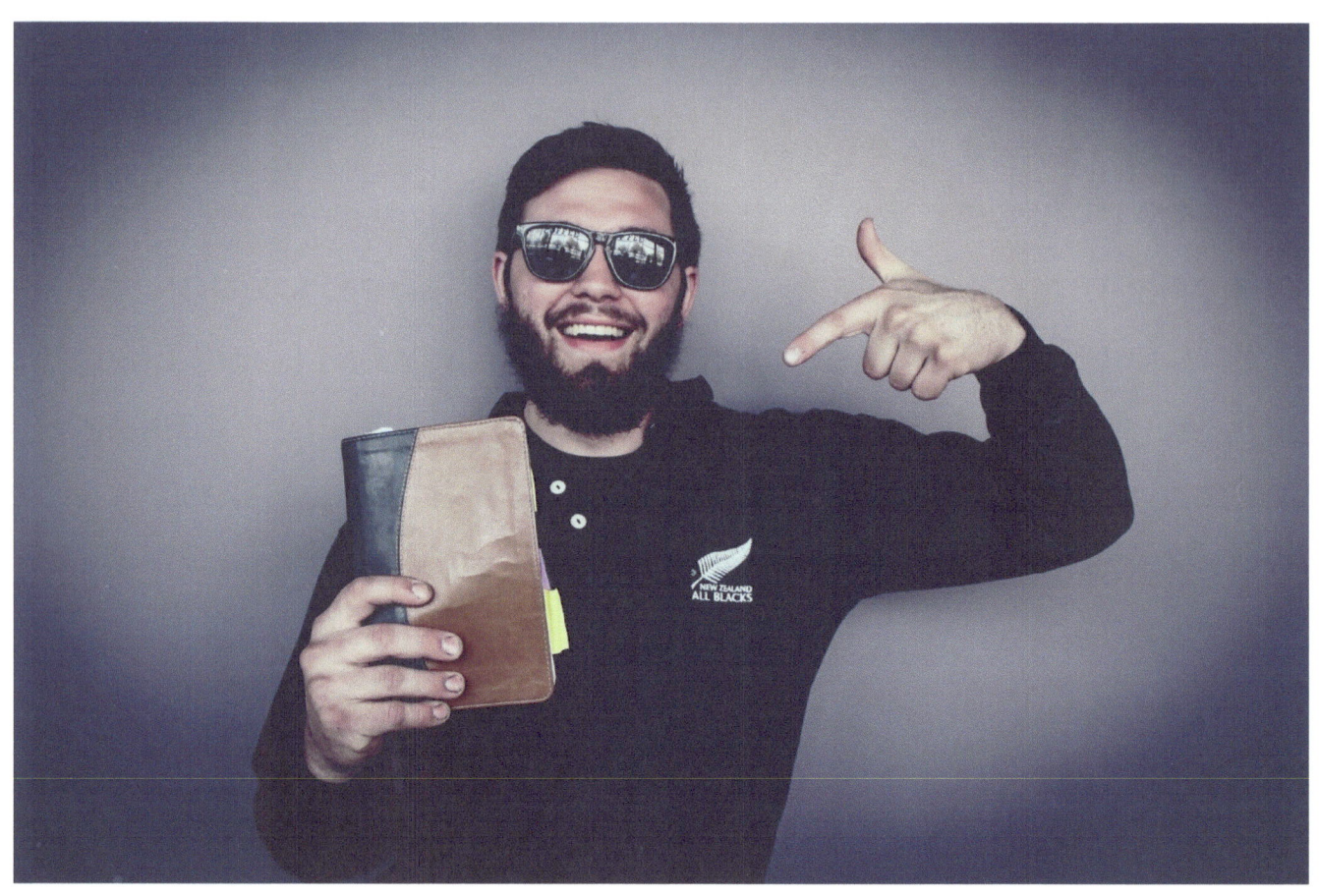

OBJECT:

BIBLE

WHY IS IT IMPORTANT TO HIM?

"MY HEART AND DESIRE IS TO KNOW GOD AND SERVE HIM WITH EVERYTHING I HAVE. I'VE LIVED A LOT OF MY LIFE FOR ME AND REALIZED THAT IT WAS PRETTY DEPRESSING. WHEN I STARTED SERVING GOD, I STARTED GETTING THIS UNREALISTIC SENSE OF JOY AND FULFILLMENT. THE REASON WHY I CHOSE THE BIBLE IS BECAUSE THE FIRST COUPLE OF VERSES IN JOHN IS, 'IN THE BEGINNING WAS THE WORD. THE WORD WAS WITH GOD. THE WORD WAS GOD.'

SO IF I WANT TO GROW CLOSER TO HIM, THEN THE WORD IS A GOOD PLACE TO START."

Kasey

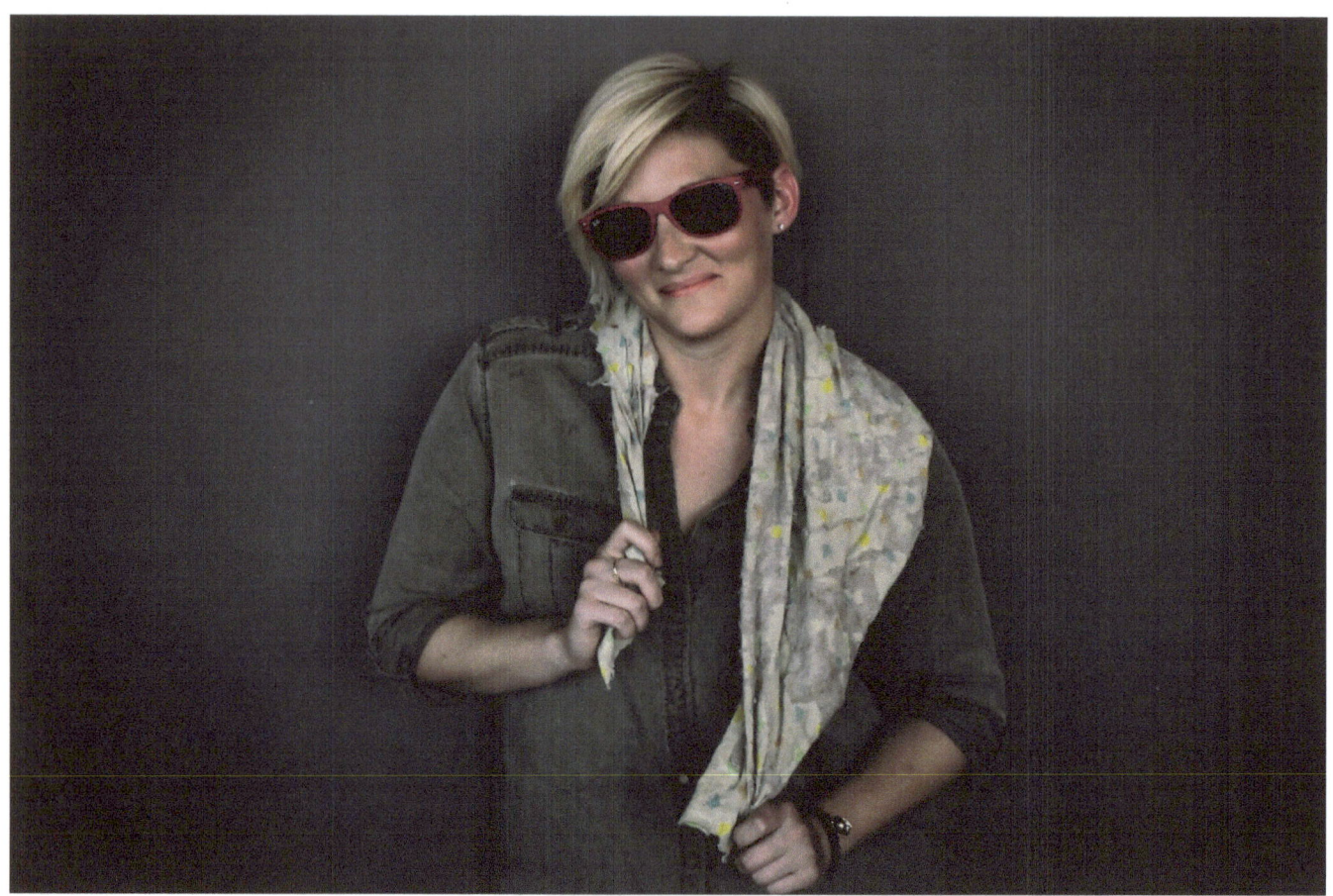

OBJECT:

CHILDHOOD BLANKET

WHY IS IT IMPORTANT TO HER?

"MY GREAT AUNT DORIS MADE IT FOR ME. IT'S ALWAYS GIVEN ME A SENSE OF SECURITY AND A SENSE OF SAFETY SINCE I'VE BEEN A KID. EVEN AS AN ADULT, IT PROVIDES ME WITH A SENSE OF SECURITY AND A SENSE OF SAFETY. IT GOES WITH ME EVERYWHERE. I HAVE MY FAVORITE LITTLE CORNER THAT I RUB ON WHEN I GET STRESSED OUT. I'M 30 NOW, SO THIS THING HAS MADE IT THROUGH 30 YEARS. IT'S NOT THE PRETTIEST THING EVER, BUT IT'S DEFINITELY SOMETHING THAT'S REALLY SPECIAL AND I HOLD DEAR TO MY HEART."

MAC DEVILLE

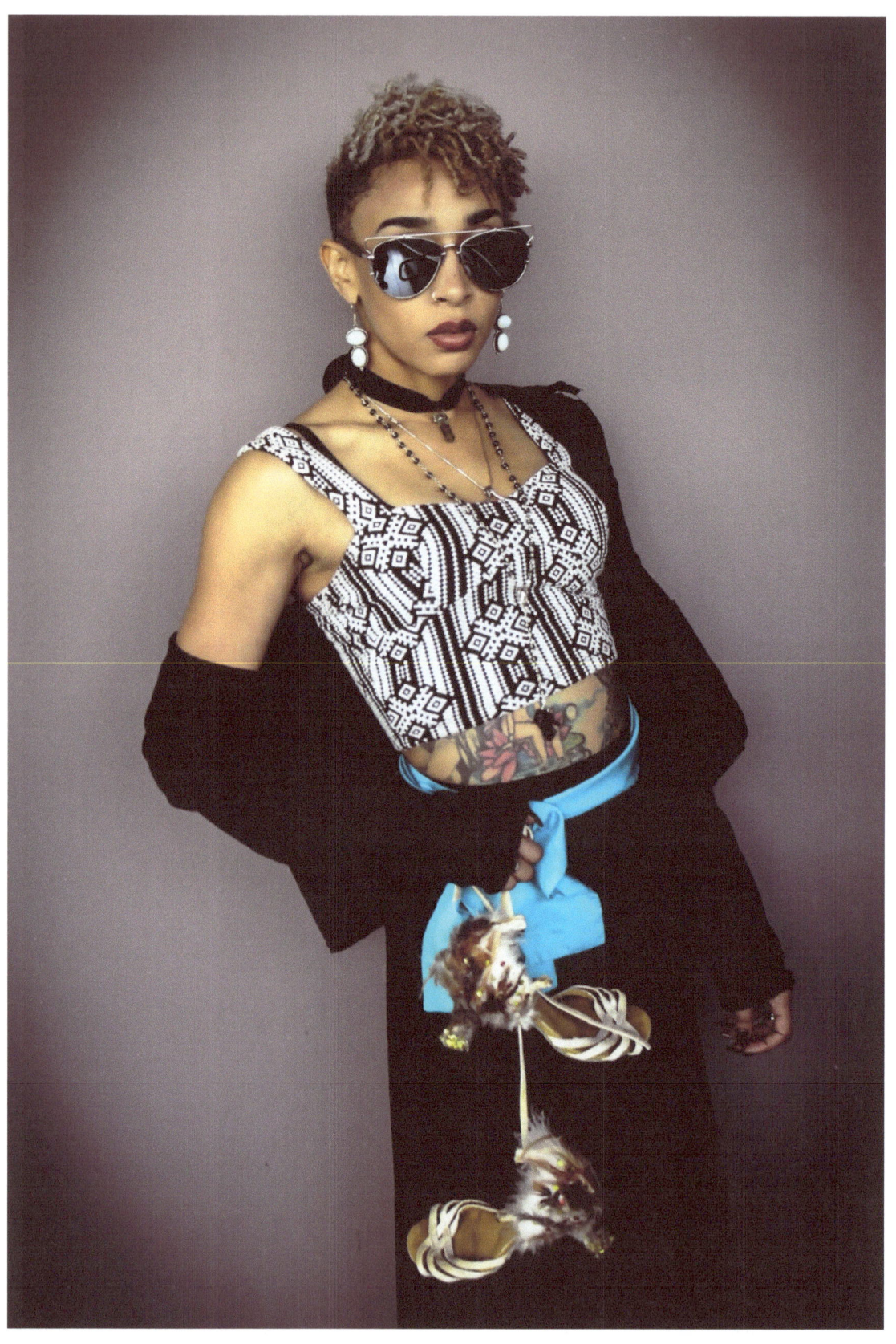

OBJECT:

BALLROOM DANCE SHOES

WHY IS IT IMPORTANT TO HER?

"I GREW UP ON THE WEST SIDE OF CHICAGO AND WE DIDN'T HAVE A LOT OF MONEY, SO THERE WAS NEVER CABLE. MY MOM WAS DETERMINED THAT I STAYED YOUNG AND YOUTHFUL SO THERE WASN'T A LOT OF T.V. THINGS THAT I COULD WATCH, AND THE DANCE COMPETITIONS WERE ALWAYS SOMETHING I COULD WATCH THAT WAS EXCITING AND GLAMOROUS AND KIND OF RISKY AND ALWAYS INTERESTING AND I ALWAYS WANTED TO BE ONE OF THEM.

SO, IN HIGH SCHOOL, I SNUCK AND AUDITIONED FOR A BALLROOM TROUPE AND I GOT ON AND I HAD TO TEACH LESSONS AND CLEAN THE DANCE ROOMS AND THE MIRRORS AND PAINT ALL KINDS OF THINGS TO HELP PAY FOR TUITION. MY PARENTS WOULD ONLY PAY HALF.

THEN I HAD TO BUY THESE SHOES, WHICH WAS THE MOST EXPENSIVE PAIR OF SHOES I'VE EVER BOUGHT AND I WORE THEM FOR YEARS ON A REGULAR BASIS. I WAS MY WAY OF GETTING INTO PERFORMING AND EXPRESSING MYSELF ON STAGE."

DELYN

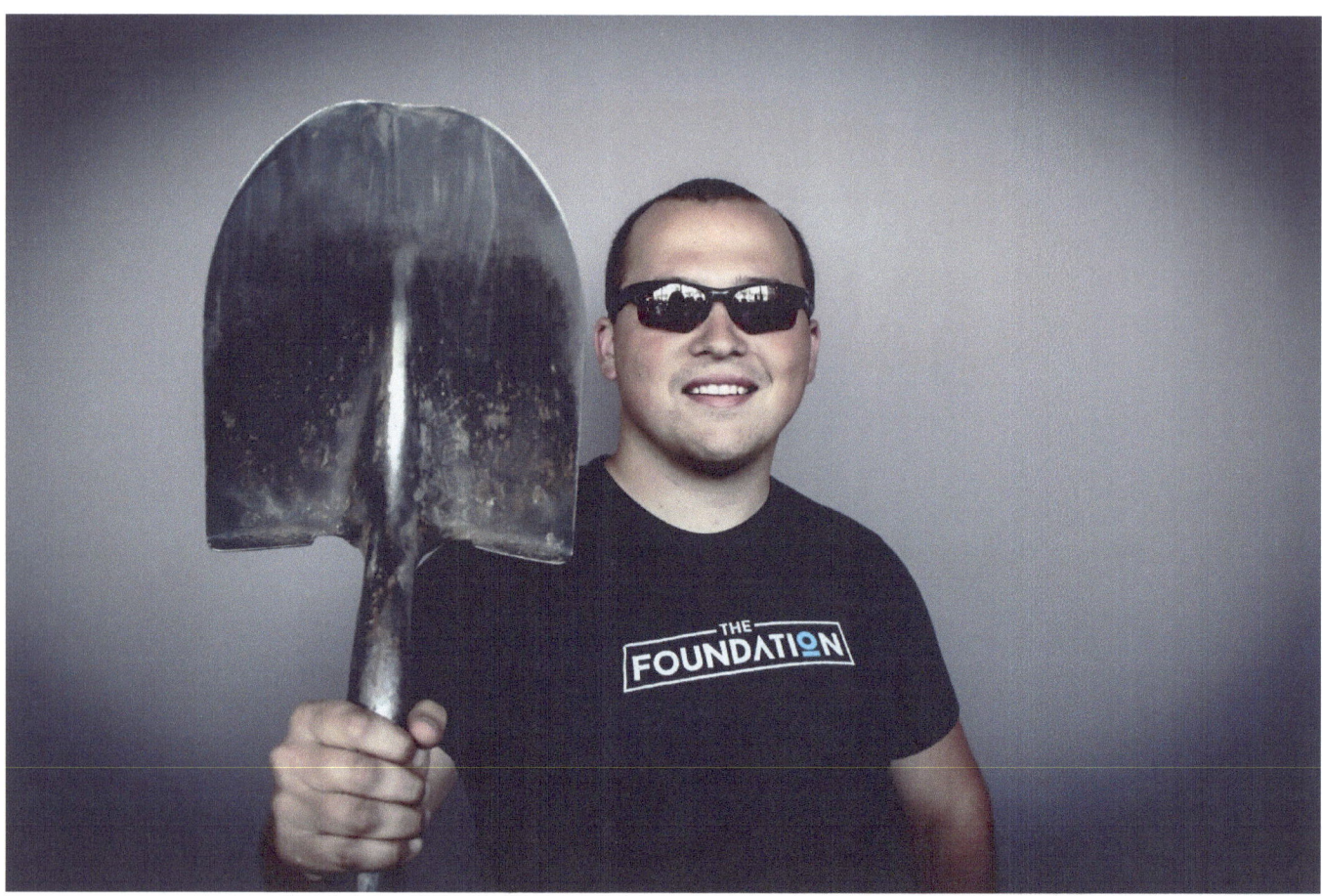

OBJECT:

SHOVEL

WHY IS IT IMPORTANT TO HIM?

"A PROFESSOR OF MINE AT UNI (UNIVERSITY OF NORTHERN IOWA) TOLD ME THIS STORY ABOUT A SHOVEL. THAT IF YOU CAN'T MAKE IT HERE, JUST GRAB A SHOVEL. JUST START WORKING MANUAL LABOR. SO THAT STRUCK A CORD WITH ME. THEN, MY SECOND YEAR AT UNI, MY GIRLFRIEND BROKE UP WITH ME AT FOUR AND A HALF YEARS. SO, THAT SHIFTED MY WHOLE LIFE. I ENDED UP FAILING OUT OF COLLEGE.

OVER SPRING BREAK, I APPLIED TO A LANDSCAPING COMPANY, WHERE I'M AT FIVE YEARS LATER. BUT THEN I DECIDED TO BASICALLY PICK UP A SHOVEL AND START WORKING. INSTEAD OF BURYING MY OWN GRAVE, I BUILT MYSELF A MOUNTAIN AND GOT ON TOP OF IT!

THAT'S WHERE I'M AT NOW AND NOW I'M CLOSER TO MY FAMILY. I HAVE A HAPPY RELATIONSHIP WITH COURTNEY CRABTREE, WHO IS MY GIRLFRIEND. CLOSER TO GOD. I'M GOING BACK TO SCHOOL IN THE FALL, THAT'S THE PLAN. AND THAT SHOVEL, JUST GRAB THE SHOVEL AND START WORKING. INSTEAD OF DIGGING MYSELF A HOLE, I JUST USED IT TO BUILD MY WHOLE LIFE BACK AND NOW I'M AT A BETTER PLACE."

JESSICA

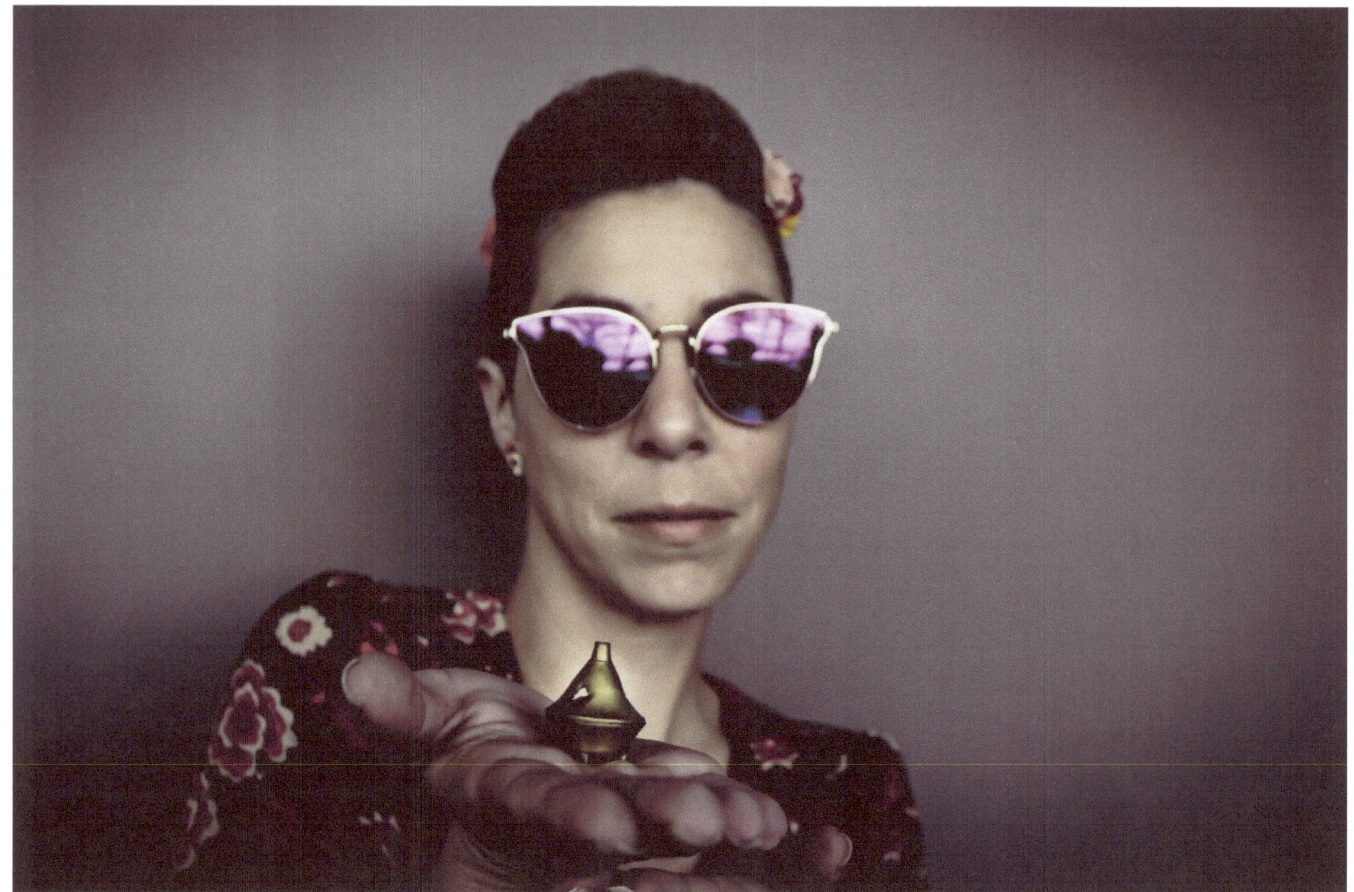

OBJECT:

INCENSE BURNER

WHY IS IT IMPORTANT TO HER?

"THIS IS MY MOTHER'S INCENSE BURNER AND SHE BURNED SANDALWOOD INCENSE MY ENTIRE CHILDHOOD. SO, WHEN I LOST HER WHEN I WAS 18. 18 YEARS AGO. I IMMEDIATELY TOOK IT, SEALED IT, PUT IT IN A BOX AND STUCK IT UP. HOPING THAT IT WOULD RETAIN HER SMELL AND FORTUNATELY IT DOES. SO, WHENEVER I'M MISSING HER TERRIBLY, I CAN OPEN UP THAT BOX AND IT'S LIKE BEING WITH HER ALL OVER AGAIN."

DUSTIN

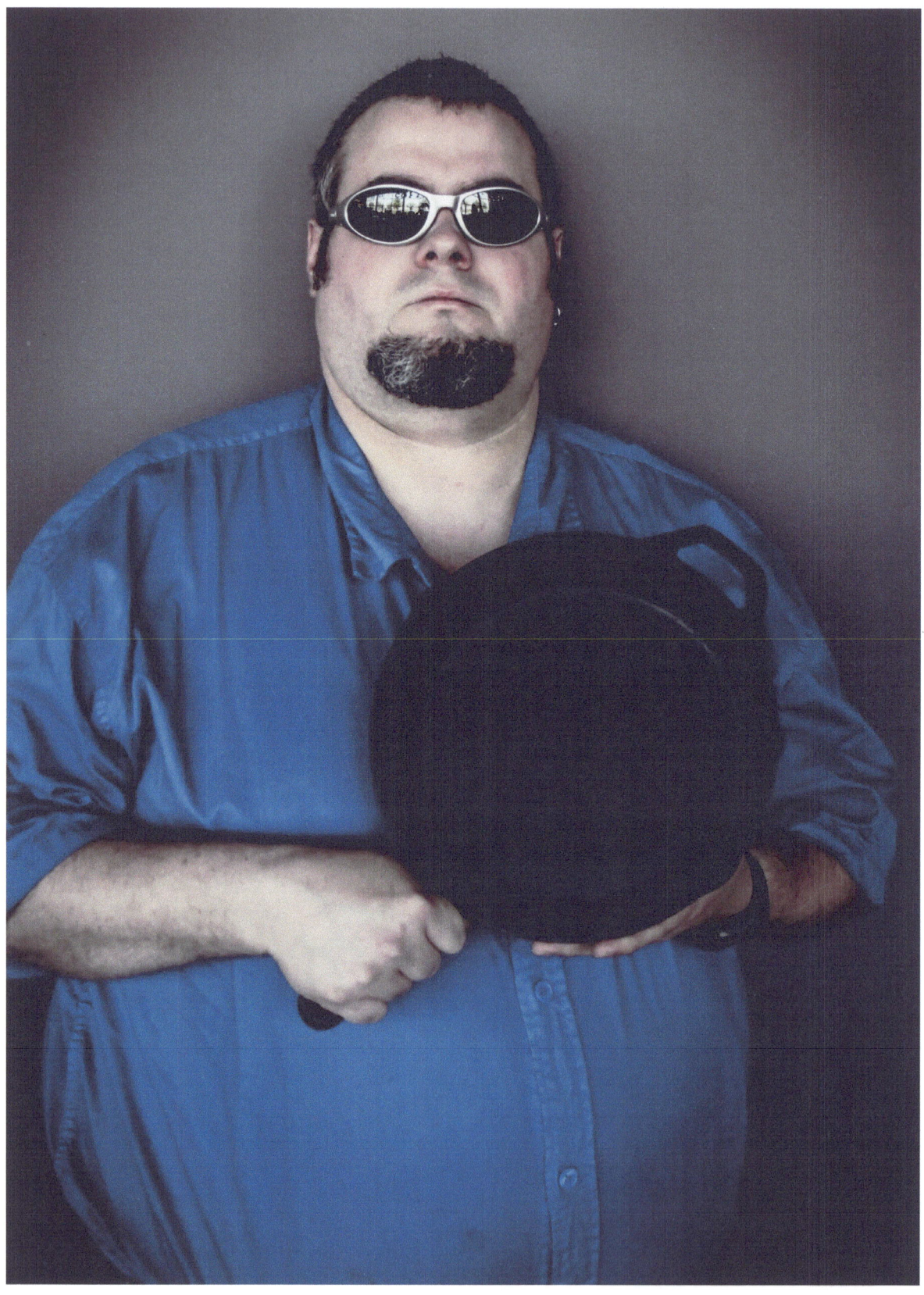

OBJECT:

CAST IRON PAN

WHY IS IT IMPORTANT TO HIM?

"I WAS BORN AND RAISED IN ALABAMA BEFORE I MOVED TO THE QUAD CITIES ABOUT 15 YEARS AGO. I DID A LOT OF COOKING IN THE CAST IRON GROWING UP WITH MY PARENTS, MY MOM, MY GRANDMOTHER. I DON'T HAVE ANY OF THE STUFF THAT I COOKED WITH THEM. A LOT OF DIFFERENT THINGS HAPPENED. GOING TO COLLEGE, DIFFERENT MOVES AND STUFF. SO I DON'T HAVE ANYTHING FROM MY CHILDHOOD THAT REMINDS ME OF THAT, BUT THE CAST IRON IS SUCH A BIG PART OF SOUTHERN COOKING.

ONE OF MY DREAMS, EVEN THOUGH I'M 35 YEARS OLD, IS ONE DAY OWN A RESTAURANT. COOKING FOR MY FAMILY HAS ALWAYS BEEN IMPORTANT FOR ME. COOKING FOR FRIENDS. COOKING FOR PEOPLE, AND THAT CAST IRON SKILLET IS SUCH A BIG PART OF SOUTHERN CUISINE AND THAT'S WHAT I GREW UP WITH. IT'S THAT TIE BACK TO MY CHILDHOOD, TO MY HOME. SO NO MATTER WHERE I'M AT, I HAVE THAT CAST IRON I CAN COOK IN AND IT'S JUST LIKE BEING BACK AT HOME AGAIN."

KATE

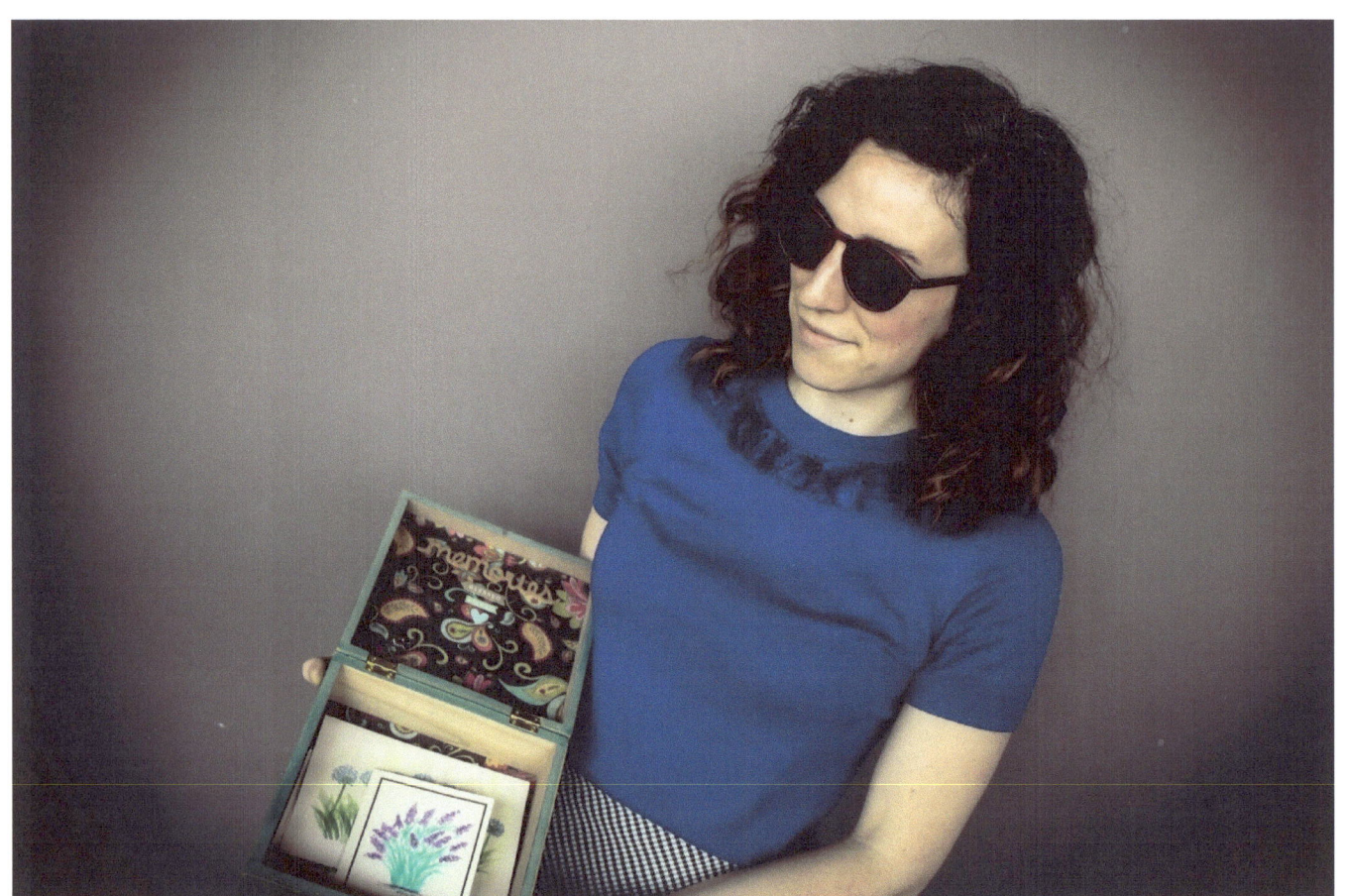

OBJECT:

Memory Box

WHY IS IT IMPORTANT TO HER?

"It's a memory box that my mom made me that is full of cards from my grandmother. She passed away almost five years ago this May. The day before her 97th birthday. She was widowed pretty early. My grandpa died in his 60's. Instantly had a heart attack. So she lived 30 plus years on her own as a single woman. That's when she really started to hone back in to her artistic side and she would always send us all of our birthday cards. Everything was hand painted cards by our grandma.

That's what this box is full of is a lot of cards and there's some other non hand painted stuff in here. All the cards that she sent me over the years, over my life time and notes from her and she also wrote poetry. I don't have any specific poetry in here, but that was a big part of who she was as well. Being artistic and writing poetry and making cards and paintings.

This means a lot to me because my grandma and I were very close. We were kind of kindred spirits. It's sometimes hard to find people who really just understand you and know you and I felt like my grandma did. When I really needed encouragement or good advice, I could call her. I'm also artistic and like to write poetry and so we share that. So I just have a special bond with her. She was a woman of faith and I admire her and I still talk to her like she's my guardian angel and that's why this box means a lot to me. If I really have a low moment, I can go through this and read her cards and it just means a lot to me."

JUNIOR

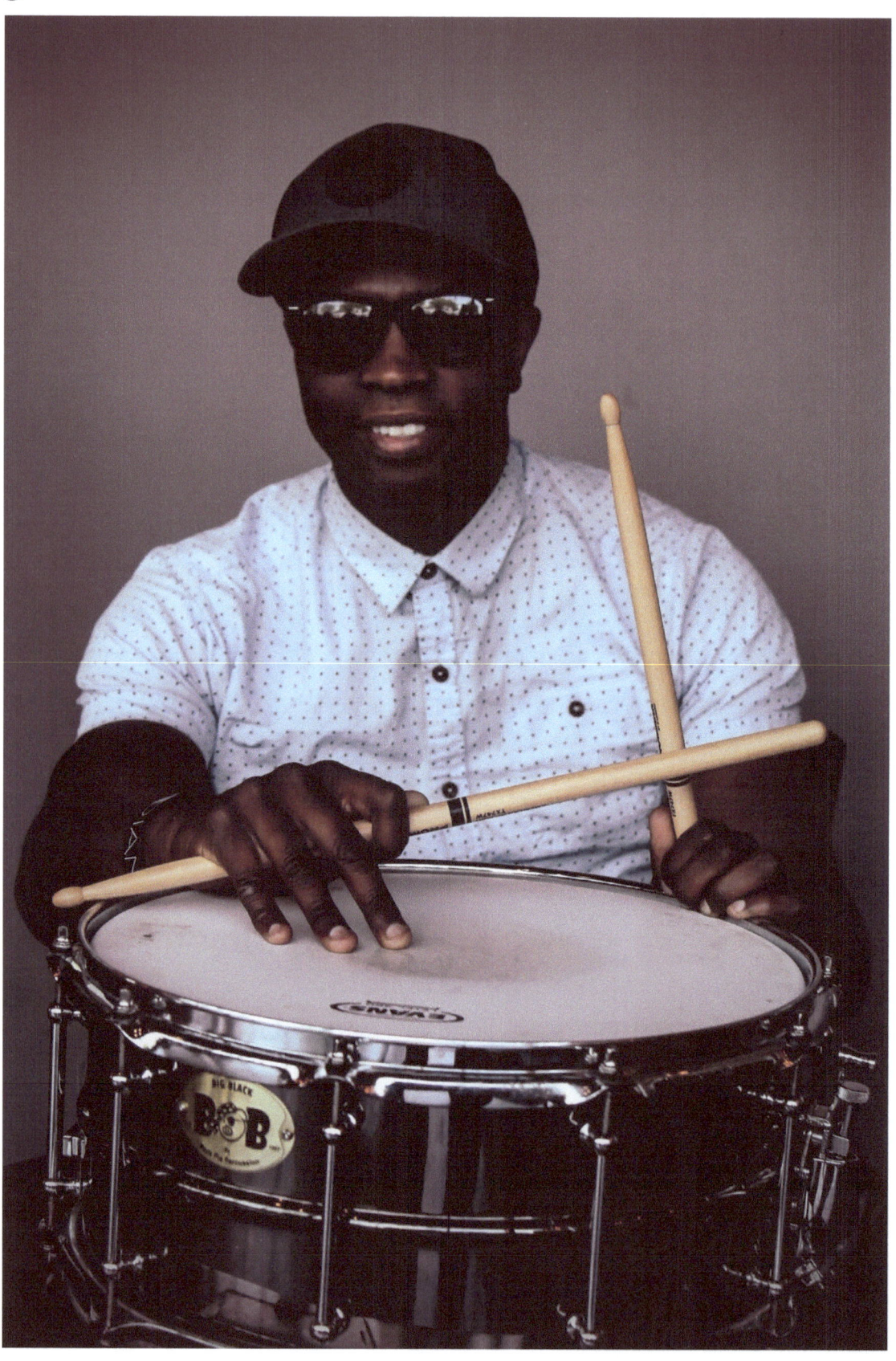

OBJECT:

DRUM STICKS AND DRUMS

WHY IS IT IMPORTANT TO HIM?

"I'VE BEEN DRUMMING EVER SINCE I WAS THREE. I STARTED DRUMMING IN CHURCH WHEN I WAS 12. IT'S FUNNY BECAUSE WHENEVER I GO WHETHER IT'S HERE AT MILLTOWN OR EVEN WHEN I GO TO MICHIGAN OR PLACES, PEOPLE ALWAYS KNOW ME AS A DRUMMER. THEY'RE LIKE, 'HEY! YOU STILL DRUMMING?'

TO TELL YOU THE TRUTH, THAT'S KIND OF LED, I WOULDN'T SAY TO VANITY, BUT IT'S MADE ME QUESTION 'DO I REALLY WANT TO BE KNOWN AS A DRUMMER? IS THAT THE IDENTITY I WANT PEOPLE TO KNOW ME AS?'

BECAUSE THERE ARE OTHER THINGS I DO. FOR EXAMPLE, I'M AN ACCOUNTANT, BUT PEOPLE DON'T KNOW THAT. PEOPLE ARE LIKE, 'HEY! YOU'RE A DRUMMER, BUT WHAT DO YOU DO IN YOUR REAL LIFE?' OR, 'YOU TOUR DON'T YOU? YOU PLAY HERE. YOU PLAY HERE.' AND I'M LIKE NO MAN! I HAVE A REAL JOB JUST LIKE YOU. THE DRUM STUFF IS HONESTLY A HOBBY. IT'S A HOBBY THAT SOMETIMES I GET PAID FOR BUT IT'S NOT A JOB. SO THE DRUM PART OF IT HAS LED ME TO LOOK AT MYSELF AND BE LIKE, 'DO I REALLY WANT TO BE KNOWN AS A DRUMMER PER SE?'

IT'S FUNNY BECAUSE THIS PAST CHRISTMAS I DID A BIG EVENT AT THE iWIRELESS CENTER CALLED 'ONE VOICE.' IT'S FUNNY BECAUSE I JUST REMEMBER FRIENDS AND EVEN PEOPLE I DON'T KNOW COMING UP TO ME WITH THEIR KIDS AND BEING LIKE, 'MY KIDS SAW YOU AND THEY'RE SO INSPIRED AND NOW THEY WANT TO BE A DRUMMER.' OR THEY WENT ON MY FACEBOOK AND POSTED A VIDEO OF THEIR KID HITTING ON THEIR TOY DRUM SET OR THEIR TABLE SAYING, 'MY SON LOOKS UP TO YOU. MY DAUGHTER LOOKS UP TO YOU AND THEY WANT TO BE A DRUMMER BECAUSE THEY SAW YOU DRUMMING.

SO I LEARNED THAT HAVING THE IDENTITY OF A DRUMMER ISN'T NECESSARILY A BAD THING BECAUSE IT CAN GIVE ME A PLATFORM TO ENCOURAGE OTHER KIDS."

TETRA

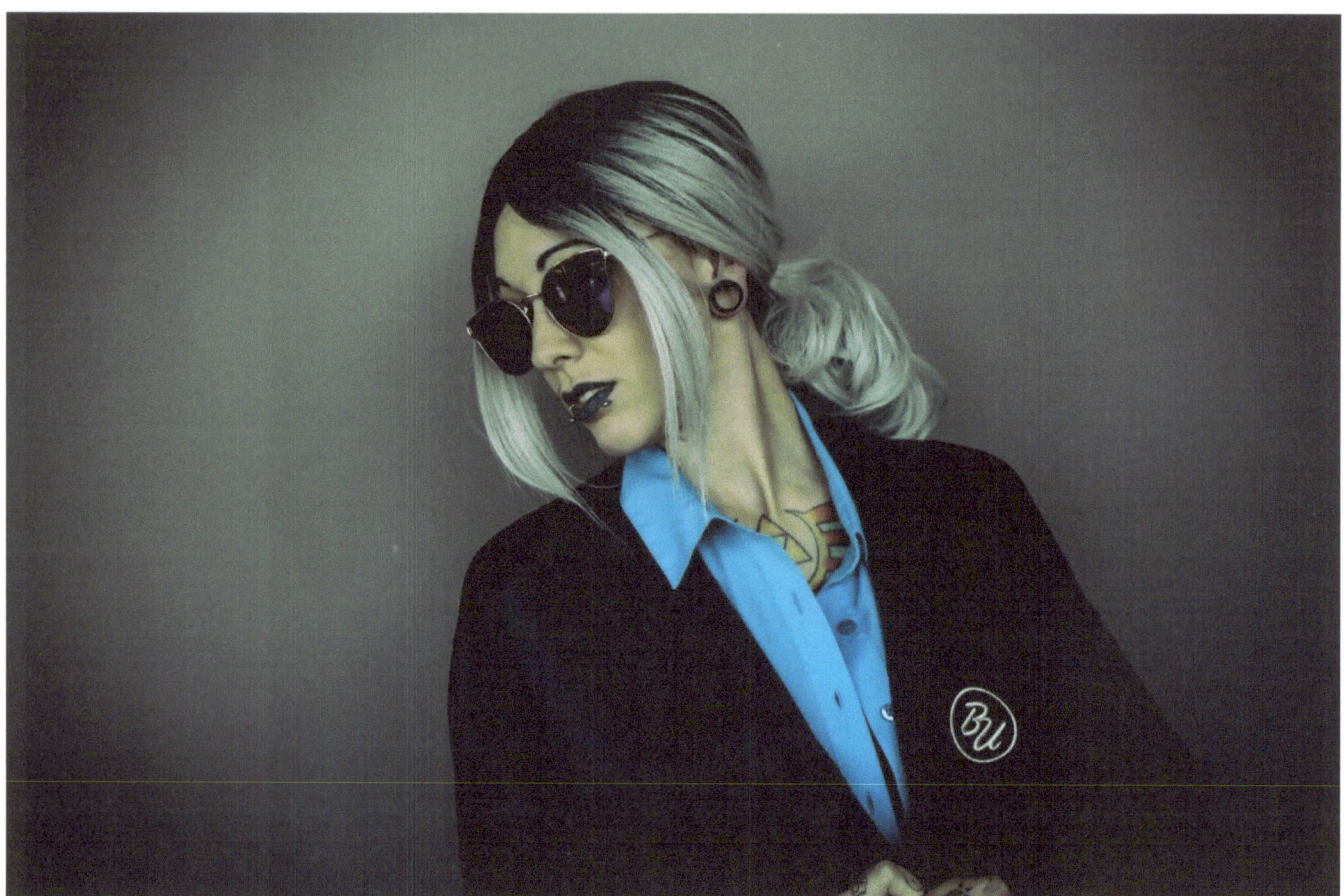

OBJECT:

Performance Robe

WHY IS IT IMPORTANT TO HER?

"Growing up, I never really felt like I had a lot of friends or a lot of close friends. I always wanted to be the popular person and I didn't know how to do that. I would look through social media and be like, 'Oh! Everyone's doing all this stuff and I'm sitting at home by myself.' Nobody really understood me. I've always been super different. Relationships never worked with anybody. I've been in and out of relationships since I was 14. I never really understood myself until I went and I saw my first burlesque show because I had no idea what burlesque was at all.

When I saw them for the first time, I was like, 'Wow! That's what I want to do with my life. This is it.' It took me probably close to two years, following them around, not taking no for an answer. Until they finally were like, 'Ok. We'll make you an apprentice.' And I apprenticed for a while, and then when I finally became a member, they gave me this robe.

Being able to create Tetra is like finding another part of myself. Every kind of made sense after that. Once I found her, I started to learn who I really was and the relationship I was in, I was actually engaged not to long ago. That actually ended. I don't want to say, Oh, I was Tetra's fault,' but finding out who I really am kind of had a part in it, because I changed completely. I wasn't afraid of myself. I wasn't afraid of the part of me that I kept locked away. I wasn't ashamed of it anymore. I embraced it and I think that probably threatened him and he just didn't understand it and he kept trying to turn me into something that I wasn't. That's what any boyfriend I ever had did. Never really found anybody who wanted me for both sides of me. Rhiannon and Tetra.

So when I finally became a member, I was like I found out who I really was and I know sometimes that takes people years to figure out, but I'm extremely grateful to be able to figure out who I am at 24. But getting this is probably the most important thing that I own. Just being able to finally have both sides of myself and now I have a new boyfriend that is more proud of me than anything and actually accepts both parts of me. Not just Tetra. Not just Rhiannon, but both of them.

The family that I have through Bottoms Up is ridiculous. Nobody's ever been more welcoming and loving and caring and understanding about all the deep dark parts of me. Not even my family, because I've always been the black sheep of my family. When they handed me this, I cried, because it's there in print and being a part of burlesque especially is an amazing, beautiful thing. A lot of people don't understand it. They're like, 'Oh, so you're a stripper right?' No. Burlesque is not about teasing men. It's about empowering women, and how beautiful of a thing that is especially with all the different kinds of women that are in the troupe. Big, tall, skinny, overweight, underweight. It doesn't matter. We show girls you're beautiful no matter what you look like and I've always believed in that and wanted to do something to show women that. Through this, this is an amazing outlet to be able to do that."

COLE

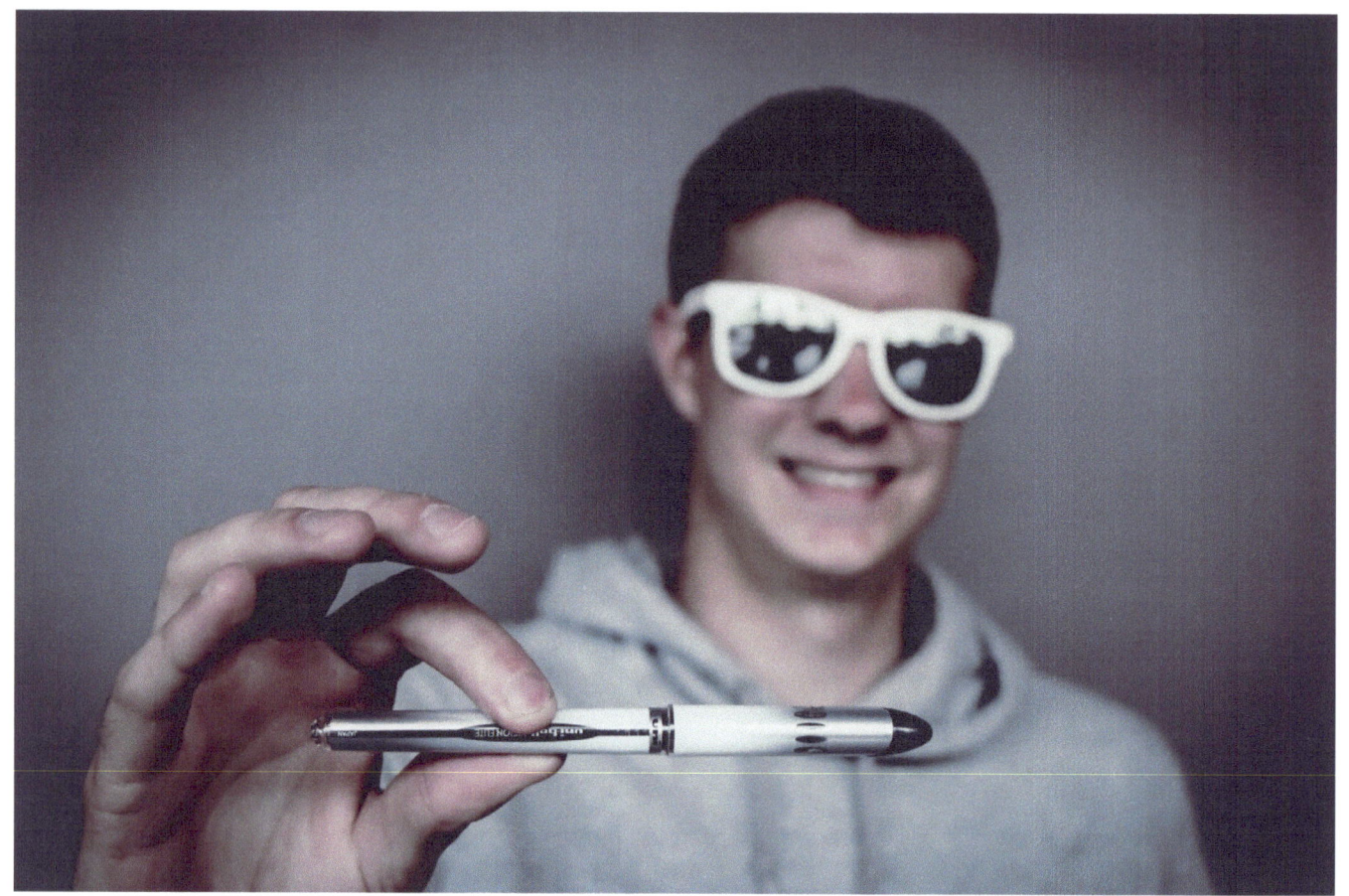

OBJECT:

PEN

WHY IS IT IMPORTANT TO HIM?

"THE PEN ITSELF IS A MASSIVE SYMBOL TO ME. THE REASON WHY IS BECAUSE I'VE BEEN ABLE TO ACTUALLY START AND LAUNCH MY FIRST COMPANY OFF OF THIS PEN. THE WRITER'S FIX. I'M ACTUALLY A WRITER. I CONTRIBUTE TO PUBLICATIONS. I HELP PEOPLE WRITE ARTICLES AND BLOGS. I LOVE WRITING. I'M ABLE TO EXPRESS MYSELF. I'M ABLE TO HELP OTHER PEOPLE THEMSELVES AS WELL IN THIS WORLD WHERE WE'RE SO CLUTTERED WITH ALL OFF THESE DIFFERENT OBJECTS AND THINGS AND VIDEO GAMES AND THINGS THAT AREN'T NECESSARILY REAL.

THE PEN IS ABLE TO BE MET WITH THE PAPER WHERE I CAN ACTUALLY GET THOUGHTS THAT ARE REAL AND GENUINE OUT OF PEOPLE AND MYSELF AND REALLY BE ABLE TO BRIDGE THAT GAP BETWEEN ALL THOSE DIFFERENT THINGS. SO THAT'S WHY I PICKED THE PEN, BECAUSE EVERYDAY I PICK ONE UP AND WRITE STUFF DOWN OR WRITE DOWN IDEAS. I WRITE DOWN WHAT I FEEL. I WRITE DOWN WHAT I WANT. I WRITE DOWN WHAT I'M GOING TO DO AND HOW I'M GOING TO DO IT AND IT'S AMAZING WHAT JUST A SMALL INSTRUMENT CAN DO FOR ME AND MY LIFE AND FOR OTHER PEOPLE IN THEIR LIFE TOO."

BRITANIE

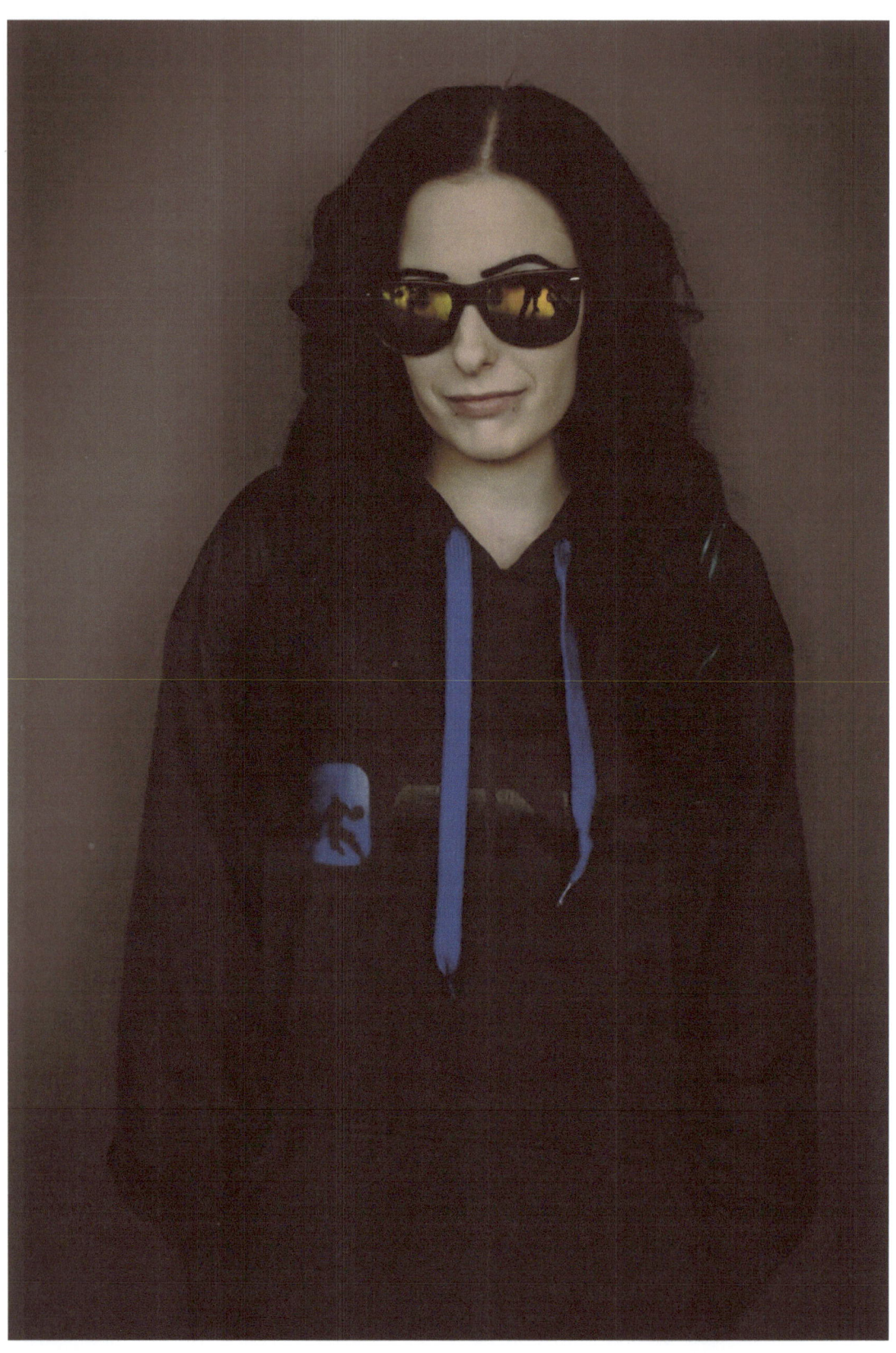

OBJECT:

Her Brother's Hoodie

WHY IS IT IMPORTANT TO HER?

"It's the only thing that I have left from him. He was 17 when he passed away, and he was wearing this hoodie in the pictures from when I took him to Missouri and in his obituary picture. He was the youngest of us three. He was very close to me. I took care of him for a little while for my mom over the summer last year and I think he was happier being with me than he was living with her."

JESSE

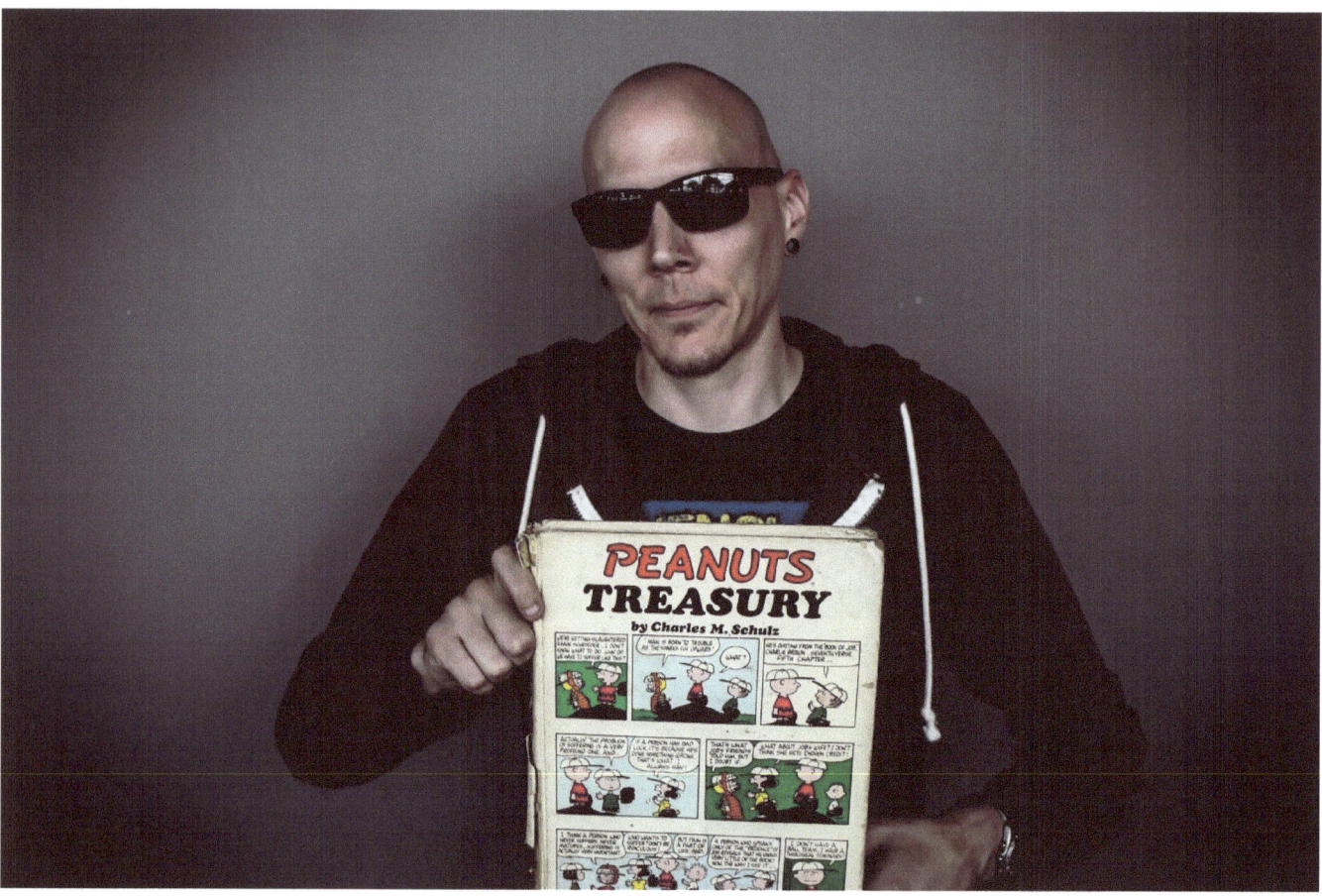

OBJECT:

PEANUTS BOOK

WHY IS IT IMPORTANT TO HIM?

"MY PARENTS DIVORCED WHEN I WAS REALLY YOUNG, AND SINCE MY MOM GOT CUSTODY OF ME, I DIDN'T GET TO SEE MY DAD VERY OFTEN. EVENTUALLY, WE WOULD EVEN FIND OURSELVES SEPARATED BY SEVERAL STATES, WHICH MADE SEEING ONE ANOTHER EVEN MORE STRENUOUS.

MY FATHER GAVE ME THIS BOOK WHEN I WAS VERY LITTLE. NOT ONLY WAS IT JUST A FUN AND FASCINATING CARTOON TO READ, BUT THE BOOK ITSELF MEANT THE WORLD TO ME SINCE IT CAME FROM MY DAD. I WOULD STAY UP LATE AT NIGHT, AFTER BED TIME, AND READ IT UNDER A NIGHT LIGHT. IT BROUGHT COMFORT, AND SOMETIMES MADE ME FEEL AS IF MY DAD WAS THERE. IT WAS ONE OF THE THINGS THAT SPARKED MY LOVE OF READING THAT LASTS EVEN TO THIS DAY.

THIRTY SOME YEARS LATER, I STILL OWN IT, AND STILL PERIODICALLY READ IT COVER-TO-COVER. TO THIS DAY MAKES ME FEEL CLOSER TO MY DAD, AND BECAUSE OF THAT, I WILL TREASURE THIS BOOK, ALWAYS."

KATE

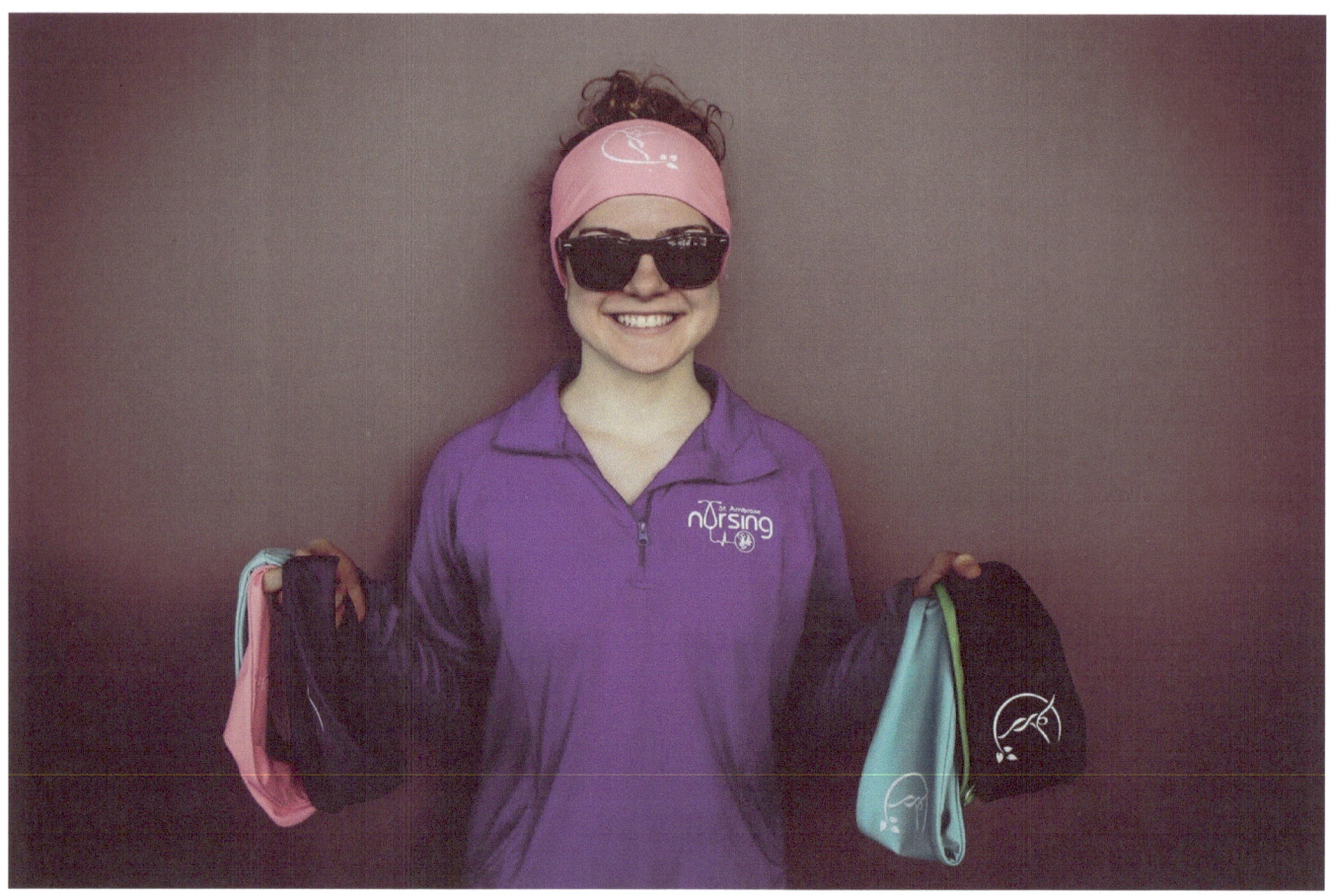

OBJECT:

HEADBAND

WHY IS IT IMPORTANT TO HER?

"They're a fun project for me and my husband and I to work on.

My husband, Elijah and I got married last august and we wanted to find something that we were both passionate about and that is health and fitness for us.

Elijah is an entrepreneur and I'm a nurse and we both work very hard and wanted to create something from our past experiences. We wanted to create something that would encourage other people to live healthy lives and get out there and try something new too. So we went through a lot of trial and error with these headbands. We've tried lots of different materials and colors and manufacturers. So this is the best product we've come up with so far. We want to expand into a whole athletic apparel, but this is where we're starting right now, so it's pretty exciting!

Right now we have five different colors and haven't yet put it online for actual sales, but it's an exciting process an something we get to work on together and I think it represents an opportunity to make your life whatever you want. You can do whatever you want in life. I'm a nurse, but I like to work on a lot of other side projects in my free time. So this is one of those things that is fun and really important to me."

MICHAEL

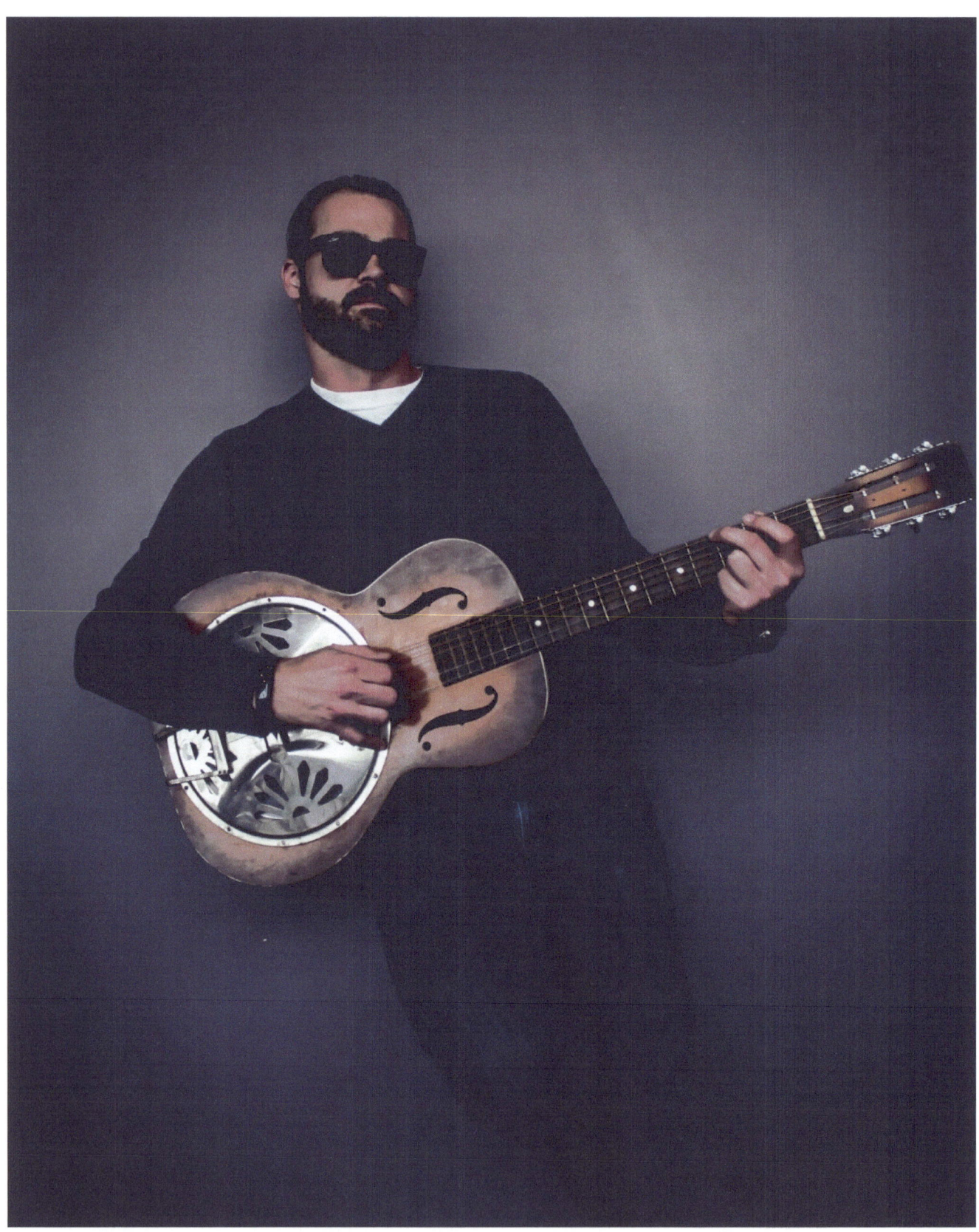

OBJECT:

GUITAR

WHY IS IT IMPORTANT TO HIM?

"THE GUITAR REPRESENTS MY PASSION AND LOVE FOR MUSIC.

LEARNING THE GUITAR AT A YOUNG AGE AND MOVING ONTO OTHER INSTRUMENTS AS I GOT OLDER, HELPED ME GROW INTO THE PERSON I AM TODAY. CREATING MUSIC IS MY PASSION IN LIFE AND THE GUITAR WILL ALWAYS BE MY FIRST LOVE IN LIFE.
I USE INSTRUMENTS AND MUSIC TO EXPRESS MYSELF WHEN MY WORDS FAIL TO COME TO ME. ONE STRUM OF THE STRINGS CAN CHANGE A WHOLE MOOD OR TELL YOU HOW I AM FEELING AT ANY MOMENT I PICKUP THIS GUITAR. BOB MARLEY SAID IT BEST, "WHEN THE MUSIC HITS YOU. YOU FEEL NO PAIN". IN A LOUD WORLD I USE MUSIC AS MY VOICE TO SILENCE THE NOISE SO THAT PEOPLE THAT TRYING TO LISTEN CAN HEAR MY SONG.

PLAYING GUITAR AND MAKING MUSIC HAS BEEN A BIG INFLUENCE IN MY LIFE THANKS TO MY DAD AND MY BROTHER FOR SHOWING ME MY PASSION AT AN EARLY AGE. AS I GOT OLDER I GOT INTO THE LOCAL BAND SCENE PLAYED IN A FEW BANDS, MADE SOME GREAT FRIENDS IN THE MUSIC COMMUNITY, AND HAVE GREAT MEMORIES TO CARRY WITH ME IN LIFE. NO MATTER WHERE LIFE TAKES ME I WILL CONTINUE TO PLAY MY SONGS, THE STORY, THE SOUND TRACK TO MY LIFE."

ALEESHA

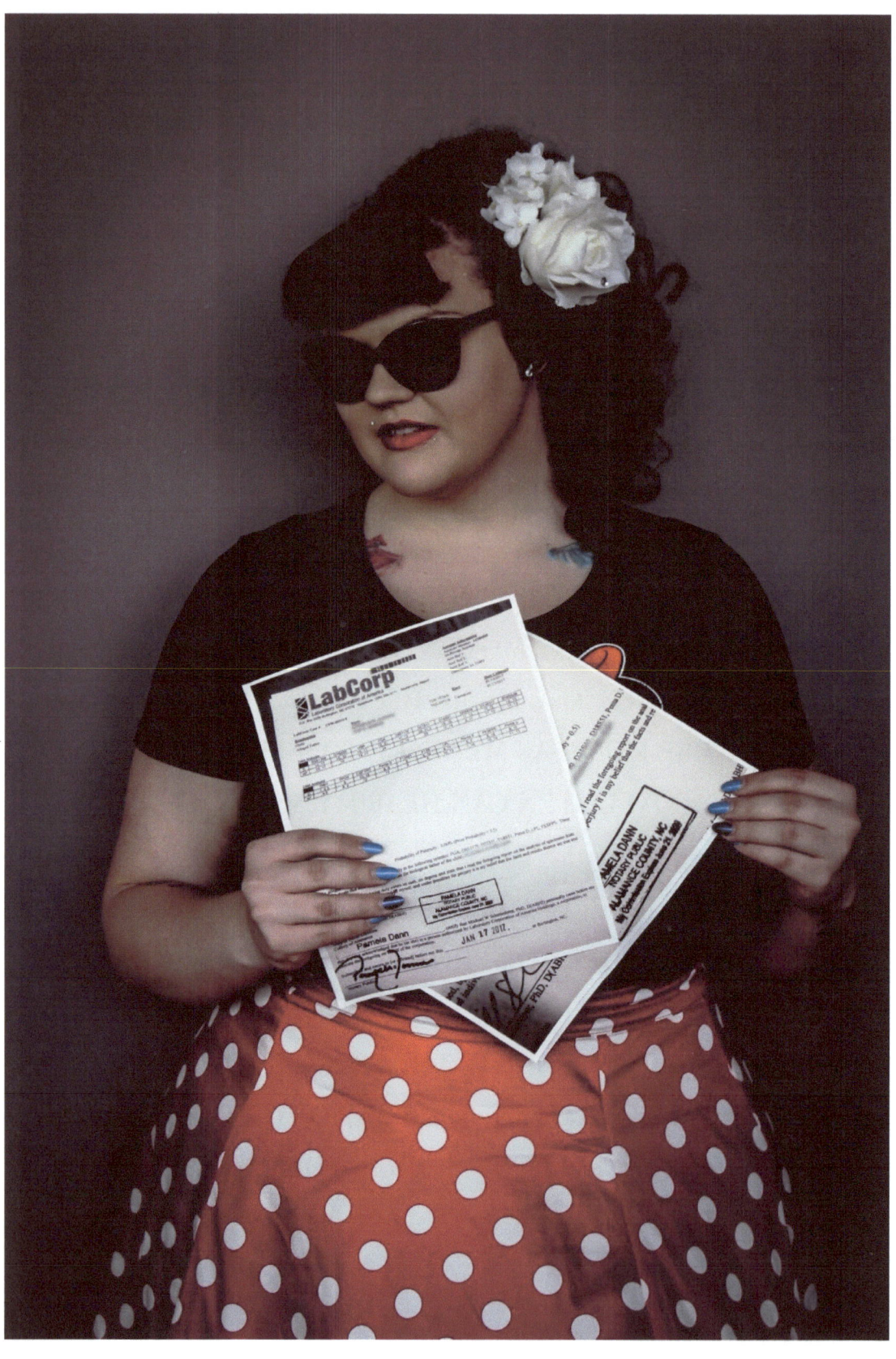

OBJECT:

PATERNITY PAPERS

WHY IS IT IMPORTANT TO HER?

"EARLIER IN THE YEAR, THE GENTLEMAN THAT I'VE KNOW MY WHOLE ENTIRE LIFE TO BE MY FATHER FOR THE LAST 26 YEARS, ASKED ME TO DO A DNA TEST. I BROUGHT THE RESULTS OF THAT DNA TEST THAT'S SHOWING THAT I'M ALLEGEDLY NOT HIS DAUGHTER. AFTER HE HAD GOTTEN THE DNA TEST RESULTS, HE HAD COMPLETELY DROPPED ME FROM HIS ENTIRE LIFE. TOLD ME HE DIDN'T WANT ANYTHING MORE TO DO WITH ME AND MY CHILDREN, WHICH WOULD ESSENTIALLY BE HIS GRANDCHILDREN. EVEN THOUGH HE'S KNOWN FOR THE PAST 26 YEARS THAT I POSSIBLY WASN'T HIS DAUGHTER, THAT HE JUST DIDN'T WANT ANYTHING MORE TO DO WITH ME.

HE GOT A STORAGE UNIT, PUT EVERYTHING INCLUDING MY SENIOR PICTURES, MY SENIOR RING, EVERYTHING INTO THE STORAGE UNIT. TOLD ME I HAVE 30 DAYS TO GET IT. IF NOT, TO JUST LEAVE IT THERE AND LET THEM THROW IT AWAY. SO I'M TRYING TO TURN THIS NEGATIVE THING INTO A POSITIVE AND SHOW THAT MY CHILDREN AND I AND ANYONE CAN COME AND BE BUILT FROM SOMETHING SO NEGATIVE IN YOUR LIFE."

PRESTON

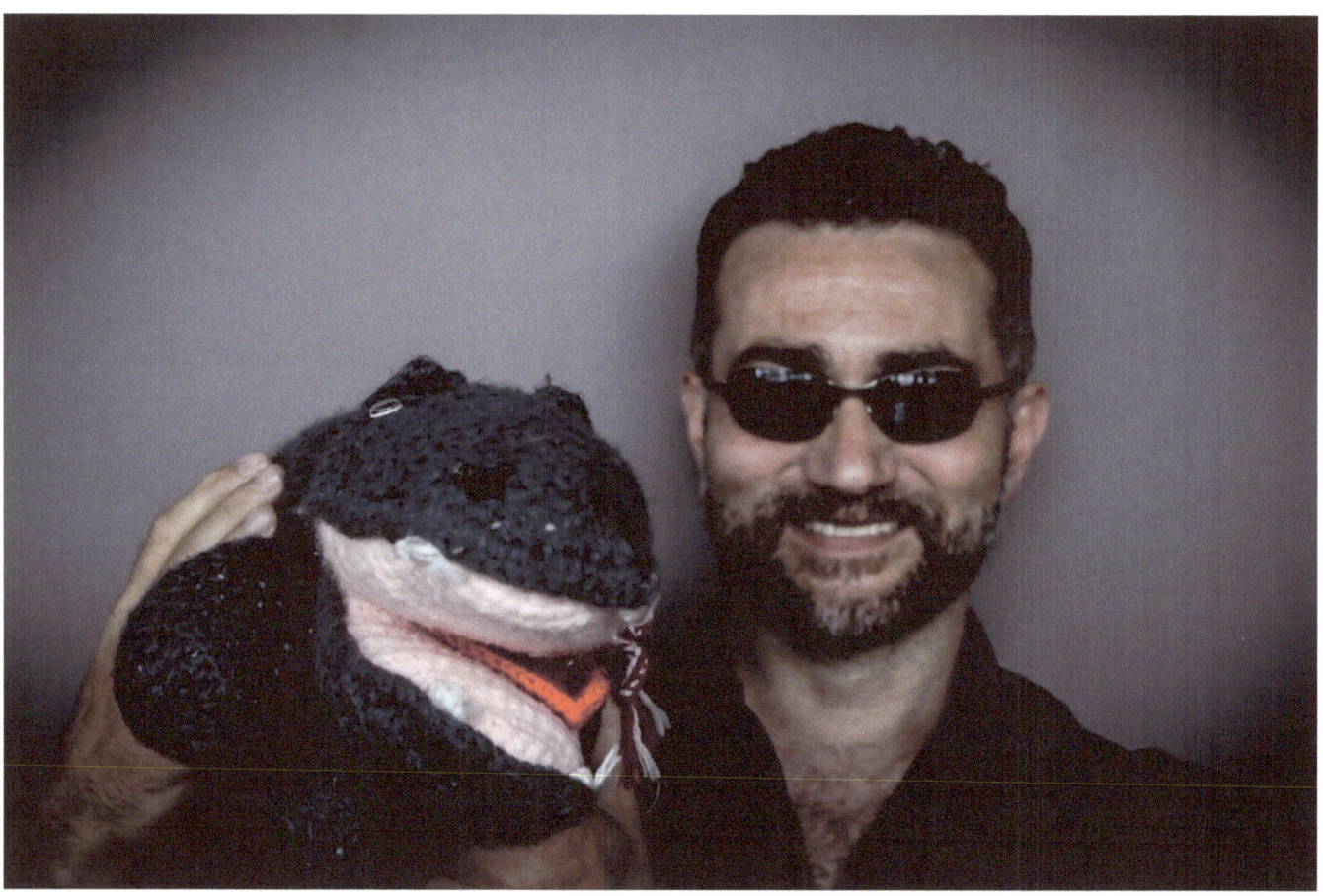

OBJECT:

CROCHETED HIPPO

WHY IS IT IMPORTANT TO HIM?

"IT'S A HIPPO MY GRANDMOTHER AND I MADE WHEN I WAS FOUR YEARS OLD. MY GRANDPARENTS LIVED A BLOCK AWAY FROM US, SO I WAS DOWN THERE ALL THE TIME. I WAS KIND OF A BIT OF A SPOILED CHILD, AS THE FIRST BORN GRANDSON, FIRST SON. SO I HAD PLENTY OF TIME WITH GRANDMA AND GRANDPA. THEY ALWAYS TOOK ME TO DO DIFFERENT THINGS AND ONE OF THE THINGS MY GRANDMA DID WAS CROCHETING AND SHE ACTUALLY TAUGHT ME HOW TO DO IT WHEN I WAS A CHILD.

I HAVEN'T DONE IT A NUMBER OF YEARS, BUT THIS OLD THING IS A HIPPO I MADE WHEN I WAS FOUR YEARS OLD AND I CAN REMEMBER...SHE HAD HER HANDS RIGHT ON MINE AND TEACHING ME HOW TO DO THE NEEDLES AND IT WAS JUST ONE OF THOSE CHILDHOOD MEMORY THINGS. AT FIRST I THOUGHT ABOUT SOME DIFFERENT THINGS. THE TATTOO, THE WATCH, MY FATHER'S NECKLACE AND STUFF, BUT AS FAR AS MY CHILDHOOD AND JUST SOME INCREDIBLY GREAT MEMORIES WITH MY GRANDPARENTS AND AUNTS AND UNCLES AND EVERYBODY... THIS CAME TO MIND."

KAYLA

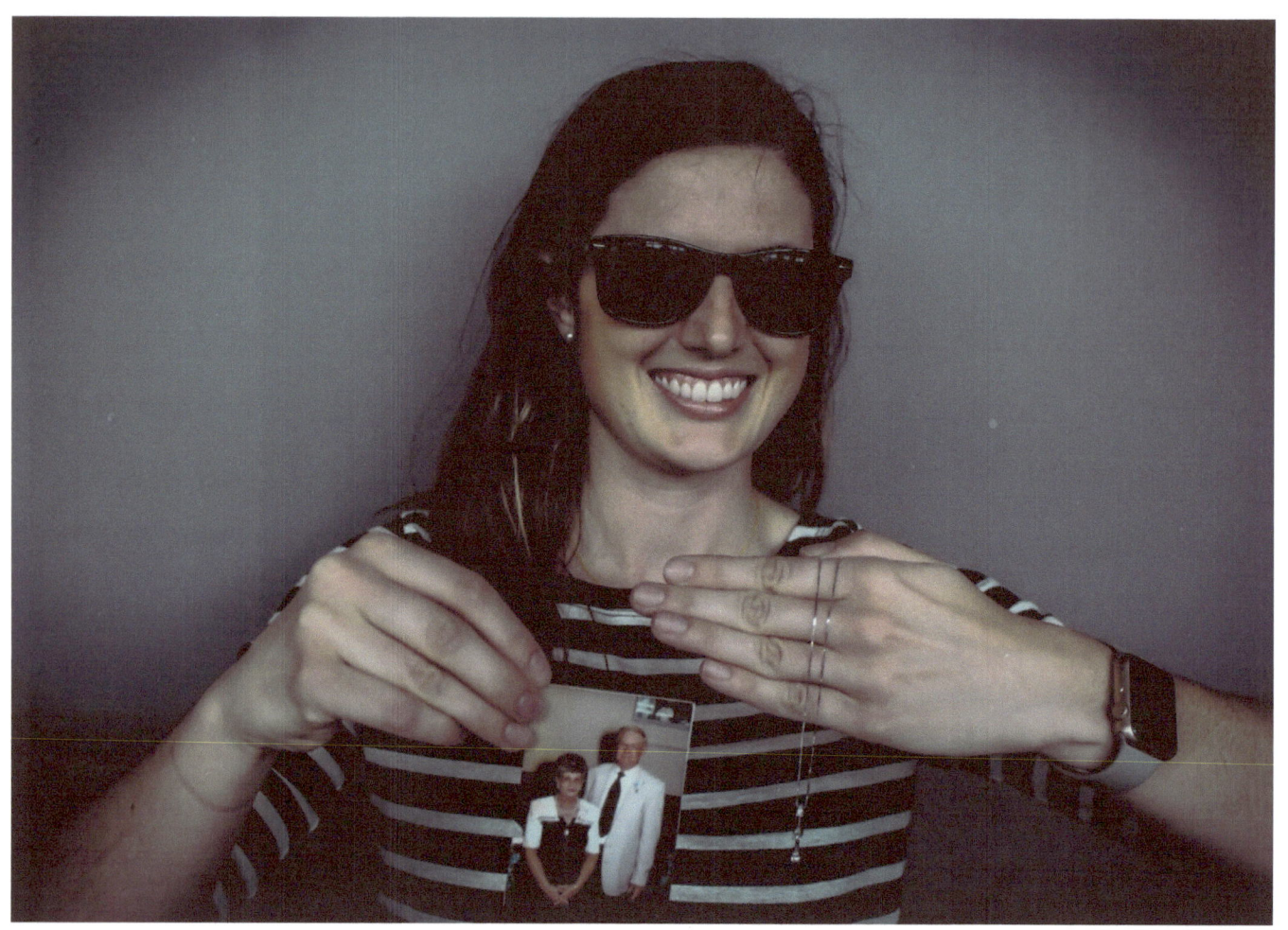

OBJECT:

Her grandma's necklace

WHY IS IT IMPORTANT TO HER?

"This necklace is important to me because it is a necklace my left for me when she passed away, this necklace was a gift from my grandpa to my grandma when he was still alive. This necklace is not only important to me because it is a special piece of jewelry that I have to remember my grandmother, but this necklace represents "past present and future". Therefore, it also serves as a reminder to be grateful for memories of loved ones, life experiences, and memories in my past, and to continue to live my life in the present moment with gratitude, thankfulness and intention so in the future I can live the life I've always dreamed of and imagined living!!

I only wear this necklace on some special occasions, but it mostly sits in a frame next to a picture of both of my grandparents. I hope it is a piece of jewelry that I can pass down to loved ones in the future! "

TRACEY

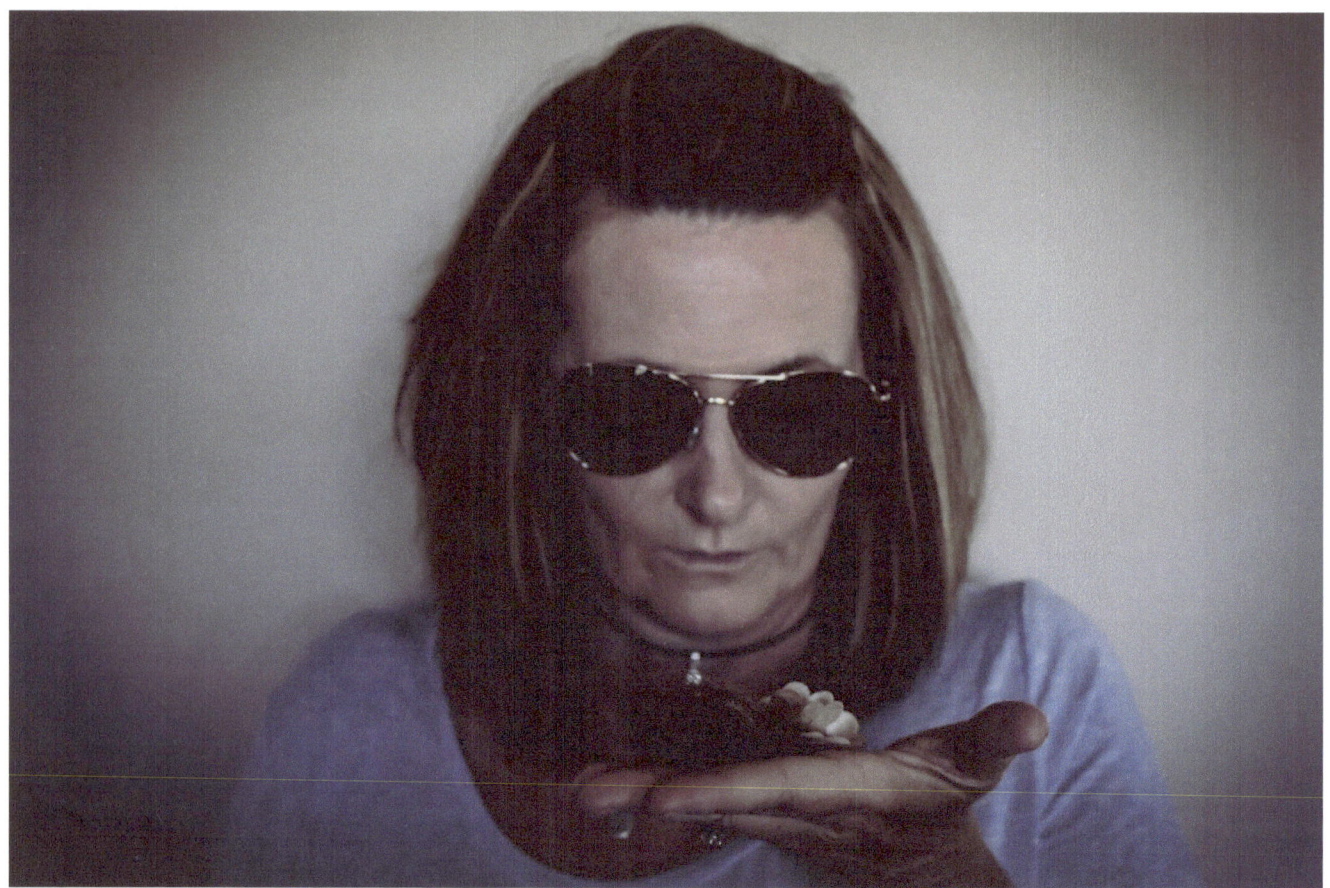

OBJECT:

HER DAUGHTER'S HAIR

WHY IS IT IMPORTANT TO HER?

"I CAN TOUCH IT AND IT'S THE ONLY THING LEFT OF HER. I CARRY IT WITH ME. IT HELPS ME TO GET THROUGH MOST DAYS BECAUSE I MISS HER SO MUCH. IT'S THE ONLY PHYSICAL THING THAT I HAVE LEFT. NOT VERY MANY PEOPLE KNOW THAT THAT'S SOMETHING THAT I DO.

BUT I STILL HAVE THOSE DARK TIMES WHERE MY MIND TRAVELS IN PLACES THAT IT SHOULDN'T AND FOR WHAT EVER REASON, THAT (HER DAUGHTER'S HAIR) IS SOMETHING THAT HELPS PULL ME FROM MY DARK SPOT.

IT'S NOT REALLY SOMETHING THAT I CAN EXPLAIN. IT'S JUST THE LOSS OF YOUR CHILD IS BEYOND ANYTHING THAT CAN BE EXPLAINED. IT'S SOMETHING THAT YOU DON'T GET PAST. IT'S SOMETHING THAT YOU DON'T GET OVER. IT'S SOMETHING THAT YOU DON'T MOVE ON FROM. IT'S JUST SOMETHING THAT YOU HAVE TO PUT ON A MASK AND PLAY PRETEND FOR EVERYBODY ELSE'S SAKE.

SO HER HAIR...IT JUST HELPS ME TO COPE WITH DAY TO DAY SITUATIONS. I DON'T NEED A REMINDER BECAUSE SHE'S ALWAYS THERE. SHE'S ALWAYS IN MY DREAMS."

JAAWAN

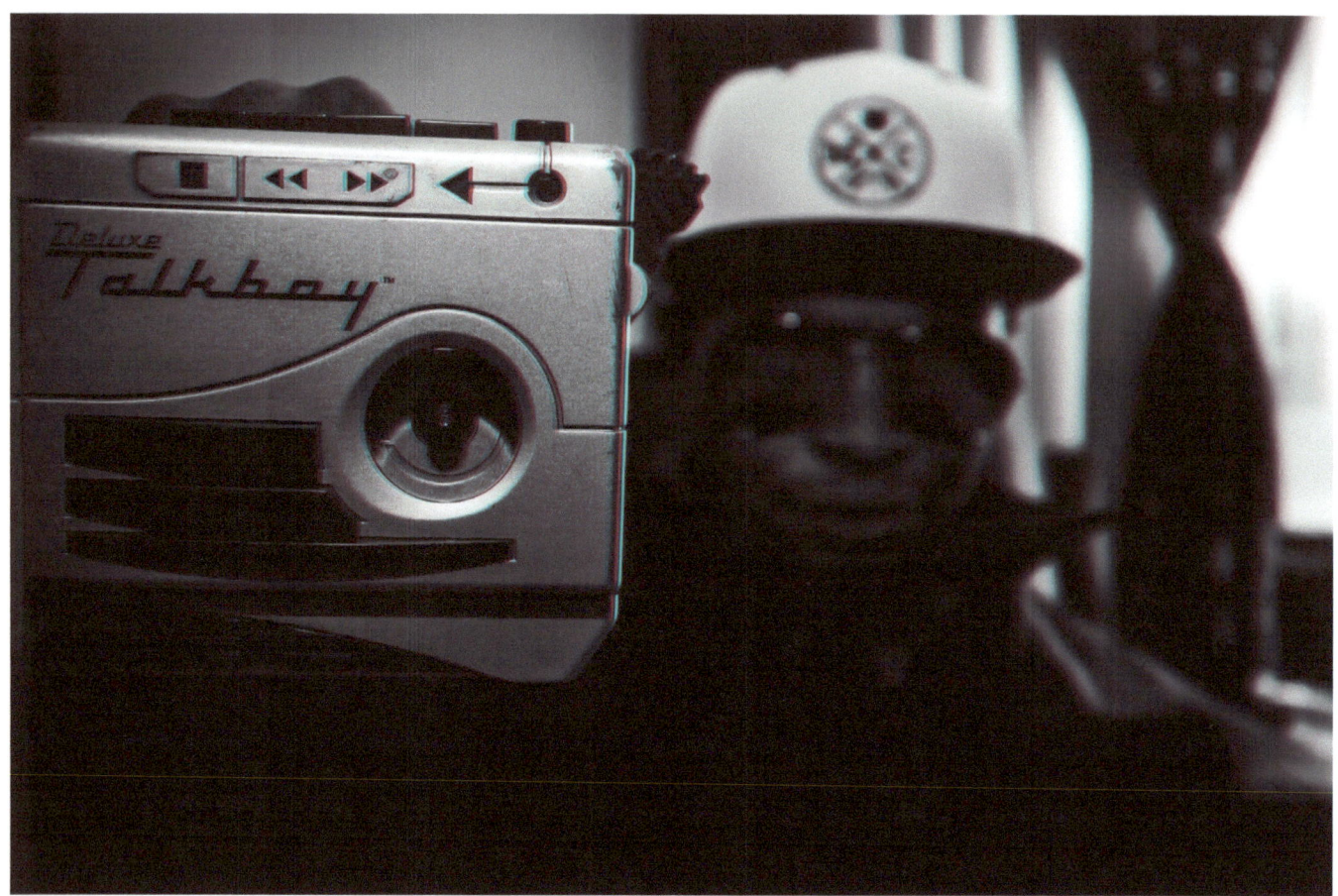

OBJECT:

CASSETTE TAPE RECORDER

WHY IS IT IMPORTANT TO HIM?

IF I HAD TO PINPOINT ANY OBJECT THAT HELPED LEAD ME TO BECOMING THE PERSON I AM TODAY, IT WOULD BE THIS CASSETTE RECORDER. IT'S ACTUALLY CALLED A "TALKBOY." YOU MIGHT REMEMBER IT FROM THE MOVIE "HOME ALONE 2." MY PARENTS GOT ME ONE FOR CHRISTMAS AND I ABSOLUTELY LOVED IT.

IT WAS GREAT BECAUSE NOT ONLY DID IT PLAY TAPES, BUT IT ALSO RECORDED YOUR VOICE AND COULD PLAY IT BACK IN SLOW MOTION OR SUPER FAST! I WOULD SPEND HOURS RECORDING MYSELF AND PLAYING IT BACK.

I ALSO GOT A BOOM BOX (REALLY DATING MYSELF NOW) AND IT HAD TWO TAPE DECKS, SO I COULD MAKE MY OWN MIXTAPES. I WOULD EVEN RECORD MYSELF INTRODUCING EACH SONG LIKE I WAS RADIO DJ!

THOSE WERE JUST A FEW PIECES OF TECHNOLOGY THAT INSPIRED ME TO BECOME WHAT I AM NOW. A CONTENT CREATOR. NOW, AS AN ADULT, I LOVE MAKING THINGS THAT MOVE AND INSPIRE PEOPLE, JUST LIKE HOW I WAS MOVED AND INSPIRED AS A KID. I FIND IT ENCOURAGING NOW HEARING FROM PEOPLE HOW SOMETHING I MADE INSPIRED THEM, OR THAT THEY WERE ABLE TO INTERPRET AND CONNECT WITH IT IN A WAY I NEVER THOUGHT OF.

I APPRECIATE YOU ALL FOR YOUR ENCOURAGEMENT AND I WILL MAKE A DEAL WITH YOU ALL. IF YOU PROMISE TO KEEP SHARING THESE STORIES WITH ME AND YOUR FRIENDS AND FAMILY, THEN I PROMISE TO KEEP GOING OUT, FINDING THESE STORIES, AND CREATING CONTENT EVERY DAY FOR THE REST OF MY LIFE. SO, DO WE HAVE A DEAL?